W9-AFU-505

THE GATORS

A Story of Florida Football

THE GATORS

A Story of Florida Football

by
Tom McEwen

THE STRODE PUBLISHERS
HUNTSVILLE, ALABAMA 35802

Photographs Courtesy Of
The Tampa Tribune
and the
University Of Florida Sports
Information Office

Contents

Foreword

Over its long history Florida football has had its ups and downs, its great moments and its frustrations. Yet Gator devotees, and how many of them there are, have never lost faith nor the hope of the great championship ahead, the Southeastern Conference championship and the so-far elusive all-winning season. I am convinced that "waiting til next year" has prolonged the lives of thousands of Gator supporters.

Whether measured by personal interest, first-hand knowledge as a Gator-watcher, depth of research, or sheer writing ability, no one could be better qualified to chronicle the Gator football story than the talented, and frequently humorous, Tom McEwen. His reputation is to report as it is, but wryly.

Tom McEwen's brother, Red, was a Gator great on one of the great Gator teams. Tom attended the University of Florida, and there I have determined rose to his athletic acme when in his junior year he made intramural all-Campus softball short-fielder, a position no longer in the lineup. Furthermore, Tom's son, Rick, attended the university.

Tom has followed and written factually and interestingly about Florida football fortunes for most of his adult life. On occasions he has acted as both self-anointed coach, and as quarterback, yet he has never called a bad play or lost a game.

In this volume Tom McEwen has brought to bear all of his many talents, his humor, his insight based on experience, and an always close proximity to the fountainheads, and the product of ferret-like research in a way that will please the readers, and make us all wish he will be around to record the many more chapters as time unfolds them.

Stephen C. O'Connell
Past President, University of Florida

Blessed Is He That Waiteth.
—Daniel 12:12

"To all those who have worn the Orange
and Blue on and off the field."

Preface

ONLY AT FLORIDA

*After the intriguing 1973 Gator season, Defensive Coach
Doug Knotts was talking to a friend about the year past, about
how the Gators had barely won the first two games, then lost
four in a row, but steadied and won the final five, to turn it
around. Coach Knotts suggested that that could happen "only
at Florida," and the thought triggered other thoughts of events
in Gator history that could have happened "only at Florida."*

*He had heard, he said, that once just before the unusually
tense Florida-Georgia game everyone noticed a great block of
empty seats at about the 30-yard line, on the east side of
Jacksonville's Gator Bowl. They were good seats. A check
around the pressbox first drew the word that they belonged to
passengers on a Gator Special train from South Florida, for the
game was figured to be a cinch sellout. But when the seats
stayed empty throughout the game, more checking determined
that the tickets were unsold, that they had been left by the
ticket boss, by mistake, back in the athletic business office in
Gainesville.*

*Knotts said he had heard it about that way and, when his
friend confirmed it positively, then Knotts shook his head and
said again, "Only at Florida."*

Knotts, of course, is right.

*Only Florida could produce a football team that would
beat another 144-0, and then produce one that could lose 75-0.*

*Only at Florida could history turn up a team that had to
play around a stump, and may have lost the game because of*

that unlikely hazard.

Only at Florida could a team be produced that would have to flee Cuba just in time to avoid jail.

Only at Florida could the best known cry of them all be "Wait'll Next Year," and only at Florida could a halfback have his pants very nearly fall to his knees as he completed a 90-yard touchdown run in the Orange Bowl, on national television.

Only at Florida could the best known of all alumni-player organizations be one whose members participated in a 13-game losing streak and have the brass to call themselves The Golden Era.

Only at Florida could the head of defense be moved to the head of the offense and the head of the offense be moved to the head of the defense just before a big game.

Only at Florida could there develop in the stands a 40-year-old self-appointed cheerleader who would make it his responsibility to race about rallying the fans, especially during the grim moments, and earn the admiring name of "Two-Bits" for the cheer George Edmondson, Jr., leads so often, so loyally, so enthusiastically.

Only at Florida would three key players cut off a piece of the mascot's tail, on prankish impulse.

Only at Florida can there be so many natural rivals on one schedule—Georgia, Florida State, Auburn, Miami.

Only at Florida could all head coaches in history except less than a half dozen be fired, or encouraged not to seek new contracts.

Only at Florida could a head coach work part-time for the WPA.

Only at Florida could there be so many spring game phantoms who somehow disappeared from the scene before assuming the stardom their spring performances suggested.

Only at Florida would athletes try to organize into a union.

Only at Florida would a race horse be honored at half time and receive a letter blanket. But, that happened in 1956 after the first Florida-bred, Needles, won a Kentucky Derby. With jockey David Erb up and owners Bonnie Heath and Jack Dudley beside him at the 50-yard line, midfield, the great thoroughbred, Needles, drew a standing ovation and was draped in a track letter blanket.

Only at Florida could such a lasting nickname be acquired so accidentally as was that of Alligators.

And only at Florida would players suddenly flop on their backs to permit the other team to score.

Well, all these things have happened, in Florida's rich, fascinating, often funny, often dramatic, very special football history. All these and more.

And so it is this that follows here, a narrative history of that—of Gator football from its very beginnings, of the players, the coaches, the administrators and the fans; of the intrigue, the hirings, the firings, the touchdowns, the fumbles, the great plays, the not-so-great plays, but most of all, of the whole package that makes so unshakeable the magnet that is Gator football to all it touches.

This compilation tells you how Doug Dickey was hired.

It tells you how Ara Parseghian of Notre Dame came within the asking of becoming the head Gator coach.

It tells you of the very first game, and the first game with "Florida State," played long before most think.

It takes you through the 8-1 season, the 0-13 stretch, the 9-2 year and all the attached drama, and it takes you through the 9-1-1 of 1969.

It tells you of the origination of "Wait 'til Next Year."

It details the win that broke that 13-game losing streak, and of the game that may have kept the Gators out of the Rose Bowl.

It tells you how Heisman Trophy winner Steve Spurrier wound up at Florida, and charts his career. It tells you of the frustrations of Bob Woodruff.

It takes you through the special drama of a young Gator playing a game the day after he had buried his first-born. It tells you of the Cracker General who coached the Gators. And it goes behind the Voice of the Gators.

It is as accurate as records and time permit.

It is as objective as school tie and years of also waiting tolerate.

It is a work designed for that special breed who is a Florida partisan.

The qualifications for membership are to be of great

devotion, as well as of great impatience; to be of great faith, but capable of instant disappointment; to reserve the right to criticize his coaches and his team, but to deny that right to those not aligned.

It is a work designed for all whose vocabulary includes these must phrases: Whasmatter with the Gators, Year of the Gator, Wait'll Next Year, and, of course, always, Go Gators.

As I was saying, only at Florida...

President W. F. Yocum, when "first team" was organized, 1899.

The Inauguration

In the late summer of 1901, when Theodore Roosevelt was sworn in as successor to assassinated President William McKinley, another inauguration was making news in the north Florida town of Lake City. Dr. T. H. Taliaferro became president of Florida State Agricultural College. While hardly so grave an occurrence as the inauguration of the president of the United States, the event had an impact on the college and to this day affects how thousands of Floridians spend their fall weekends.

Dr. Taliaferro was a vibrant and progressive man who liked, appreciated, and approved of the new, if somewhat brutish and mysterious, sport of football. His predecessor, the late W. F. Yocum, and Dr. Yocum's board of trustees, had tolerated the formation of a football team at Florida State Agricultural College in 1899, but no games were played and there was no team at all in 1900. Dr. Taliaferro saw to it that there was a football team his first year of 1901 and by that deed saw to it that there are University of Florida football Gators today.

The college that Dr. Taliaferro headed, FAC as it was called, had been chartered 17 years before along with six other state-supported institutions of higher learning. The entire higher education system in Florida reaches back to January 6, 1853, when Gov. Thomas Broome signed a bill that created East Florida Seminary at Ocala. That followed the state legislature's passage in 1851 of an enabling act which provided for two seminaries of higher learning—one to be located east of the

13

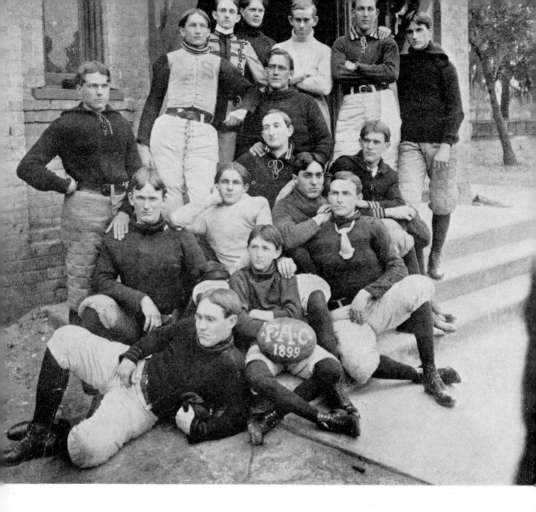

Campus scene at Florida Agricultural College, Lake City, in 1900.

Florida's very first organized team, 1899, at Lake City, was undefeated. Coach Cox could find nobody to play.

Suwanee River and one west. The legislature became practical and took over a private school already operating in Ocala to serve as its east-of-the-Suwanee seminary. The school struggled and suffered during the Civil War but truly was Florida's very first higher education institution.

In 1862 the Morrill Act provided each state up to 30,000 acres of public land for each U. S. Senator and Representative to be used for schools of mechanical arts, agriculture, and military science. Florida accepted her share of 90,000 acres in 1870 land script, which was sold for revenue-producing bonds. The Florida Legislature moved then and accepted an offer from Lake City to establish the Florida Agricultural and Mechanical College there. When it opened in 1884, that marked the beginning of land-grant colleges.

Lake City was a thriving place even before the turn of the century. It was built on the vital east-west railroad across north Florida and was situated only 13 miles from the great Civil War battleground of Olustee, where on February 20 the Confederates under Joseph Finegan defeated a large Union force moving west along the railroad, and drove the Bluecoats back to Jacksonville. Lake City in those days was a booming city of 5,000, the home of men influential in business, government, and letters. It was as proud of its college as its contributions to the great victory at Olustee. The town's social and recreational activities centered around Florida Agricultural College, a coed institution of just under 200 students who came from all over Florida.

FAC's turn of the century bulletins advertised this predecessor to the present-day University of Florida as a place for the education of: "Young men under military discipline, and young women under refining care."

FAC's Yearbook for 1899-1900, when Dr. Yocum was president, carried a photograph of the very first football team, one that played nobody, and this account:

"The history of football is very young in connection with FAC.

"...Never until this past season has a team been organized with the expectation of meeting an adversary on the gridiron. This past season the Board of Trustees, for the first time in the history of the college, consented to the playing of some

16

intercollegiate games. Heretofore, as in many other institutions and in a great many localities, football has been regarded as a kind of legalized fighting.

"But, in this latter day of enlightenment it has come to be recognized that 'all work and no play makes Jack a dull boy' and the general public is coming to see that for the best development of the intellect a certain amount of physical training is indispensible. Among the vast number of sports which are cultivated among the students of the most renowned colleges of today, football occupies a place that will never be occupied by any other game.

"It is true that many men were injured in the early history of the game, and this is what gave the game the bad reputation it bears in some localities. But advancement has been made in this line just as it has in everything else during the last few years.

"The football player of today is so well protected by modern rules of the game, as well as by his equipment, that his chances of being hurt are no greater than those of the average bicycle or horseback rider. This season, our Commandant took charge of the training of the squad and personally conducted their exercises, and to say this, is to guarantee that the work was done thoroughly. To show that the training was not done with intent to kill anybody, let us add that, in addition to the work of Lieutenant Cox (Battalion Commander), we were very materially aided by the advice and coaching of two members of the Faculty, Professors Blair (A. W., chemistry) and Miller (H. K., also chemistry), and of a minister of the Gospel, the Reverend Mr. Tims, of the Presbyterian Church," making it official that the first pre-Gator team was head-coached by Lieutenant Cox, and assistant-coached by Professors Blair and Miller and Reverend Tims.

The 1899-1900 FAC Yearbook also reported that "the team entertained very strong hopes of meeting some other teams during the past season, but owing to circumstances over which we had no control we were unable to get the games we so desired, but we have hopes for the future."

The members of that first, if untested, team were:

Center H. A. Laycock; right guard Hardy Croom; left guard E. Porter; tackle W. E. Hensley; tackle B. Cone of Lake

Lieutenant N. H. Cox (upper left) organized and coached the first team in 1899, but no intercollegiate games were played.

City; end Norman Ives of Lake City; end J. Layton; quarterback Oliver Kinnison of Lake City; halfback Harvey Waugh of Lake City; halfback J. J. Finley; fullback Ed Clute; and substitutes W. B. Cone of Lake City; David Craver of Tarpon Springs; Rudolph Lanier of Lake City; Lloyd LeBaron of Jacksonville; Tebrough Morgan of Churchill; J. M. Nilson of West Palm Beach; F. W. Price of Manatee; and T. Saussy.

There is no record of any football activity in the fall of 1900, or until Dr. Taliaferro became president for that historic year of 1901.

The *Lake City Reporter* described Dr. Taliaferro "as a man of broad culture, sound judgment," and as being "thoroughly abreast of the times." His work before going to Lake City had carried him for teaching and study into the Ivy League where Yale, Princeton, Brown, and Harvard were playing the sport of football intercollegiately. Dr. Taliaferro was fascinated by it. He studied it, and had a desire to try his hand at, at least, part-time

18

coaching of the game.

As soon as he was inaugurated, Dr. Taliaferro enlarged the academic curriculum and approved a football program. He was an aggressive, outgoing man. He went after students instead of having them come to him. He advertised heavily, his ad declaring that Florida Agricultural College offered in the classroom: "One year courses in business, stenography, typing, and telegraph. We offer also a prep course of one or two years for those who wish to prepare for more work at other universities and we offer post-graduate work."

The school term of 1901-1902 was just begun when Dr. Taliaferro agreed that James M. Farr, professor of history, should be the head coach of football. He would assist him as time permitted, but Dr. Farr would be the head coach. He was, and as it turned out he was the first coach of the first intercollegiately competitive football team to which the Florida Gators of today are traceable.

The First Game

Florida Agricultural College had been chartered in 1884, along with six other state-supported institutions of higher learning, such as East Florida Seminary, 50 miles south at Gainesville, and Florida State College, 110 miles west in the state capital of Tallahassee. FAC was set up for educational purposes, not for supporting intercollegiate football, so its resources in that area were few. In fact, as it turned out, the college's total contributions to the program in that first year were President Taliaferro's approval of the team and his offer to assist in coaching.

Acquisition of uniforms and equipment was up to the team. Each player scrounged for his own quilted pants, jersey, and football shoes. Farr organized what was called "The College Gridiron Club" which was responsible for necessary financing and team management. Somehow the team was organized and practiced, and arrangements were made for the first game.

On November 15, 1901, the *Lake City Reporter* carried, between notices of the latest in constipation remedies, this item: "The College Gridiron Club has arranged a series of football games to come off in the near future. The first of these will be played at Jacksonville on the 21st, during the Fair. On that day, they will contest the honors with Stetson University."

Some of the other colleges in the state had organized football clubs, but now, on November 22, not November 21, as it turned out, intercollegiate football history was to begin in Florida.

The press buildup for the game was surprising, considering the newness of the sport. But the *Lake City Reporter,* in announcing that first game, went into some detail: "The lineup will be as follows: Rice, cent; Keen, Bates, guards; Henderson, Maguire, T., tackles; Ives, Mitchell, H., ends; Maguire, H., Simton, halfbacks; Brown, F., quarterback; Helveston, fullback."

Then the *Reporter* threw down the gauntlet to Stetson: "The Lake City players are made of good stuff and the DeLand boys will have to hustle if they are to carry off the Honors."

On November 21, the *Florida Times-Union,* in Jacksonville, delighted with the addition of this new sideshow to the Fair, headlined:

COLLEGES TO MEET ON GRIDIRON
SPECIAL GAME EXPECTED BETWEEN
CADETS AND STETSON
* * * * *

COLLEGE YELLS AND COLLEGE COLORS WILL
BE A FEATURE

The newspaper listed both starting lineups that day, its version of *Lake City*'s starters different from that of the *Reporter* a few days before:

Lake City		Stetson
Rice	C	Pope
Keen	RG	Keller
Bates	LG	Caimes
McGuire	RT	Dunkin
Henderson	LT	Botts, H.
Mitchell	LE	Botts, E.
Ives	RE	Oates
Simmonton	RHB	Pounds
Porter	LHB	DeCottes
Brown	QB	Haynes
Dougherty	FB	Compropst

The next day, the day of the game, the *Times-Union* headlined:

STETSON AND AGRICULTURAL COLLEGE
MEET THIS AFTERNOON
* * *

GREAT FOOTBALL PROMISED

Dr. James M. Farr coached Florida (at Lake City) in first game in 1901.

* * * *

THE GAME WILL BE HISTORIC
* * * *

IT WILL MARK THE BEGINNING OF FLORIDA INTERCOLLEGIATE FOOTBALL

"This afternoon the first great football contest between two leading colleges of Florida will take place at the Fairgrounds. The Blue and White of Florida Agricultural College goes against the Green and White of Stetson.

"It is the first battle in the royal game, the game that calls out the best resources, the pluck, the endurance and speed of lusty young manhood between these two great colleges.

"It inaugurates what will be a long-continued and generous, manly rivalry between them. It is a game that will mark the beginning of a new growth of college spirit, not only in these two colleges but in all the schools of Florida.

"In short, this gridiron battle promises to be historic in Florida college athletics.

"The game will be in halves of thirty or thirty-five minutes. That will be decided today. Stetson is coached by C. Seton Fleming, a football player of this city thoroughly familiar with the game."

So the stage was set. The Fairgrounds, on Jacksonville's Northside, bristled with activity of crowds on a holiday at the fair. (The site of the old fairgrounds is now about split by I-95 North and is divided into many parts, including some sections of Golfair Manor, Bentwood Golf Club, and Gateway Shopping Center.)

Stetson arrived in its green and white. Florida, wearing the blue and white which eventually gave way to today's orange and blue, was late. There was no explanation for the tardiness, but the game was delayed for an hour—from 2 until 3 p.m.—and the halves were reduced to 20 minutes of playing time each.

The great game was played, and it is recorded that the pre-Gators bowed in their first formal competition. The score was 6-0. As the season would go by, there would be extenuating circumstances contributing to the outcome of many games, but few would match the special interference in the very first game.

Deep into the game, with the score 6-0, the FAC Boys were driving, the *Times-Union* post-game story reported: "The ball is now only eight yards from Stetson's line (goal). A stump in the field interferred with the play and the ball had to be carried to one side, to Lake City's disadvantage. That stopped the drive."

The newspaper began with these headlines:

STETSON WON BY
SIX TO NOTHING
* * * * *

GREAT CROWD SAW SPLENDID GAME
* * * * *

THE INTEREST WAS INTENSE
* * * * *

CADETS MADE FINE SHOWING,
ESPECIALLY IN GROUND GAINING

"With thousands to witness the first great intercollegiate football match in the history of Florida, the Florida Agricultural College went down to defeat before Stetson University in a gallant fight at the Fairgrounds yesterday, which even now has not finally settled the question of supremacy for football honors between the state's two leading educational institutions. Yesterday's game marks the beginning of intercollegiate athletics in the state. It was the first in a series of games that the

The 1902 East Florida Seminary Team of Gainesville.

Agricultural College and Stetson will play. The best two out of three games this season will make either college the champion.

"Nothing could have been more auspicious for the inaugural day of intercollegiate athletics than the circumstances that attended the game between Stetson and Lake City yesterday.

"The immense crowd seemed to be impregnated with a part of the enthusiasm and the college spirit that followers of either school displayed, and the Green and White and Blue and White were worn by many besides those who actively represented the two schools. Everyone wore a bunch of colors.

"And the women! They watched the game with shining eyes and eager faces. Of course, they had their favorites and applauded as well.

"Long may the Blue and White and Green and White prosper in future athletic rivalry."

The first half went scoreless after Stetson won the state of

Florida's first intercollegiate coin toss. Sometime during that half Simmonton registered the first ground gain of any size in the pre-Gators intercollegiate competition by dashing 20 yards.

His feat was surpassed, however, in the second half when Stetson's Pounds circled left end to set the stage for Stetson's touchdown.

"It is near the Lake City goal," according to the *Times-Union.* "DeCottes is given the ball and behind splendid interference circles left end for the remaining space and a touchdown (which counted five points in those days). Goal is kicked by Compropst and the score is 6-0."

It was then the pre-Gators began the drive that was stumped.

Afterwards, "pandemonium reigned among the Stetsonites. Lake City also received a standing ovation.

"Dr. Taliaferro and members of the Agricultural College faculty were on the grounds congratulating the boys for their fine showing, considering the disadvantages they labored under. The Cadets are confident they can win the next game."

In the first "locker-room interviews," Captain Compropst of Stetson said, "I think our superior team speed is what gave us the game."

Pre-Gators Captain Simmonton of Lake City said: "I am greatly disappointed at the result of the game but I believe our team has not yet been thoroughly tested."

Apparently those other two games never came off, or, at least, there is no record to indicate they did.

Thus, Florida's pre-Gators began with the 0-1 record, and there would be at least one game played annually from then on, save 1943.

Start Of The Florida's "FSU Series"

After that one-game season, Florida's football program did not spring forth overnight. The next few years were to be troubled and confused. Rules and eligibility were uncertain, coaches and players came and went. Games were scheduled and cancelled, and few records were kept. Even the newspapers failed to report all the games. Yet, FAC appears to have played three games in 1902, two with Stetson, and one with Florida State College at Tallahassee.

The Florida State game did not come until after a scoreless tie and a 22-5 loss to Stetson. After the game that ended without a point, the *Lake City Reporter* noted that:

"The Stetson boys are somewhat taller and apparently larger." The paper also reported that one of the spectators was J. M. Gulliam, president of East Florida Seminary at Gainesville. A game scheduled with that school in 1902 somehow did not come off.

But the pre-Gators, in their fourth game in history, finally recorded a victory.

The *Lake City Reporter* headlines read:

THE FAC BOYS WIN
* * * *

HARD FOUGHT CONTEST ON THE GRIDIRON
* * * * * * *

SCORE WAS 6 TO 0

The account of the first win went like this:

"On last Friday afternoon, the people of Lake City

witnessed a game of football between the teams of Florida Agricultural College of this city and the Florida State College of Tallahassee.

"The game was called promptly at 3 o'clock at the Fairgrounds. Although the game was hotly contested from the very first, it was plain that the local team was the stronger, and the ball moved steadily through Tallahassee's field. A touchdown was made by a 20-yard run by C. H. Maguire and a 10-yard run by McCaskell. The first half ended in a score of 6 to 0 in favor of the local team. No points were scored by either in the second half."

That game began the fierce rivalry between the University of Florida and Florida State University. That rivalry has continued unabated through the years except for a period when Florida State became Florida State College for Women and abandoned football. But State became Florida State University in 1947, and football and the rivalry returned.

The roster of those pre-Gators playing for the first time against the pre-Florida State Seminoles, and engaging in first victory ever FAC, was: center, Fidley; left guard, Bates; right guard, Bridges; left tackle, Maguire, T. C.; right tackle, Christenson; left end, Helvenston, W.; right end, Mitchell, J. T.; right half, Maguire, C. H.; left half, McCaskell; quarterback, Taylor, C. D.; fullback, Cone, W. B.

The pre-Seminoles from Tallahassee playing in that historic game were W. W. Hughes, C. W. Peters, G. McCord, W. Mullin, W. Dickey, Ed Watson, Lawrence Murray, H. Sheats, H. Provence, D. Williams, F. Buckholz, A. B. Clark, F. F. Rawls, J. T. Howard, B. Belcher, W. McLin, and W. Van Trunt.

Thus, after two seasons FAC footballers had a composite record of 1 win, 2 losses, and 1 tie, and after that second season in 1902 FAC was not again known as FAC, or Florida Agricultural College.

On September 23, 1903, the start of the 1903 school term and three days after Lake City voted dry by 51 votes, President Taliaferro referred to the college as "The University of Florida."

The truth is, the name change did not do much for the Florida football fortunes right away. In that year of 1903 Florida lost two and won but one. It is noteworthy that in the

27

The 1905 Fightin' Florida Band.

lone victory they sort of beat themselves. The win was over East
Florida Seminary, moved from Ocala to Gainesville, a team
those pre-Gators of Lake City eventually would absorb.

But at the start of the 1903 season Stetson beat the
University of Florida again, 6-5, and so did Florida College at
Tallahassee, 12-0. It must have been particularly embarrassing
even then for Florida to lose to a team from Tallahassee because
after the loss the coach, Fleming, quit and "returned to
Jacksonville to resume his law practice," an account reported.
His replacement, who guided Florida to that lone win, a 6-5
season-ending victory over East Florida, was A. B. Humphreys
"of Jacksonville, who has coached many of the leading teams of
the South." Notably, a record of the game also shows that the
name of the referee for Florida's only win was: "A. B.
Humphreys."

The lineup for the first team ever called the University of
Florida was: Appleyard, center; Daniels, right guard; Bates, left
guard; Jeffrey, right tackle; Christensen, left tackle; Kirkland,

right end; Dougherty, left end; Grubb, quarterback; Bridges, right half; Maguire, C. H., left half; Buck, fullback. C. H. Maguire was team captain.

The pre-Gators had been in business three seasons and had a record of 2 wins, 4 losses, and 1 tie. But the worst was yet to come.

If You Won't Slug Me, I Won't Slug You

The year 1904 was a turning point in Florida football history, not in terms of victories, for there were none. But a reorganization of the athletic club assured a smooth-operating football program for the university, and with good administration football began to mature as an intercollegiate activity. Games were played all over the South in a business-like manner rather than being limited to the brotherly competition of challenging a Stetson or a Florida State.

It began with a revamp of the athletic club on September 30, 1904, as the *Lake City Reporter* recorded:

"The University Athletic Association was reorganized last Friday afternoon in the chapel hall by the election of Capt. C. H. Maguire as president; James W. Dougherty of High Springs as vice president; Frank Weller of Lake City, secretary; J. C. Jeffrey of Syracuse, N. Y., treasurer; P. S. McClung of Duneding, B. F. Bridges of Holt, and A. M. Jackson of Inverness were selected student board managers.

"The meeting was very enthusiastic. President Andrew Sledd (who had succeeded Dr. Taliaferro) congratulated the students upon their interest and gave them an encouraging talk. He was followed by Professors Blair and Jeffrey and students Bridges, Jackson, and Coach M. O. Bridges. One hundred and eight were enrolled as members, paying far in excess of membership fees, the contributions ranging from $10 down to the fee. So, the boys have a cash footing to begin life upon. The team, headed by Capt. Bridges, was present and was heartily received as they marched down the aisle."

That 1904 season Florida played four of its games on the road, losing to Auburn, Alabama, Georgia, and Georgia Tech. The far-ranging trips were made by train. The pre-Gators lost all five of its games that season without scoring a point.

Proud Captain William M. Rowlett of the 1905 Gators strikes a challenging pose. Rowlett went on to become a leading Tampa doctor and civic leader.

One of the regulars on that team was William Morrow Rowlett, Jr., now 91 years old and for many years a respected physician and governmental leader in Tampa. Rowlett went to high school in Bradenton, and while he was there the school began playing football. He came to love the game.

When it came time for college, "My daddy wanted me to go to a state school, so he sent me to the University of Florida at Lake City. First thing I wanted to do, of course, was play football on the team there, but even though I tried I didn't make it the first two years," in 1902 and 1903. "Stetson was the big rivalry. Those fellows had good teams. In 1903, I remember playing against a big fellow named Pounds.

"I remember," said Dr. Rowlett, interviewed at his home in Tampa, "that when the game began, with Pounds opposite me, I suggested to him that if he would not slug me, I would not slug him."

And, though the program made great strides toward maturity in 1904, Dr. Rowlett recalls difficult days, in terms of facilities and competition.

"At Lake City we didn't have any stadium, just played in the open. The games were well attended, particularly when Stetson played.

"Our equipment I remember was quite sparse. We wore those clumsy nose guards that came down across your cheeks and you held them between your teeth. Quite uncomfortable. And I remember the rules were a bit sketchy. Ben Bridges played next to me in the line, and on one occasion at Alabama when the going got particularly tough we resorted to grabbing each other by the belt to prevent the runner from coming between us."

"Why we played Alabama, I recall. And we played in Alabama and then at Auburn, Georgia and we played Georgia Tech," said Dr. Rowlett. "I remember we were the first University of Florida team to play those schools, to travel so far."

On these points Dr. Rowlett's memory was better than any previous written history and led to some correction of records at Alabama and Florida.

"Oh, I remember some of the players, like Ruey Cason, John Lykes, and the Bridges boys. It all meant a great deal to me. They elected me their captain, and I hold that very dear, though we played little in 1905. I left the university after 1905 to go to medical school at Emory."

Dr. Rowlett was big for his day, 6 feet and 175 pounds, and he needed all the size and endurance he had for that 1904 season.

It was, point-wise, the worst season in the history of the pre-Gators, and Gators. But it was the first to travel widely and play established Southern powers.

First, there was the trip to Alabama by train. The *Reporter* covered two ball games and hundreds of miles of travel in two paragraphs.

"The University football team returned home Tuesday morning and although suffering defeat in the two games played, are to be congratulated on what they accomplished. The first game was with the University of Alabama at Tuscaloosa on last Saturday, resulting in a 29-0 final score in favor of the University of Alabama. Bridges did some excellent playing for Florida.

"On Tuesday, a game was played at Auburn, Alabama, resulting in a 44-0 final in favor of Auburn. The game was hard-fought by both."

Coach Bridges practiced his team hard, then put them back on the train for a two-game series in Georgia. The *Reporter* told it this way in its October 12, 1904 issue:

"The University of Florida football team played the University of Georgia at Macon Saturday, and the latter won by a score of 51-0. Monday they played Georgia Tech at Atlanta, Tech winning by a score of 77-0. The boys returned home Tuesday morning. They will play Florida State College here on Saturday and a good game is anticipated."

But the game provided the final indignity, a loss to Florida State, resulting in what is believed to be the first editorial grumble. From the *Reporter* of October 28, 1904, came this:

"The football team of the State College at Tallahassee and the team of the University of this city met on the local gridiron on last Friday afternoon, the former winning 23-0. The people of Lake City had expected at least one victory after a long series of defeats encountered by the university and were greatly disappointed. The university should be made stronger before it attempts to play again."

And thus Coach M. O. Bridges and the pre-Gators of 1904 lost all five games they played and scored not a point. Their average yield of almost 45 points a game stands as a record, and except for the first, single-game season, no other Florida team has gone through a year scoreless. Two others ahead in history would yield more total season points, and two others would go winless.

Finally Coach Bridges and his pre-Gators were the first of Florida to feel "alumni" pressure and the first to be criticized by the press. They would not be the last.

The pre-Gators of 1904 had gained distinction—not only with their train tours of the South to play schools from other states, but because they were the only Florida team to go scoreless through the season, and because they yielded more points per game than any team to follow.

Buckman Gets Into The Act

While those who cared were considering the repair necessary for the Florida football team of 1905, state government in Tallahassee, under progressive Governor Napoleon Bonaparte Broward, was considering sweeping legislation that would change the state's college system completely. It was called The Buckman Bill.

A major point was that it would reduce the number of state-supported colleges from seven to four. One would enroll white men only, one white women, one blacks (the bill specified "Negroes"), and the other would train deaf, dumb, and blind. The bill also would establish a Board of Control which would administer the system. The bill became law on May 20, 1905.

The first responsibility of the Board of Control, on which sat Governor Broward, was to select the locations for the four different universities. The lobbying was vigorous, the newspaper and political campaigns unrelenting. Name-calling was not uncommon.

The biggest fight was for the location of the university for white men. Finalists were Lake City, home of "The University of Florida," formerly Florida Agricultural College, and Gainesville, site of East Florida Seminary. Each city offered land and $40,000 cash. The Board of Control voted 6-4 to relocate the University of Florida in Gainesville. The decision was made July 6, 1905.

Governor Broward led the unsuccessful fight to keep the University in Lake City. P. K. Yonge, for whom the experimental high school at Gainesville later would be named, and T. B. King fought successfully for the move.

In effect, Lake City's college would lose its state financial assistance, and full support towards building a major men's university would go forward at Gainesville. Public school buildings and whatever could be built quickly would be used the first year.

The University of Florida would move to Gainesville for the 1906-07 term. A side effect would be that the 1905 Florida football team would be a lame duck operation. As it turned out, it was that and worse. It was lame duck, confusing and troubled.

It appears that only one half to one and a half games were played, one half for sure under the leadership of captains Rowlett and J. W. Lykes, fullback and member of the pioneer Florida family that would found Lykes Steamship Company, Lykes Meat Packing, and the Lykes Ranches.

First, a new coach, C. A. Holton, tried to schedule a final "state championship" game with Stetson. They could not agree on a site. Stetson objected to Lake City, Gainesville, and Tampa but finally approved Palatka. Florida planned to tune up with Rollins College of Winter Park first.

But another first struck the pre-Gators. The *Savannah News* reported: "Some time ago, eight of the best men on the University of Florida team were barred from playing by the faculty because they were behind in their studies."

Next Coach Holton scheduled games with Columbia at Savannah, as well as contests with Gordon Military in Barnesville, Georgia, and Alabama Medical at Mobile, but all were cancelled for the same reason—not enough eligible players. Savannah was rescheduled, but there is no account of the game coming off.

Only known result in 1905 was a 6-0 halftime victory over Julian Landon Institute of Jacksonville before academics claimed its first Florida football victims.

On October 27, before those eligibility problems, the *Reporter* said: "The football game played here on Monday between the University and JLI lasted for only one half. The University boys refused to play the second half as the visiting boys wanted to play Yancey, who is a professional. The game stood 6-0 in favor of the University. Quite a number came down from Jacksonville."

And as if that were not enough, there was another tragedy. George Frederick, an 18-year-old from Brooksville, died of pneumonia.

Despite the season and despite the Buckman Act and its consequences, the Athletic Association met late in 1905 and prepared for its first season as Columbia Athletic Club, of Columbia College, named for the county in which Lake City is located. Lykes was re-elected captain, unanimously, and a decision made to apply for membership in the Southern Intercollegiate Athletic Association.

It was a game but futile effort. They would field a football team on the Lake City campus the next year and for some years after that. They would even play the University of Florida at Gainesville four times off and on through 1911, but win none of them, indeed not score a touchdown. The lingering resentment among townspeople in Lake City over the loss of the university eventually led to a dissolution of relations.

With the end of the school year of 1905 the University of Florida, its name, its state support, President Andrew Sledd, and one known football player (tackle William W. Gibbs) moved fifty miles downstate to their new home at Gainesville.

Pee Wee's Boys

From the football standpoint, the year of 1906 was ideal to relocate, and begin anew: The rules of the game had been rewritten during the off-season, pretty much on demand of President Teddy Roosevelt.

A *Chicago Tribune* survey in 1905 showed that 18 had died and 159 were seriously injured in the "sport." Until the rule changes of 1906, the game was one of pure brute strength. Grace, agility, and deception were lost on it.

President Roosevelt was so outraged that he declared he would outlaw the sport unless it was cleaned up. He called a panel of leading coaches to the White House and told them that "Brutality and foul play should receive the same summary punishment given to a man who cheats at cards."

Some schools—California, Columbia, Northwestern, Stanford, and Union—suspended the sport for a time.

In December of 1905 a group met that eventually would become the powerful National Collegiate Athletic Association (NCAA) of today. In 1906 a rules committee was formed and new regulations devised that wholly revolutionized and saved the game.

The greatest single innovation coming out of that meeting was the legalization of the forward pass. Two 30-minute halves were devised too, a neutral zone at the scrimmage line created, and the distance for a first down advanced to 10 yards. In addition hurdling was outlawed.

A bit later, in 1909, the field goal value was dropped from

4 points to 3 and a minimum of 7 men on the offensive line was ordered. In 1912 a fourth down was added, a touchdown was to be worth 6 instead of 5 points, the field size reduced from 110 yards to 100, the 20-yard limit first imposed on a forward pass eliminated, and the kickoff point moved from midfield to the kicking team's 40.

It was but shortly after these first major rules changes in early 1906 that interviews were conducted for the hiring of the new coach of the first University of Florida football team at Gainesville. C. A. Holton, who had coached at Lake City the year before, applied but was turned down. In late summer the decision was made for J. A. Forsythe, Jr., nicknamed Pee Wee.

Forsythe was a North Carolinian who played his football at Clemson, and it is a matter of record that the first coach of Florida at Gainesville had previously coached, for a time, at Florida State College at Tallahassee. He also had experience at Stone Mountain College, before landing the Florida job.

It was no easy task. At the first convocation of University of Florida students, held in an incomplete building on the new campus, only 60 students showed up. The number grew in a few days to 75, but in Lake City the newspaper chortled that "they'd hoped for 125, and of the 75, some 25 were from Gainesville and Alachua County."

But Pee Wee Forsythe put his team together, installing the Minnesota Shift. He would remain as head coach the first three years, leaving in a huff for Jacksonville towards the end of the first, but returning in 1907. The team played on in 1906 despite his departure and wound up with a 5-3-0 record. The most prized win came in the third game, a 6-0 decision over Rollins of Winter Park. It also was Florida's first home game in Gainesville.

The *Gainesville Sun,* in advance of that game, announced: "The first real football game of the season, where football sure enough will be featured, will be the game between the University of Florida and Rollins College which will occur at the Baseball Park in the city today.

"The people of Gainesville are dedicated to football, and since the university has been established here and there is a good team with the prospects of witnessing some fine games, the interest increases."

Admission was 50 cents.

The post-game *Sun* reported:

"The first game of football of the season resulted in victory for the University of Florida. A great deal of interest was exhibited. The result of the action was victory for the university by six to nothing over Rollins College. Neither team scored in the first half, which lasted 20 minutes. But in the second half, 20 minutes more, the University Boys scored six points which gave them the game."

The 1906 team defeated Riverside Athletic Club of Jacksonville 19-0, lost to Savannah 27-2, and played another game with Rollins, losing that one 5-0. The other games of the eight apparently were played but without great attention paid them by chroniclers.

The roster of that first team of Florida at Gainesville, included: Captain Thomas Guy Hancock, fullback from Tallahassee; Roy Corbett, R. M. Whidden, Albert Baars, James Kirk, Pat Johnson, Ralph Radar, C. Thompkins, Jim Shands, H. B. Coe, A. C. Bennett, A. I. Roe, D. S. Bryan, Arthur Albertson, T. C. Thompson, Alf Neilsen, J. B. Earman, Guy McCord, Charles Puleston, Pat Graham, Kent Johnson, and William W. Gibbs, who had played at Lake City the year before. Coach Forsythe played end.

Corbett became the captain the next year. As a side benefit to the team, he was athletics editor of the *Florida Pennant,* campus publication of that day. In the *Pennant* the next year, in a biography of Coach Forsythe, Roy Corbett wrote: "This is now his second year as coach of the U. of F. Again did he have to make a team out of green material. Only four of the 1906 team returned and showed up for practice. The fact that he won the State championship his first year in 1906 is all that will be said on that subject."

The Rollins College yearbook, describing the 1906-07 season, wrote: "Although it has not been a victorious one for us, we feel pleased with the good showing we made, especially in view of the fact that this is the second year we have played football," thus establishing the beginning of Rollins football as 1905.

The article went on, affirming the two meetings in 1906 of Rollins and Florida: "Before school opened the squad was out under our coach, Professor W. F. Buck, and practicing new plays, which proved successful later on.

"Four games were played, two with the University of Florida and two with Stetson. The first game against U. of F. was hotly contested from the start and neither team scored until nearly the end, when a university back got away with the only score of the day. The score was 6 to 0 in favor of the U. of F.

"The next game was played at home with the same team, this time resulting in a victory of Rollins, 5 to 0. Again the score was in the last few seconds, but all through the game our team showed marked superiority in material and coaching." Stetson beat Rollins twice, 15 to 0, and 2 to 0, but "Stetson outweighed our team 15 pounds to the man, and appeared a better team," the Rollins account went.

Roy Corbett, the captain of the 1907 team, in a letter to his friend Rex Farrior, captain a few years later, wrote these memories on November 7, 1956: "I have just looked over an itemized list of things purchased by Pee Wee Forsythe, football coach in 1906 and 1907, for which the university owed him nearly $100.

"You know that very first year in 1906, we fell heir to the used football suits, shoes, etc., that came over from the Lake City squad of 1905. Anything we needed bad enough, we bought individually and personally. When we played Riverside in Jacksonville there must have been 50 paying customers there. Tom Hancock of Tallahassee, I believe, captained the 1906 team, me the '07 team. I also served as trainer and was re-elected captain for 1908, but I did not return to college."

As it turned out, the captain of the 1907 Florida team would play against future Florida teams. He wrote Farrior:

"In 1908 and 1909, I promoted, financed, coached and played right halfback on the Riverside team of Jacksonville. About equal to the usual semi-pro city teams of today, made up of ex-college players and local talent. A fair squad. We played home and home with the U. of F. We practiced at night. No lights except on the street corner, so I painted the ball white."

In 1907 Corbett captained the Florida team that upset Columbia of Savannah 6-0 and enjoyed a 4-1-1 record. On the team was a newcomer named Bill Shands, who played quarterback, and would become one of the state's foremost legislators.

On the 1908 team, Forsythe's last, was a talented Gainesville youth named Dummy Taylor. Forsythe's 1908 team with Shands, Taylor, big Jim Vidal, and the veteran transferee, Gibbs, would have its ups and downs but would wind up respectable with a 5-2-1 record, including a precious first—a win at last over Stetson, 6-5, on Taylor's extra point after a Charlie Bartleson touchdown run. The nickname, Alligators, also developed in 1908. Pee Wee Forsythe in the first three years of Florida at Gainesville put together a record of 14-6-2 for a .636 percentage. Not too many of his successors would improve on his start.

The Nicknaming

Football was so new at Florida in 1906-07 it still lacked a nickname. At times the team was referred to in print merely as "Pee Wee's Boys" for Player-Coach Pee Wee Forsythe. But in a Gainesville sundries shop—an off-campus student hangout— owner Phillip Miller was contemplating buying pennants for the new team, and he wanted a picturesque nickname.

Off Miller went to Charlottesville, Virginia, where his son, Austin, was enrolled at the University of Virginia, to visit the Michie Company, which manufactured pennants and banners and such paraphernalia. Miller and son were shown by sales-people at Michie Company that college football teams had nicknames, such as Yale's Bulldogs and Princeton's Tigers. Young Miller immediately associated alligators with Florida, but the Michie people did not know what an alligator looked like. It was not until he went to the library and found a picture that an order was placed.

"I had no idea it would stick," Austin Miller told the *Florida Times-Union* years later when he was practicing law in Jacksonville.

The alligator emblem first appeared in the Miller store as the 1908 season began, and before long Miller found himself having to order all manner of pennants and banners—six-foot long banners with orange alligators (the colors had by then been changed to orange and blue), small ones with full-length alligators, some with just alligator heads like the one in the book from the Virginia library.

43

The Alligator name caught on and is still unique in major colleges. For years "Alligator" and "Gator" were used interchangeably, though fans in the South shortened it to "Gator" much quicker than those in the North.

Phillip Miller died in 1941, thirty-three years after almost accidentally nicknaming the Florida Gators.

The Pyle-Driving Years

G. E. Pyle was described by Tom Bryant, who managed a couple of Pyle teams and went on to become a member of the state board of control and devoted alumnus, as "a hard-driving man who worked night and day at his job. He was a technician and a man who could draw great response from his players. He also was able to find players who could produce."

Pyle was the Gator head coach for five years, from 1909 through 1913. Those were formative years for the program, and it was the hand of this wiry, far-sighted man that guided the program into competition against the giants of Southern football and into the prestigious Southern Intercollegiate Athletic Association. Against formidable opposition Pyle compiled a record of 26 wins, 10 losses, and 3 ties.

When he took over the program, Florida was playing what virtually amounted to prep school football. The 1909 schedule he inherited included two colleges, Stetson and Rollins. The remaining games were with town teams developed in Jacksonville and Tallahassee.

Before he was through Pyle had toughened the schedule, adding Georgia Tech, Auburn, Clemson, Mercer, and South Carolina. Too, by the time he left, Florida football was a paying proposition. He had the athletic association reorganized and somehow managed to be sure of drawing his salary, even though the 1912 season began with the school owing him $132 in back pay. But in 1913 Pyle's salary was $410.87, and he received $120.37 in expense money.

45

The seven-game Florida season of 1913 took in a total of $3,082.17 in gate receipts, including a high of $988.50 at Jacksonville for the Georgia Tech game.

Pyle's first-year Gator record, 1909, was 6-1-1, but four of the victories were over those hometown teams scattered around the big cities of Florida. Pyle's charges beat Rollins twice and played one loss and one tie with Stetson.

In 1910 the Gators went 6-1, losing only to Mercer, 13-0, while including Georgia A&M, The Citadel, and Rollins among its victims. Other than Mercer, only The Citadel scored on the Gators, getting two points.

The high point of 1910 came in the season's finale when the Gainesville Gators returned to their old homeplace, Lake City, to play Columbia College, created when the University of Florida pulled out of town. Manager Bryant of the Gators remembers the game:

"The people of Lake City hated the people of Gainesville because they felt Gainesville had taken the university away from them. Another fellow and I went up to Lake City a couple of days ahead of time to make arrangements for the team. We went by excursion train. When we got there we were like a couple of foreigners, and it was worse when the team got there. We beat them 33-0 and as quickly as the final whistle blew, the Lake City people behind our bench broke through and we had to run for our lives.

"We escaped to a building on the campus assigned to us, and the police watched over us. We were escorted to the train station. We did not even eat.

"Then," said Bryant, "the next year in Gainesville we beat Lake City 9-0 when Dummy Taylor dropkicked three times for field goals and all the points."

The next year Columbia College's administration formally apologized for the treatment accorded the Gators in 1910 in Lake City. The Florida athletic association, by a close vote, agreed to accept the apology, but there were no more games between the schools.

Florida's season of 1911 was lustrous enough as far as records go, a 5-0-1 final tally being built on victories over The Citadel, Clemson, Stetson, and Charleston, in addition to the multi-field goal triumph over Columbia.

But it was 1912 when the Gators really ventured out into big-time football. At the same time they compiled a respectable 5-2-1 record. The season included two important firsts: the start of the Auburn series, and the first win over an established, major out-of-state college.

An encounter with the Plainsmen opened the season—at Auburn—and a reporter for the *Alligator,* the student newspaper, wrote that the town "is not a very inviting looking place, being only a small town built around the school. The students board and room with town people, and only a few stay at the dormitory. It must be a very good place, as there is not even a moving picture show in town."

It was not a good place for Gator football that day, as it rarely has been since. Auburn, which finished the season 6-1-1, did the Gators in 27-13, but, as was written later "the team, the coach and the University are happy over this honorable result, and grant cheerfully that Florida is not master; but only the worthy opponent of that Southern team, which, with Vanderbilt, claims the Southern pennant."

A hallmark victory came when the Gators beat South Carolina, 10-6, the next Saturday, October 19, 1912, for its first win over a major out-of-state opponent. It was a contest later labelled by a writer "the most thrilling and hardest fought game ever played on University Field." It could not be said "that Florida outclassed the Gamecocks as can easily be seen from the score. In fact, the teams were very evenly matched and it was a neck-and-neck race from kickoff until the final whistle blew at the end of the interminable fourth quarter."

It was 6-3, South Carolina, late in the game when "Dummy's failure to make his dropkick go over the bar (and it was short by only a couple of feet) was a very lucky event, for South Carolina fumbled and Pounds (Hoyle of Winter Park) fell on it for a touchdown."

Pyle lost to Georgia Tech, 14-7, the next week and thus had fallen twice to the only teams he would not beat in his five years at Florida. After that, though, the Gators romped through three of the remaining four games on the schedule, settling for a scoreless tie with Mercer.

The Stetson game spotlighted Dummy Taylor, who became legendary as a side-stepping broken field runner, a master

47

of the hidden ball trick, and the dropkick. Florida drubbed Stetson 23-7 that year in Gainesville "before the largest and most enthusiastic crowd that ever witnessed a game in the state. Florida upheld her enviable record of never having lost at home."

Along the way, "from an impossible angle Dummy kicks goals, with that good right boot of his, which by the way, was never in better form, and that is saying that his booting was as good as was ever pulled off a gridiron. Pretty strong dope, that, but his booting average was just exactly one thousand, three dropkicks out of three attempts, and twice he successfully kicked goal—going some, eh?"

And, looking back at 1912, the *Alligator* on page one founded the most famous of Florida prayers. It read:

"Another secret of those off days was an overdose of confidence, a pleasing dope to have in one's system before the game, but which is rather apt to 'go bad' about the first five minutes of play. It appears to be especially fatal to the Gator race. But who could help taking a swig from its delectable depth after the wonderful Auburn contest (a 13-27 loss)?

"The comparative dope overcame the strongest ones and we had dreams of beating Vandy in but a season or two, and as for those insignificant insects from Tech, who cared about them? But they stung us. Let us now bow our heads in prayer and join in quoting Stetson's motto, 'Wait till next year!'"

It was a typical example of Florida fans' optimism at the start of the year and patience at the end.

That very year, a few days before the season began, the *Alligator* had predicted:

"But with the man-size schedule we have this year, we can only hope for, not expect, a clean slate.

"The four games with South Carolina, Charleston College, Stetson, and Mercer belong to us. Auburn and Georgia Tech, however, will give us games the outcomes of which cannot be safely prophesied."

The *Alligator* had proved amazingly prophetic.

But the season of 1912 was not quite over.

The First "Bowl"

Florida's first post-season spectacle was not against Tulsa in 1952 in the Gator Bowl in Jacksonville but in Havana, Cuba, on Christmas Day, 1912. And there were fireworks that would make the modern-day Orange Bowl affair seem tame.

For a few years the Vedado Athletic Club of Havana had invited an American football team there for a Christmas Day game or two. This year the invitation went to President Murphree and the University of Florida. He agreed, as did Coach Pyle, anxious for one more opportunity to coach that team of Dummy Taylor, Harvey Hestor, Louis Tenney, Sam Buie, and Hoyle Pounds.

Taylor had been acclaimed by the student newspaper as being one who "has stood out as such a pre-eminent star as none has heretofore. To Dummy (real name, Earle, of Gainesville) must go the credit more than to any other one man, of putting Florida on the football map, and it is with regret that we realize that his football days for us are a thing of the past."

But, that was written December 17, 1912, and was not quite true. The Cuban invitation came. Pyle wisely contacted alumni in Tampa, from where his team would embark overseas, and asked that a practice game be worked up. It was, on old Plant Field there against what the record book calls the Tampa Athletic Club. There was some irony there. Rex Farrior, who would go to Florida the next year, play four years of football as center and fullback and be captain in his senior year, played against those 1912 Gators in that game as a Plant High senior.

The 1912 Gators, first "bowl" team, played a game and a half in Havana, Cuba, after the regular season. Florida President A. A. Murphree is at right and Coach Al McCoy at left.

51

His presence, however, did not affect the outcome. The Gators won handily 44-0, then were all-aboard to Cuba.

The story of that trip is best told in terms of the time. Here is an account, untouched:

"We are all Southerners and Democrats, anyhow—which means that we are anti-imperalists and believe in Cuba for Cubans and These United States for all white men. We have believed all that for one long time; but we gripped our principles anew, and with a new heartiness—some of us during the Christmas vacation.

"Cuba isn't so bad—if it is hot, and if the talkers do all talk a Chop Suey sort of language, and if they are shocking free and public about arrests, Cuba isn't so bad; but 'E Pluribus Unum' is one sight a better place to live in.

"The Alligator squad migrated from Gainesville Friday noon, Dec. 20th, and coiled up for the night in the Tampa Bay Hotel in Tampa. Saturday afternoon three or four Tampans rustled out to the Tampa Bay Grounds in automobiles and mourned at the funeral of the Hyde Park Pick-me-ups. The score was Florida 44 and Hopkins 0. Somebody kicked for the other side and Hopkins did the rest of the playing. It is said that Hopkins played on the Yale team—anyway, and this is no sarcasm, he delivered all charges prepaid, the best football of the game. Taylor and Hester were the shiniest Alligators in the aquarium. Teamwork was the point-winner in that shindig.

"Sunday night the gang, plus Bullock and Sutton, who were not afloat in Saturday's firmament, hoisted anchor for Cuba. Tuesday morning, the day before Christmas, the boat 'made' Havana. Representatives of the Vedado Club esconced the Alligators in the Plaza Hotel, the city's best, and later took the crew avoyaging around the place. In the afternoon, the 'string' was transported to the athletic grounds. The weather was terrifyingly hot, however, and Coach only ran the team through a few signals.

"The Christmas game was a gift to Florida 27-0. The Vedado Club, nevertheless, had a 'scrumptious' aggregation and Plant, one of the two Americans on the team, and the Cuban right end starred. Tenney, Merritt and Baker were the Alligators who found room in the showcase.

"Between games, the Florida fellows enjoyed various social

fol-der-ols. They were entertained as guests at 'an affair' at the Vedado Club, and numerous individuals 'put themselves out' to make Havana agreeable to them, including a cousin of the King of Spain, who floated them around in a yacht.

"A part of the second game 'came off' on the thirtieth— the other part hasn't been played yet. About fifteen hundred people spectated—the same number were present at the first contest—and half were policemen. It was the Cuban Athletic Club which offered the feed for the Gators in the second gridiron battle. The team is the champion one of Cuba, and a lively hand-me-out for the Florida eleven. Three years ago it lost to Tulane by a respectable margin only, and two years ago Tulane hauled down its pennant to it. Mississippi A&M, ranked third in the S.I.A.A., won over this bunch of Havana smokers by 11 to 0 merely.

"Florida outplayed the Cubanites during the first quarter, Taylor getting loose twice and making two almost-touchdowns. The referee fought hard, however, and managed to keep the score scoreless by earnest penalization of the Alligators. Finally, when the Florida team had stopped a man at the line on fourth down, and Cuba was in possession of the ball, the Havana Leaf gentlemen continued to drag their bucker forward and onward regardless of the rule. Coach (Pyle) protested, and asked for the legal penalty of fifteen yards. The referee offered him five; but Coach wouldn't bargain with him. Thereupon the referee said he might take five or none. Coach refused to play his team, the referee declared the game forfeited and police inundated the field.

"Coach Pyle was arrested and had a Spanish trial, or part of one—the rest was postponed. During the postponement, Coach and his retinue took ship across the 'glassy sea' for home.

"Lest the uninformed do injustice, be it stated that the Vedado Club, whose guests the Alligators were, acted in shipshape and seamanship fashion.

"Still, Hurrah for These United States."

Pyle was not extradited, nor indeed was his extradition sought by Cuba.

Official Florida Gator football records show only the 27-0 win against the Vedado Club and ignore the part-game played with the Cuban Athletic Club. In Cuba that second one is recorded as a Cuban Club win, by forfeit.

What happened was that the ref in the questionable game was a former coach of the team Florida was playing, and he spoke no English. Pyle, who was excellent at protesting, protested repeatedly the Cuban use of the outlawed flying wedge, as well as pulling and pushing the ball-carrier. It was that latter objection that forced the showdown between Pyle and the ref, when Pyle refused to bargain for the penalty in yards. The police came into the picture because there were paying customers, and a Cuban law said such a game cannot be forfeited but must be played. Pyle and the team went to the station, pleaded, and were released until the trial the next day. They did not wait, but booked passage aboard the *Olivette* about an hour before the trial was scheduled.

The Gators have not been invited back to Havana, nor have they since sought invitation.

One Hundred Forty-Four To Nothing

Surely the high point of Coach Pyle's final, 1913 season came explosively early. It was on Monday afternoon, October 6, the opening game, against Florida Southern, a newcomer to the schedule and opponent of unknown quantity.

The game, played at Gainesville, had W. A. Shands, the former Gator who later became a Florida legislator, as the referee and was played under high school rules. That meant twelve-minute quarters, and as it developed that may have been the best decision Florida Southern made all afternoon.

This was the first Gator team without Dummy Taylor and talented quarterback R. W. Shackleford and menacing Hoyle Pounds. Captained by Louis Tenney, it had some promise, but was still a question mark.

Still, it did not take long to convince Southern what the latest version of the Gators was like. The Moccasins won the toss and did nothing else right all day. As quickly as Southern punted, Florida was on its way. Tenney passed to Harvey Hester for the first touchdown, and Tubby Price kicked the first of 12 extra points.

Tenney passed to George Moseley of Lakeland for a second touchdown, ran over from the 15 for another, and Frank Swanson went 40 for 6 more points. It was quickly 27-0.

That was only the beginning. Before the long afternoon was over, Florida had scored 144 points while holding the visitors scoreless and without a first down. The Gators made 22 touchdowns, losing another on a holding penalty. Four of the

These 1913 Gators set a record that will stand forever. They, under Coach G. E. Pyle at left, beat Florida Southern 144-0!

Gators' six completions were good for touchdowns.

When the massacre was over, Harvey Hester had scored seven touchdowns, a record that still stands. Tenney added five counters, Swanson three, Moseley, J. B. Sutton, James Miller, Roy (Puss) Hancock, Sam Buie, and Rex Farrior one each.

It was the biggest score ever for the Gators, though their confidence was deflated the next week when Auburn won 55-0.

"I must say," said Farrior, a freshman playing in his first game, "I thought after that 144-0 game that college football was a piece of cake. Auburn instructed me otherwise."

56

McCoy's Years

The University of Florida president from 1909 through 1928 was one Dr. Albert Alexander Murphree, a man of high moral standards, social graces, and excellent speaking ability. In the words of one of his students he "knew every student on campus by name and had a way of making each one think he was his best friend. And he may have been."

During his presidency he figured in the selection of seven head coaches, and he intensely wanted a winning team. He always remained close to the squad.

When G. E. Pyle resigned suddenly in the spring of 1914, Dr. Murphree went looking. Everything pointed to Charles J. McCoy, then coach at Sewanee Military Academy. McCoy played football, baseball, basketball, and ran track at the University of Miami in Ohio, and was on a championship football team there in 1908.

In print he was described as "a man most highly recommended in every case. His personality is pleasing but forceful, and he is well able to control men. He has no bad habits, and his heart and ambitions are with his team. Florida should be congratulated on his acquisition."

McCoy began his career in October, 1914, with the newspaper prediction that: "Never before at this stage of the game has the athletic outlook been as bright as now." Then, in qualification, "It is true that the majority of the candidates are light, but they make up for this in speed. Already the line is charging like a veteran and holding like a wall."

Not quite.

McCoy's debut was a 20-0 loss to Auburn at Jacksonville. But one newspaper regarded it as such a moral victory against the defending champions of the South that beneath a picture of McCoy the next day was the caption: "Coach C. J. McCoy—The man who made the football world sit up and take notice last Saturday."

The Auburn game was costly for the Gators. Captain John Sutton left his left tackle position feeling poorly, and a complete physical examination later disclosed a weak heart, ruling out further competition. It was the first of many turns of fate which would be McCoy's undoing, even though he had no control over them.

The new coach brought his team back to whip Kings College 36-0 before falling to Sewanee 26-0. He then won the rest of his games for a 5-2 first year in one of the strangest statistical seasons in Florida history. Those 1914 Gators shut out all five of their victims, but were shut out themselves in both defeats.

Optimism prevailed as prognosticators looked toward the

Coach C. J. McCoy 1914-1916.

The Gators of 1914 move against Sewanee.

next season. The *Alligator* wrote: "It is conceded by football authorities that Florida has the best flightweight team, at least in the South, and one of the very best in the country. With our rapidly growing student body and the whole state to draw from, we shall soon be able to put on the field teams of greater weight."

But it was not to be—at least for 1915. The Gators under McCoy went 4-3, suffering shutouts at the hands of Auburn and Sewanee (both scores were 7-0), and Georgia, 37-0. The only thing resembling a respectable victory was a 14-7 defeat of Tulane.

McCoy, dreaming of winning the S.I.A.A. title, was convinced that he had the basis for a truly great Gator team for 1916. He would not have the kind of team he thought, but he would certainly make history—and it would cost him his job.

1916 — A Special Season

After the 1915 season McCoy had the S.I.A.A. championship in mind. He decided that Florida needed a tougher schedule (schedules were made from year-to-year in those days). So he dropped from the Florida schedule old favorites like Florida Southern, Sewanee, Wofford, and The Citadel. In one of the toughest schedules ever, McCoy assembled a slate of Georgia at Athens, Alabama at Gainesville, Tennessee at Tampa, Mercer at Gainesville, Auburn at Jacksonville, and Indiana at Bloomington, Indiana. There were no breathers.

Things began to go haywire almost immediately. McCoy had found a potentially great quarterback in A. Wakefield (Rammy) Ramsdale, a versatile four-sport athlete. Ramsdale broke his leg playing baseball at Auburn and would not be the same. There was no substitute for the triple-threater.

Then, J. Ham Dowling, a top tackle, chose to move to Georgia Tech, where he sat out a year and became a member of a great 1917 Tech team. When trouble developed on the Mexican border, Everett Yon, the other tackle, was called up by the National Guard and headed southwest for the season.

Rex Farrior, moved from his three years at center into the fullback position because of the loss of personnel, was selected captain of the team. "Everything went wrong," said Rex many years later. "Besides losing some of our key men, we lost numbers. We had almost no substitutes in those days. Coach McCoy was unable to cope with the situation. And while he was not a man given to profanity, I dare say he was tempted."

J. Rex Farrior, Captain 1916.

Instead of the greatest season, the year 1916 became a disaster. The Gators not only lost all five games, they went scoreless in four. Georgia beat them 21-0, Alabama did it 16-0 for Florida's first loss ever at University Field, Tennessee won 24-0, and Auburn outdid them 20-0. All had good teams.

Then came the last game, at Indiana.

"I remember the game well," said Farrior. "We outplayed those fellows. Paul Baker (a sophomore) kicked a field goal, and we led at the half 3-0. Then our best lineman, Orryl Robles, got into a fight with several of those Hoosiers, and the referee, unfriendly to us all day, threw Liza—that was what we called Robles—out of the game and penalized us as well. We did not have a substitute of the quality of Robles, and it led to our defeat by Indiana." The score was 14-3.

Mercer cancelled its game, depriving Florida of its best bet for a victory that season. Florida had gone 0-5 and scored but three points. Not until 1946 would the Gators again go through a season without triumph. In the *Seminole* (yearbook) of that year, there was the consolation:

"All stood shoulder to shoulder and responded with the best they had. While victory never smiled on them, they have the admiration and satisfaction of a loyal student body (of about 300 boys at that time), a student body that supported them through all the trials and troubles of defeat."

Of Coach McCoy the yearbook said: "Coach McCoy has been with us now for three years, during which time we have had countless opportunities to judge his worth. His choice of material is infallible, and under his able direction Florida has become a factor in the S.I.A.A. He has built up an organization which each year proves a greater stumbling block for the crack teams of Auburn and Georgia Tech."

But regardless of the backing from the yearbook, McCoy followed the path of so many other coaches. He was asked not to come back even though "it was not his fault he did not win more," said one of his players.

"Florida had not learned yet that it took more than a coach to win. We still had no scholarships at all. The only thing was that now and then a few of the better players would be found jobs to help them pay their way through school."

"Puss Hancock," said Farrior, "I remember he had a job.

Dr. A. A. Murphree, 1909-28.

They put him in charge of the heating plant for the dormitories, and he got paid for that. Occasionally we could get help. I know I went to Dr. Murphree once and told him I required some assistance. He got me a job selling insurance. I sold one policy, and Dr. Murphree bought that."

Farrior went on to become a coach and administrator, then a lawyer, serving terms as state attorney in Hillsborough County. He and former quarterback W. R. Shackleford eventually formed one of the state's outstanding law firms. Farrior was almost as tough at 70 as he was at 22. Once, after he had reached his 70s, he was accosted in a parking lot by a man who sought to hold him up. Enraged at the man's nerve, Farrior struck the would-be robber, withstood some blows himself, and drove the stunned thief off empty-handed.

Also praising McCoy was Jim Sparkman who played halfback from 1914 through 1916, then went to France with the 82nd (Rainbow) Division during World War I. Sparkman returned in 1919 to captain the team.

"Coach McCoy was a real gentleman. He used no profanity off the field or on it and would not tolerate its use by his players. He also taught you before the game and then left all signal-calling to the quarterback. I remember once after we'd worked and worked on a series of downs, Rammy Ramsdale was quarterbacking his first time as a starter. It was against The Citadel. He called for me to go off tackle. He called it again and again and again, until we'd marched the full length of the field with only me carrying the ball.

"I asked him why he'd not called any other plays, and urged that he do so. But he said he couldn't think of any of the others."

Said Farrior, speaking of the 1916 season: "I realize we won no game on the record, but it is the conclusion of many that without the problems that befell us we could have been the greatest."

The *Seminole* said only: "We fought a good fight, and that can be our satisfaction."

A Gator's Best Friend

During these years of Florida football, the student newspaper was the very best off-the-field friend of the team and coach. Editorials repeatedly berated those who would not attend the games ($1 for a season), or subscribe to the *Alligator* for that matter. It editorialized on the benefits of athletics in general and in particular at Florida, under whomever was coaching at the time. It urged students to try out for the team, "older students" to help coach, carried detailed accounts of the athletic association meetings (the total receipts from football in 1914 were $1,997.50, expenses $2,816.90, thus a loss of $819.40).

The *Alligator* carried long stories on the "scrub" team, as the non-varsity unit was called quite unabashedly, and reported President Murphree's pre-game speech before a contest with Mercer as being "a regular Give Me Victory or Give Me Death" exciter. It gave great play to rule changes, such as after the 1914 season when the S.I.A.A. ruled that a fourth down pass out of bounds went over to the opponent not at the point where it left the playing field, but back at the scrimmage line. Other rule changes covered by the *Alligator*: it was unlawful to run into and knock down "the fullback" after he had punted the ball; a center would have to snap the ball with a continuous motion instead of faking the snap to lure the enemy off sides; and numbers were required on the backs of players.

And as the *Alligator* was the critic of its students and team, it also was their public defender. After Auburn had

A Florida game at Gainesville in 1917.

beaten Florida 20-0 in Jacksonville in the opener of the 1914 season, Jacksonville authorities wrote a letter to the *Alligator* notifying students that there would be no betting allowed in the stands at games there, noting that "during last Saturday's game there were a great many arguments that resulted in a good deal of bad language being used." The authorities then said they did not imply that the students were guilty of past misdeeds but were simply putting them on notice. *Alligator* editor H. L. DeWolf, a devoted football fan, wrote this stirring editorial:

"Now the *Alligator* does not wish to seem didactic or radical in our statements but we have an apology to make for in our opinion this habit of betting on major sports in schools and colleges is the greatest evil that the promoters of amateur athletics here in the South have to contend with; that rather than being a manifestation of true college spirit and sportsmanship, it forms an almost insurmountable barrier in the path of these two elements—these elements without which we might far better have no athletics at all. At the Auburn-Florida game in Jacksonville we noticed the very things that have caused the complaint to the authorities there. We saw an Auburn alumnus tauntingly waving money in the face of our crowd, and we saw former students and supporters of Florida openly and loudly negotiating bets on every hand. In all fairness to our readers we will say that we saw nothing of the kind on the part of any student at present registered for work, but still to be fair we will say that betting is occasionally carried on among a few of our constituency. We realize that only in a few cases is that betting carried on purely for the sake of making money, but even at that when it reaches the stage that it reached at the Auburn-Florida game, we can conceive nothing that will so damn the progress of an institution of learning as does the same gambling spirit.

"When viewed from the outside it makes little difference whether the guilty party is student or merely an ardent supporter. He wears the Florida colors and to all appearances is a Florida man, and in every case, the stamp of disapproval is placed upon the entire institution and the vilest slander is spread broadcast.

"It seems to us that in the face of these facts it behooves every Florida man to cast the eye of disapproval upon all betting at games in the future thus not only avoiding the possibility of arrest and consequent embarrassment to any of our own party or of our friends but also that the face of amateur athletics may be cleaned of this blot."

DeWolf then encouraged 100 percent turnout at the upcoming Sewanee game, promising that "if we beat their rooters then the Gators will romp on the Tigers, chew their ears, and add a few knots to their tails, as well as markings to their bodies."

Apparently the rooters did not root hard enough. Score: Sewanee 26, Florida 0.

The Best Of Buser

It was 1917 and war clouds were hanging over Europe. Football's future looked uncertain at Florida, but Dr. Murphree went out and found a new coach anyway. A. L. Buser was hired from Wisconsin to pick up the pieces of the disheartening 0-5-0 1916 season, trying to build around a few veterans from that outfit.

The 1917 Gators began well, beating South Carolina 21-13. But then they lost four of their next five games by lopsided scores, 52-0 to Tulane, 55-7 to Clemson, 52-0 to Kentucky, and 68-0 to Auburn for the worst defeat in the school's history. The only other 1917 win was over Florida Southern 19-7.

World War I joined forces with an influenza epidemic that hit the college and the team to ruin the football program for 1918. The only game played was a 14-2 loss to Camp Johnson.

In 1919 Buser began his third year with a few veterans returning from the war to play out their eligibility.

"Even after that war there was some friction between us returning vets and non-vets," confessed team Captain Jim Sparkman. "We'd win some games, but we still couldn't compete with schools like Georgia."

And that Buser-coached team of 1919 suffered the ultimate indignity: It lost to Florida Southern 7-0.

The game was scheduled for a high school field in St. Petersburg. "We were so confident not all the regulars started," said Sparkman. "We were already in trouble by the time we got

These seven ex-Gator captains attended the 1955 Homecoming Game. Reading left to right: Jim Sparkman, 1919, of Tampa; Alfred Marshall, 1917 of Clearwater; Arthur H. Fuller, elected for 1918, of Gastonia, North Carolina; J. Rex Farrior, 1916, of Tampa; Louis Earle Tenney, 1913, of Palatka; Sam Buie, 1912, of Ocala; and Neil S. (Bo-Gator) Storter, 1911, of Brownsville, Texas.

into the game.

"I remember the Southern touchdown came on a play mixup by us. In those days the center had to lead the tailback as he began to break to the right or left with the play. Our center, Tootie Perry, got mixed up. The play went right, and he centered the ball left. A Southern man rushed through and picked it up and scored the touchdown. It was the worst kind of humiliation. It was our lowest point in Florida football history to that time—losing to Southern." Florida had beaten the same school 144-0 in 1913.

There was one favorable note. Several of the best Southern players were recruited and played for the Gators the next year. But, though the Gators wound up 5-3 for the season, they beat nobody of note, winning over Georgia A&M, Mercer, Stetson, South Carolina, and Oglethorpe, while losing to Georgia, Tulane, and, in the final blow, Southern.

A 7-8 record for three years meant that Buser had to be on his way, though a *Seminole* yearbook consoled, regarding the 1919 season: "Each man deserves credit for the part he played. The student body unites in thanking the team."

The teens were gone, the Twenties ready to roar. Florida football at Gainesville was 14 years old. Its record, manufactured by four coaches, was 56-31-5, with the best mark the 5-0-1 of 1911, the worst the 0-5-0 of 1916.

G. E. Pyle had the best scoresheet with a record of 26-7-2 for a win percentage of .771 during 1909-1913.

President Murphree went looking for another G. E. Pyle for 1920.

The Twenties Roar In

Florida football in the Twenties, 1920-1929, under four coaches would win 64, lose 23 and tie 8 for a .621 percentage, reaching peaks not to be matched for three decades. Yes, the Florida fans of the Twenties were treated to undreamed of glories, their first genuine all-Southern, their first all-American, their first, in America, post-season game, and the first 11-game schedule. They saw one Gator team come within a point of the Southern title, and another within two points of a trip to the Rose Bowl. They saw their Gators beat Alabama, Auburn, Georgia, and Georgia Tech for the first time. They saw their school's enrollment triple, and begin to attract out-of-state athletes and a coaching staff with a head man and three assistants. Yes, their university and its football team were growing up.

Squads grew in size, and the sixty-minute player was no longer so necessary. Rules gained sophistication, and at last uniforms which offered genuine protection replaced the old helmetless, lightly padded, inadequate ones.

While full-blown scholarships were slow in coming, the sponsorship plan was developed and put into successful operation, especially in the Jacksonville, Tampa, and Miami areas. Under this plan, clubs, companies, or an individual would sponsor an athlete's education. The Hebrew Club in Jacksonville financed Goldy Goldstein, a talented guard. Others to engage in this practice were the Jacksonville Ford Agency, the Chevrolet agency, and the George Washington Hotel which played host to Gators on their regular game visits.

71

First Gator freshman team, 1922.

The "Good Times" began at the very beginning of the decade when university president, Dr. Murphree, who had made several trips west in the quest of men to guide his beloved Gators, decided on a successor to A. J. Buser. The choice of W. G. Kline was interesting in that he was not just a coach but a lawyer and an Elk, with contacts in the Midwest.

Kline was an Illinois graduate and ex-halfback and track star who had previously coached at a Waukegan high school, Nebraska Wesleyan, and Nebraska, where he finished his law degree. He was to produce records of 6-3 in 1920, 6-3-2 in 1921, and 7-2 in 1922. The 6-3 start in 1920 included losses to the big two teams, Georgia 56-0 and Tulane 14-0, and an upset by Oglethorpe. The wins included an unusual 1-0 victory when Rollins did not show and the game was forfeited.

Though his 1920 start was not overly impressing, Kline got everyone's attention in 1921 by (1) beating Alabama 9-7, a first for the Gators over that school, and (2) by scheduling an 11th, post-season game against North Carolina, played in Jacksonville and lost, 10-14.

His 7-2 final season in 1922 was his best in spite of an embarrassing start with a 7-6 loss to Furman, and Florida's not being able to "handle" Harvard to the tune of 24-0, on their trip east.

One of Kline's absolute playing heroes during the first two years was the late Carl (Tootie) Perry. A guard-center, Tootie was all-Southern in both junior and senior years and also captain of every game in his last two seasons. His specialty was blocking punts, and he was among the largest Gators of the day, 5-10 and 235 pounds.

Other players of gift and contribution included another Perry, guard Henry, 6 foot, 247 pounds, and nicknamed "Little Tootie;" halfback Hoyt Carlton of Wauchula; halfback Stewart Pomeroy of Tampa; end Bob Swanson of Texarkana, Arkansas; fullback Jim Merrin of Rackmore, Georgia; 6-6 center Shorty Gunn of Kissimmee; quarterback George Stanley of Jacksonville; and, of course, Captain Paul Baker.

Two actions of Coach Kline proved to be vital contributions to Florida's football progress: (1) The convincing of a Gainesville visitor, from Arkansas, to enroll and play his football for the Gators, and (2) extending an invitation to a

Coach William Kline, 1920-22.

young major assigned to the university's ROTC program to become his assistant coach.

These two men turned out to be respectively Ark (as in Arkansas) Newton, one of the most celebrated and talented Gators of all time, and Major James A. Van Fleet, who would succeed to the position of coach perhaps a little sooner than Kline would have liked, and later become one of this country's most effective generals and international statesmen.

Though Coach Kline was the one who actually convinced Ark Newton to join his team, he was not directly responsible for bringing him South. He was told about Florida by a relative whom he was visiting, and upon leaving the school after a little preliminary investigation he ran into a practice game on the school field and stopped to watch. Just the sight of Ark so impressed Captain Perry that he offered him a uniform and coaxed him onto the field. The first ball Newton kicked was so impressive that it got the attention of coaches Kline and Van Fleet, and the rest is history.

Newton played four years for the Gators. He was a superb punter and classic broken field runner, fearless and football-wise. "I'd have to judge him my best," said Van Fleet, whose 1924 team led the nation and brought national attention to the school and program. "He had an unorthodox style," continued Van Fleet, "and we tried to change it. That was a mistake. He went back to his own style, and was often a savior to us." It is recorded that he once punted 92 yards against the Mississippi College Aggies, and that in a game against the Army at West Point, that same year, "Captain Ark carved his name in the football hall of fame when he grabbed the ball behind his own goal line in the third period and dashed the entire distance of the field for the Gators lone score of the game," a 14-7 loss that was regarded as a moral victory. Van Fleet said flatly that the Gators were gypped by officials at his old school; he was not just a graduate of West Point but had been a standout player.

Though born in the North where his family had moved to avoid the yellow fever epidemics of Florida, Van Fleet was a graduate of Summerlin Institute in Bartow and a classmate of Spessard L. Holland, who later became governor and then United States senator.

As a young captain in 1919-1920, he was stationed at Kansas State as ROTC program assistant. His boss, Major Terrell, loved football and introduced him to the Kansas coach Charley Bachman, who was later to become a great Gator coach. Terrell suggested to Bachman that Van Fleet work with him. He did and after the season the athletic department voted Van Fleet a $300 honorarium for his contribution to the team, which as a captain and the father of two baby girls he needed desperately.

In 1920 he was sent to South Dakota State College to handle the ROTC program. He succeeded Omar Bradley who later became general of the armies of the United States and a major factor in the World War II victory in Europe. Van Fleet was there for several months when the military advisors job at the University of Florida opened up, a fact of which he was not aware until Dr. Murphree (president) wrote him and asked if he would like to have the job. He jumped at the chance.

Van Fleet was no sooner relocated in Gainesville in that summer of 1921, when Coach Kline, learning of Van Fleet's background, offered him an assistant coaching position.

"I agreed. I do not recall that I received any pay at all," said Van Fleet, a fine cut of a man who commanded the immediate respect of his players. He was a man destined for such great military achievements in the Korean War and such great military diplomacy in saving Greece from Communism that these feats are object lessons in the Pentagon and State Departments.

Van Fleet's 1923 and 1924 teams were outstanding. Because of his background he developed a two-game series with Army (both games regrettably lost, respective scores being 20-0 in 1923 and 14-7 in 1924), but in 1923 he tied Georgia Tech, 7-7, and in 1924 he led his Gators to their most significant victory to that date. They went to Alabama and upset that mighty team of Wallace Wade's, 16-6. An Alabama win would have given her the Southern championship. Van Fleet said that Wade never spoke to him again.

So Van Fleet's 1924 team, captained by Newton, ended up with a 6-2-2. They again tied Georgia Tech 7-7 which was impressive in itself, beat Rollins 77-0, had a controversial loss to Army 7-14, a controversial tie with the University of Texas, in Austin 7-7, and had a record of traveling more and farther than any college football team in America.

Van Fleet gave much to Florida, even his vacation time. When his four year assignment there was over in August of 1924 and he was ordered to the Panama Canal Zone, he took the four months leave he had coming and stayed to coach the 1924 Gators on to national prominence. All in all, he was a truly uplifting force in Florida football.

Three Early Biggies

Florida played three games in the 1923-24 seasons which focused real national attention on the Gators for the first time and did more to satisfy Florida partisans than anything in the previous twenty-plus years of the Gators' intercollegiate play. The first of the Big Three was in "family play" against Alabama in Birmingham.

It was 1923 and Van Fleet's Gators had built a record of 5-1-2 by tying a good Mississippi A&M team. That left only the season finale with Alabama, in its first campaign under Wallace Wade. The Crimson Tide had experienced a couple of so-so years before Wade took over, but in the 1923 season, by the time the Florida date arrived, Alabama was winging its way toward the Southern championship.

Fresh off consecutive wins of 10-8 over Kentucky, 30-0 over Louisiana State, and 36-0 over Georgia, the Tide stood at 7-1-1, having lost to rugged Syracuse in New York and played a scoreless tie with Georgia Tech.

It was a rainy, dreary day in Birmingham on November 29, 1923, and Florida was expected to offer little opposition. Even ticket sales were slow.

In an attempt to promote the contest Alabama publicity man Champ Pickens had found a stuffed alligator, photographed it, and added art work that showed tiny Crimsons swarming over the beaten, puzzled alligator. Posters were made and passed out to drum up interest in the contest. Those which fell into the hands of Coach Van Fleet and the Gators caused quite a stir.

Five times in the first half the fired-up Gators pushed back Alabama within Florida's 10-yard line. Once Alabama made it across and led 6-0 at the half.

Newton's great punting had helped keep the Gators out of trouble in the first half as the teams tried to combat each other and the ankle-deep mud created by the constant rain before and during the game.

At intermission Van Fleet came up with an idea that would make the difference in the battle.

"My players were soaked to the skin, not just with water but with mud. And we had on those old ribbed stockings. They were carrying a couple of pounds of mud each. I had my boys take off their stockings, and the regulars changed uniforms with the ones not playing. We were dry and lighter without the stockings.

"I waited until the last minute to take the team back out into the rain. Alabama was already lined up for the kickoff, and later Coach Wade would be furious. He said we left them standing there to get wet and cold while we delayed. He was so mad he never spoke to me again. But, as I remember, he had his boys play barelegged in the future in bad weather."

Quarterback Jones went 11 yards for a Florida touchdown in the third quarter, and the score remained 6-6 when he missed his try for a point-after. Moments later a Newton punt of more than 60 yards put 'Bama in a hole, and a poor Crimson Tide kick gave Florida good field position. The Gators worked the ball into a spot where Jones kicked a field goal to make it an unbelievable 9-6. Jones added another touchdown in the fourth quarter to make it 16-6.

Newton's punting was given a big role in the victory, and Van Fleet revealed a little secret about that.

"Tom Sebring helped in that game with an idea," he said. "Ark needed a little more time (to punt) than most. Sebring proposed we worry only about the kick and not the runback, leaving an extra blocker for Ark. It worked."

Though Jones scored all the points, he was not the only hero, Van Fleet said. There were "Robbie Robinson at tackle, Spec Lightsey at end, Joe Meerin at end, Goldy Goldstein and Oscar Norton at guards, Sam Cornwall at center, Brown and

James A. Van Fleet
Head Coach

H. L. Sebring
Assistant Coach

Everett Yon
Assistant Coach

Carl Middlekauf in the backfield. And remember, they played both ways. We had beaten a great coach and a great team at a great moment in their hometown. We had knocked Alabama out of the championship."

Van Fleet moved the Gators into the 1924 season with big travel plans.

The opener was at Florida's newly completed Fleming Field, a 77-0 victory over Rollins. Then the Gators went to Atlanta to tie Georgia Tech 7-7, to Tampa to beat Wake Forest 34-0, to Austin, Texas, for a 7-7 deadlock with the Longhorns, and back to Gainesville for a 27-0 win over Florida Southern.

Van Fleet's next adventure was to West Point for a bitter 14-7 loss to his old team. Then the Gators returned to the

South for a 10-0 upset by Mercer at Macon, Georgia. A 27-0 win over Mississippi A&M at Montgomery preceded a 10-0 defeat of Drake in homecoming, and the finale was a 16-6 triumph over Washington and Lee at Jacksonville.

The tie at Texas was gratifying to Van Fleet, and the game was unusual and controversial enough to put the Gators back into the spotlight they had enjoyed after beating Alabama a year earlier.

"Texas was coached by Doc Stewart," Van Fleet recalled. "He and Coach Kline (the former Florida coach) had become bitter enemies. The Florida-Texas game was scheduled before Stewart got the job in Austin. As soon as he saw it on the schedule, he began accusing Florida of having a pro team. He demanded verification of ages. He called Ark Newton a pro brought in by Kline.

"We scored on an illegal play, but it wasn't detected. Jones' touchdown pass was caught by Spec Lightsey who was actually a tackle on the play.

"But they got even. As the first half was ending, time ran out before the ball could be put in play. There was a big argument and somehow the officials gave Texas one more play. They scored. Went around right end...Damn," said the general, remembering.

The 14-7 frustration at West Point, Van Fleet's alma mater, hurt worse.

"I hate to say it but they robbed us," he said. "Twice we scored, our backs pushing across the goal line, but the officials would not blow the whistle until our boys were pushed back. The rule was as it is now. Break the imaginary barrier above the line and it's a touchdown.

"Then, later in the game on an important play, Bill Middlekauf was clipped right in front of our bench, and they did not call it. He was clipped so severely it broke his left leg.

"It was a disgrace. But it was no excuse for us going back and losing to Mercer. Damn," said the general.

The Coach And Justice

Florida is probably the only university which has had a head football coach who went on to become chief justice of the state supreme court. H. L. (Tom) Sebring did that, later was prominent in the Nuremberg trials after World War II, and finally became dean of the Stetson University Law School. Florida did not play Stetson during Sebring's coaching years, so he did not have to live with that reminder when he went to Stetson.

Van Fleet urged that Sebring be hired as assistant coach, and when he left he all but willed the head job to the former Kansas State end. Sebring had a degree in architecture so it is established that he drew the best blackboard plays of any Gator coach ever.

He had no sooner arrived in Gainesville than he enrolled in the law school and eventually received his degree before departing after the 1927 season. It was clear that he wanted a law career over coaching, though there are many who believe Florida never had a wiser football mind than Tom Sebring.

"He was a total gentleman," said Nash Higgins, "and I have been associated with the best—Knute Rockne, Bob Zuppke, Stagg, Warner—and I knew none who was any better than Tom Sebring."

Higgins and Joe Bedenk were hired by Athletic Director Everett Yon as assistants for Sebring. Formerly of Wabash, Higgins had been the head coach of Tampa's Hillsborough High, a longtime producer of Gator talent. The year he was hired he had just produced a great high school team and brought no less than seven of his players to Florida, including one of the greatest guards ever, Jimmy Steele. Higgins also coached the Gator track team to great heights, losing only one dual meeting in nearly a decade, and stayed as an assistant for Sebring's successor, Charley Bachman.

Bedenk, trained to teach the interior line play Florida needed so badly at that time, joined Florida the same day as Higgins and signed a five-year contract. With two years to go on that contract he left and eventually wound up as head coach at Penn State.

Sebring's three coaching years, 1925-27, were an unusual combination. He took Van Fleet's 1924 team that had gone 6-2-2 and extended the record to 8-2 in 1925, the first time Florida had ever won 8 games in a season.

The Gators slipped to a disturbing 2-6-2 in 1926, but strong recruiting not only produced a 7-3 mark in 1927, it

Edgar Jones of Jacksonville was the Gator quarterback in 1923-24-25, making all-Southern and serving as team captain in 1925. Jones returned to Florida to serve as athletic director in 1930.

formed the basis for a great season the next year.

Sebring's 1927 team was his best because, though it included a humiliating 12-0 upset at the hands of Davidson and losses to Georgia and North Carolina State, it also encompassed the first victory ever over Auburn and another stirring win over Alabama in Montgomery.

The triumph over Auburn, after six straight defeats dating back to 1912, was sweet indeed. Here is how it happened, as reported by newsmen then:

"Three days after the Davidson fiasco, if one should essay to call it that, yet many teams of big reputations, tumble in the face of smaller and weaker opponents, for that is the inevitable of law of sport—Florida elected a new leader in football. Frank Oosterhoudt was declared ineligible by the faculty committee on athletics. To his post by unanimous vote went Wee Willie Middlekauf, and as captain of the Fighting Gators, Bill was among the finest in Gator history.

"The University student body rallied behind the squad as they prepared for the journey to Auburn, Alabama, and gave on October 6 the greatest sendoff a Florida team ever received. It did the boys a world of good. They treked to the 'Lovely Village' with fight in their systems for Coach Sebring, for Capt. Bill, and for old Florida. It was homecoming at Auburn, and the Tiger eleven had never been beaten on the Plains under such auspicious circumstances. And though Auburn battled like the Grecian iron men of old, Florida ploughed their way to a decisive 33-6 victory—the first an Orange and Blue machine had ever registered over an Auburn eleven.

"No time did the Gators seem to play quite so well—as a team. Not a flaw presented itself. Early in the first quarter when quarterback Goof Bowyer knifed over left tackle and cut back and Willie DeHoff clipped away the safety man, there wasn't an upright figure on the field but that of Bowyer, and Goof raced forty-four yards for a touchdown. Crabtree later made two touchdowns, Middlekauf and Owens one. It was a glorious triumph."

Objectivity requires reporting that Auburn beat nobody that year, and the victory was the beginning of a five-year winning streak over the Plainsmen. Neither did Alabama have much of a season for a Wallace Wade team, and the Gators won

13-6 in Montgomery.

Sebring closed his Florida coaching career with a 7-6 win from Maryland in Jacksonville on a day so cold that only 2,000 people showed up to watch the contest.

"It wasn't long after that," said Higgins, "I came home from a scouting trip, picked up the evening paper, and saw where Sebring was out. I didn't understand it then, and I don't now."

Not only did Sebring produce two of the finest teams that Florida has ever known, he brought in much of the talent that would create a great 1928 team. Clyde Crabtree and Dale Vansickle, for instance, became Gator stars. When Sebring left after 1927, whether of his own volition to study law or because of administration pressure (the Davidson loss had been particularly embarrassing), he left a stable of marvelous athletes, the greatest ever assembled at Florida up to that day, in numbers, size, and speed.

Whatever the reason behind Sebring's departure, it was the best thing that ever happened to him, for he then turned to the beginning of a distinguished career in law.

President Dwight Eisenhower pins a third Distinguished Service Medal on tunic of Gen. James A. Van Fleet, the four-star general and onetime Florida Gator football coach.

Rise And Fall Of The Gator "Empire"

Chosen to succeed the scholarly Sebring was Charles W. Bachman, head coach at Kansas State and former boss of both Sebring and Van Fleet. A strong-willed disciplinarian of German extraction, Bachman was a great believer in exercises and all manner of off-season programs. He had been head coach at Kansas State since 1920 and at 35 was in the prime of his career.

Bachman played college football at Notre Dame and later played at the Great Lakes Naval Station during World War I with George Halas, founder of the Chicago Bears and co-founder of the National Football League. That Great Lakes team went to the Rose Bowl.

Before taking the head job at Kansas State, Bachman was top man at Northwestern for a year.

At the time of his selection for the Florida job, Bachman had already been given credit for conceiving many improvements in football pants and protection pads.

Just before the search for a new coach began, Dr. John J. Tigert took over the presidency of the University of Florida and was destined to enjoy the great 1928 season and the fruits of Dr. Murphree's long efforts to build a football team of championship quality and national notice.

But first came the task of selecting a coach.

That duty fell to Athletic Director Everett Yon, who started his search by calling Knute Rockne at Notre Dame. Rockne recommended Bachman for the job and then called him

Charles W. Bachman
Head Coach of Football

and told him so.

Bachman agreed to meet with Yon at the coaches' convention in New York in January, 1928.

"It was an interesting coincidence," Bachman recalled. "I was debating resigning. Mrs. Bachman had asthma, and we had been told to leave the climate. I had sent her to Texas. I met with Yon in New York and then accompanied him by train to Jacksonville to go look over Florida. I remember when we got to Jacksonville it was 18 degrees above zero, and we drove in Yon's open Dodge car all the way to Gainesville. I have never since been so cold, never was before, and yet Yon, the salesman, never once mentioned the weather. He didn't apologize for it or even acknowledge that it was anything but 75 degrees and sunshiny.

"I met with the athletic committee. They offered me the same thing I was making at Kansas, $7,000 a year. I got one raise before I left Florida in 1932 for the head job at Michigan State. That was for $500. Then when I went to Michigan, I got

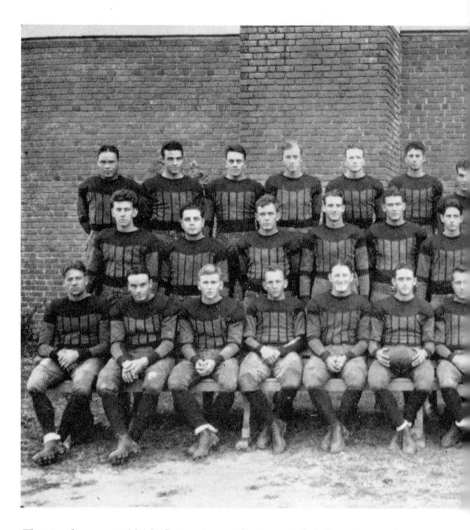

This is the great 1928 Gator team that went 8-1-0 and was the national scoring champion.

the same, $7,500.

"Anyway, the one thing I didn't like was that there already were assistants with long contracts (Brady Cowell, Joe Bedenk, and Nash Higgins) so I asked to bring along one."

Bachman accepted, put Higgins in charge of scouting and the Omelets (as the reserves were called), Bedenk in charge of the interior line, and Cowell in charge of the freshmen. Then he

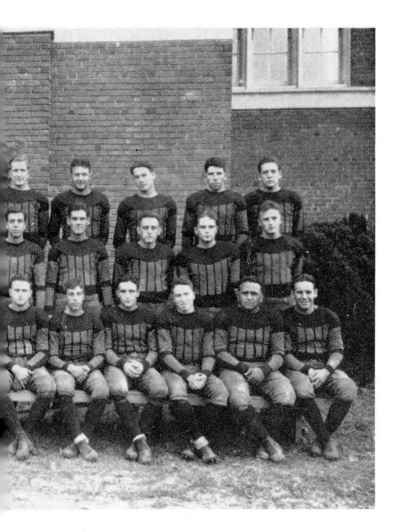

brought in Joe Holsinger to handle the backs and chose to direct the ends himself.

The stage was set to get ready for a great season. Bachman's first team was left almost intact by Sebring.

"I brought in no one," said Bachman. "They were all there when I arrived."

The few missing from the 7-3, 1927, squad were Captain

Horse Bishop, Cecil Beck, Ion Walker, Tom Fuller, Charlie Tucker, Goldstein, and Middlekauf.

It was a time for history to be made.

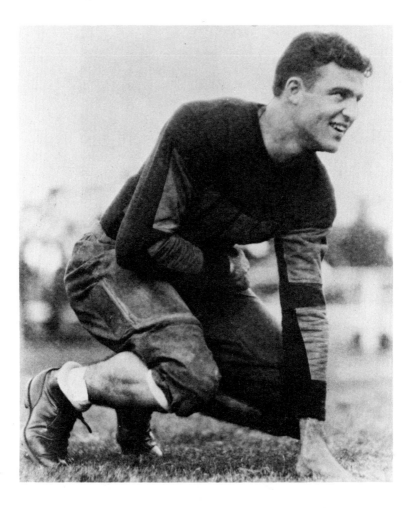

End Dale Vansickle, 1928, Florida's first all-American.

A Cold Day In Knoxville

After all these seasons, this—1928—surely was the genuine article, a Year of the Gator. Following eight straight victories, only a win over Tennessee was needed to wrap up the package. Such a win would produce a Southern Conference championship—or at least a tie with Georgia Tech—and there was talk of a bid to the Rose Bowl.

It did not seem important that starting tackle Jus Clemons was left in Gainesville for the Tennessee trip with "a lung infection," or that "in Jacksonville, Joe Bryan, the other starting tackle, got into an argument with Coach Bedenk and got off the train there and did not make the trip."

When the Gators' train pulled into Knoxville, it was bitter cold. Still water iced almost immediately.

But the future had a warming effect on the Gators.

Florida was favored over Bob Neyland's Vols after Tennessee had played a scoreless deadlock with Kentucky (4-3) a week earlier to run its record to 8-0-1.

The visitors' wins over two mutual opponents had been more impressive. Florida crushed Sewanee unmercifully 71-0 while Tennessee's margin had been 37-0, and the Gators had smacked Washington and Lee 60-6 the week before the Tennessee game, while Tennessee had won 26-7 earlier.

Only two things dampened Florida's confidence. Although it was unclear what was wrong, Neyland arrived at the game in a wheelchair and coached from it. One witness claimed that at the game's end, the Vol coach arose from his seat as if healed

CRABTREE

BETHEA

Two genuine Gator heroes of the Bachman Years and the 1928 team were halfback Red Bethea, and ambidextrous quarterback Clyde (Cannonball) Crabtree.

instantly by the contest's outcome. Florida's other problem was the weather. It was bitter cold, and the field was slushy. Florida's fleet backs depended on good footing for their speed.

"I had mud cleats for the backs, but none for the line," Bachman said.

Tennessee scored first, in the second quarter, when the great Gene McEver ploughed over. Bobby Dodd, the Vols' sophomore quarterback, had set up the score with his passing, and then his connection with E. H. Alley for the point-after made a big difference later in the day.

It was 7-0 at the half, but Florida scored early in the third period, powered by the running of Goodbread and Brumbaugh and Crabtree's pass to Vansickle at the two. Goodbread scored, but Brumbaugh's attempted pass to Crabtree for the point was not good.

No matter. Florida led the nation in scoring and was

rolling.

Then came a slipup.

"I ran out and tried to lateral to Brumbaugh," recalled Crabtree. "He was in the open. If I'd pulled it off, we'd have had a score."

It did not work that way. Dave McArthur, a Volunteer from St. Petersburg, hit Crabtree's arm at the moment of release, and the ball flew up and short and into the arms of onrushing Buddy Hackman who went 70 yards for a score. Dodd's placement for the point was no good.

The Gators stormed back, driving 70 yards only to be stopped at the two, "and as good as Muddy Waters and Dashwood Hicks played, we missed our regular tackles in there," said Bachman.

Tennessee punted only to the thirty, and Brumbaugh, the best passer on the team, hit halfback Tommy Owens at the one and Crabtree scored.

It was going to be a tie, 13-13.

No it was not. Brumbaugh's placement try was blocked.

It was going to be a loss. A 13-12 loss. A loss that would haunt Florida football history forever.

"I felt awful at the time, but I feel worse every year that passes," said Crabtree. "I never knew it would mean so much to us all."

It may have left some wounded pride, but it did not cost a Rose Bowl bid. Georgia Tech, which had completed its season before the Florida-Tennessee game and had a 9-0 record under Bill Alexander, had already received and accepted the bid.

The word was that Bachman had a wire in his pocket saying Florida would be considered for the Rose Bowl with a victory.

"I remember he waved the wire at us and said it was from the Rose Bowl and that we would be considered...I thought," said Crabtree.

"I remember, too," said McEwen. "We were lying on a hillside at a country club where we were staying, having a team meeting and he told us. Yes, I know he told us."

"Well, maybe I mentioned something. I don't remember," said Bachman, retired, in his 80s and living in Pompano. "I knew Tech had the bid. That was for certain. Maybe I thought

if we won they'd reconsider, and I said that. I can't remember."

Another story about that game has lived through the ages. Supposedly the Vols, seeking to slow the Gators backs, wet the field all day on the day before the game so the playing surface would freeze overnight, then thaw, and turn to mud.

A student and devoted fan who made the trip is certain to this day that it happened.

Bachman disagrees: "I don't think they'd do that. I think it was natural from previous snow and rain and the cold."

Was Neyland really ill? "I don't know," answered Bachman. "He was in that wheelchair."

Then he added: "Neither his being in the wheelchair nor the wet ground caused us to miss the two points or not to complete that lateral to Brumbaugh. I can see it now. I have seen it for nearly half a century."

Backs on the great 1928 Gator team.

Georgia Tech went on to the Rose Bowl and beat California 8-7.

In a few years the quarterback of the Volunteers that cold day in Knoxville became Coach Bobby Dodd at Georgia Tech.

"I remember that game. How I remember it," said Dodd. "When it began, I thought our Tennessee team could beat anybody anywhere. When it was over, I confess, we were a bit lucky to beat Florida.

"Way back when I was an assistant at Tech, Dr. Tigert offered me the head job at Florida (it was for 1940, when Tom Lieb later was hired), but Coach Alexander suggested I stay at Tech."

He stayed with the Engineers, but later sent his favorite assistant to become Florida's head coach and his own son to become a Gator—and beat him.

But if Dodd thought Tennessee was lucky that day,

UNIVERSITY OF FLORIDA EIGHTH ANNUAL FOOTBALL BANQUET

MENU

CELERY HEARTS   QUEEN OLIVES

SALTED ALMONDS

OYSTER COCKTAIL

ROAST FLORIDA TURKEY
—Sage Dressing
—Cranberry Sauce

SNOWFLAKE POTATOES   CREAMED ONIONS

BUTTERED BEETS

WHITE HOUSE FRUIT SALAD
—Mayonnaise

ENGLISH PLUM PUDDING
—Original Sauce

IMPORTED SWISS CHEESE

SALTINES

COFFEE

MINTS

CIGARS
CIGARETTES

THE WHITE HOUSE

Florida's 1928 Results

'Gators	28	Southern	0
'Gators	27	Auburn	0
'Gators	73	Mercer	0
'Gators	14	N. C. State	7
'Gators	71	Sewanee	6
'Gators	26	Georgia	6
'Gators	27	Clemson	6
'Gators	60	Wash. & Lee	6
'Gators	12	Tennessee	13
	336		44

Florida's 1929 Schedule

Sept. 28—Southern at Gainesville
Oct. 5—V. M. I. at Jacksonville, or Tampa
Oct. 12—Auburn, at Auburn, Ala.
Oct. 19—Ga. Tech, at Atlanta, Ga.
Oct. 26—Georgia, at Jacksonville.
Nov. 2—Harvard, at Cambridge, Mass.
Nov. 16—Clemson, at Gainesville (Homecoming)
Nov. 23—South Carolina, at Columbia, S. C.
Nov. 28—W. & L., at Jacksonville (Thanksgiving)
Dec. 7—Tennessee (tentative)

DECEMBER 18, 1928

Program for Football Banquet of 8-1 Gators of 1928, with autographs.

Bachman went just one step further: "We would have beaten California in the Rose Bowl," he said. "Worse than Tech did. On a dry field."

The Legend Of '28

Nothing about Florida football has ever been so celebrated as the fabulous team of 1928. The Gators went 8-1, losing only to an unbeaten Tennessee team 13-12 in the mud at Knoxville in the final game of the year.

Bachman's charges that year beat Georgia for the first time, 26-6, led the nation in points scored with 336, and produced Florida's first genuine all-American in Dale Vansickle, an exceptional pass-receiver.

Only four members of the 42-man Gator traveling squad that year were from out of state—but one of them was the quarterback, Cannonball Clyde Crabtree, a marvel of an athlete.

The sparkplug of that great Florida team was not recruited and got to Florida pretty much on luck. His name was Clyde Crabtree.

"I had enrolled at Northwestern in 1925. I had a scholarship there, as scholarships went. I waited tables and was a part-time trainer. I didn't like Northwestern so I quit. My mother and stepfather had moved to Haines City. He was going to try real estate there and maybe law. I went to visit them, and they encouraged me to go to Florida so I could be close at home. I remember, my step-dad and I drove to Gainesville to see Everett Yon. We had called him. We went to his home and asked for a scholarship.

"I want you to know," said Crabtree, "I weighed 110 pounds at the time. There trying to get a scholarship at the same time was Alex Reeves, a guard from Alabama who weighed 190. You know who got it.

"But when we got back, my step-dad said he'd send me. He did, and I went out for freshman ball. At Florida I was never on a real scholarship. I waited tables, and Royce Goodbread and I swept out the fraternity house for our room."

Few better things have happened to Florida football than that decision of Crabtree to enroll. Never very big during his career—in 1928 he stood 5-8 and played at 148 pounds— Crabtree was special. He could pass with either arm and could punt with either foot. And he could do either on the run.

"About the most frustrating thing he'd do to the opposition," said Coach Charley Bachman, "was on third down he'd run to his right or left towards the sidelines, and if the safety came up, Crabtree would punt over his head on the run, side-footed. What a weapon he was.

"He was a double-quadruple option. He could sprint out and had the option of running, passing, handing off, or punting. He also was a good receiver."

Assistant Coach Nash Higgins called him a Daniel Boone player: "He played by instinct. That's not all. He had rubberband legs. He'd bounce around. He was never on the bottom of a pile."

Contrary to stories that he learned his techniques by playing soccer in Cicero, Illinois, Crabtree says he learned to pass and kick on the run going either way "from sheer fright. I weighed 110 pounds when I played high school ball."

After college Crabtree stayed in Florida and made a career of education. He retired in 1968, spending his last 10 years as principal at Miami's Palmetto High, where his size was more appropriate to his nickname, Cannonball. When he retired, Crabtree had 220 pounds wrapped on his 5-8 frame.

Florida publicist Frank Wright thought up the name Cannonball. "First it was 'Skeeter.' Then he got going with 'Crafty Clyde Crabtree,'" said Cannonball of Wright. "Then they came up with Cannonball. I remember an Atlanta paper headline, after we got beat up there, saying, 'Crabtree Came Here a Cannonball and Went Home a B-B Shot.'"

The 1928 team was so loaded with talent, particularly in the backfield, Bachman seldom started the same eleven. While he regarded Crabtree, fullback Rainey Cawthon and halves

Royce Goodbread and Carl Brumbaugh as the first four in the backfield, he did not hesitate to start any of the other half dozen backs. Oddly, the team captain, Goof Bowyer, was the second string quarterback. Red Bethea at halfback could have started on any team in the country, but he alternated with Brumbaugh, who called signals. The backfield's average weight was about 168.

The line was talented but not quite so deep. Bill McRae, who became a Rhodes scholar and federal judge, was a brute of a guard and tackle. So were Jus Clemons, Carlos Proctor, Joe Bryan, and Dashwood Hicks. Mike Houser, Chester Allen, Louis Bono, and Bert Grandoff were stellar linemen, and Jimmy Steele and Wilbur James became one of the finest pair of guards in college football. Steele, an all-time great, made all-Southern.

That team did what all great teams do: Someone always came through. When North Carolina State moved towards an upset in the fourth game, Goodbread went on two 70-yard touchdown runs to save it 14-7.

Among the defensive standouts was the other end—Dutch Stanley, whose impact on Florida football would be felt for years and years.

The complete staff that produced that 1928 club was:
Captain Everett M. Yon, athletic director
James R. Boyd, Jr., graduate manager
Charles W. Bachman, head coach
Joe Bedenk, assistant varsity coach
Nash Higgins, assistant varsity coach
Joe Holsinger, assistant varsity coach
Warren F. Cowell, freshman coach
A. P. Pierson, assistant freshman coach
A. L. Browne, director of intramurals
Frank W. Wright, director of publicity
Dr. L. G. Haskell, director physical education
Dr. John Piombo, trainer
Bill Bond, varsity football manager
Ernest (Goof) Bowyer, captain of the team
Tommy Owens, alternate captain

A typical newspaper account—and they came from all over to see this Gator team—was written by Morgan Blake, then sports editor of the *Atlanta Journal,* on hand to see the 60-6

Florida crush of Washington and Lee.

His account began: "At this writing, it is a matter for serious debate as to which is the dizziest—the Washington and Lee football team or this groggy sports scribe from Atlanta.

"Not being equipped with the hand grenades, sawed-off shotguns, poison gas, and anti-aircraft guns, the Generals from dear old Virginia were entirely impotent before an attack that was dazzing in its sweep, crushing in its power, and merciless in its slaughter.

"Washington and Lee might have stopped Florida with the deadly weapons mentioned above. Even that is doubtful. After all, the only certain method to halt these demons is to refuse to come on to the field. If the Generals had stopped at the front gate turnstiles yesterday afternoon they would at least have gotten as good as an 0-0 tie. Their greatest mistake was in scheduling the game.

"The expert accountants in Jacksonville finally computed the score at 60-6. We take this as correct. Mathematics was always our Jonah in school, and we never learned to add that fast. Florida's second and first string men scored four touchdowns in the first half. The Gators' first, second, and third string men scored five more in the second half. Talk about pulling rabbits out of a hat, why dear friends, these Gators can pull touchdowns out of a thimble.

"Florida's great football team—magnificent in the fullest sense of the word, keen, alert, fast, and powerful—gave Washington and Lee the most crushing defeat it has encountered in many years."

Get this: Florida gained 590 yards, 240 running and 224 on passes, 87 returning punts and 39 in returning kickoffs, said statistics of that day.

Blake finished, "It is really hard to find words to do the Gators justice."

It was, 1928, a time to remember. Anything approaching it, beyond the 8-2 of 1929, would be a long time coming.

THE RECORD OF THAT 1928 TEAM

Florida	26	Florida Southern	0
Florida	27	Auburn	0
Florida	73	Mercer	0
Florida	14	N. Carolina State	7

Florida	71	Sewanee	6
Florida	26	Georgia	6
Florida	27	Clemson	6
Florida	60	Washington & Lee	6
Florida	12	Tennessee	13
TOTAL	336*	TOTAL	44

* Lead nation in points scored

THE VARSITY TRAVELING SQUAD
1928 FLORIDA GATORS

No.	Name	Pos	Age	Wt	Ht	High School
1	Bert Grandoff	G	21	204	5-7	Hillsborough
2	Muddy Waters	G	19	185	6-2	New Castle, IN
3	Chester Allen	G	24	185	6-0	Lakeland
4	Joe Norflett	T	21	175	6-0	Newberry
5	Harvey Yancey	B	20	160	5-10	Duval
6	Milton McEwen	B	19	155	5-8	Wauchula
8	Wayne Ripley	G	22	190	5-11	Duval
9	Bill McRae	T	19	172	6-1	West Palm Beach
10	Joe Bryan	T	23	182	5-11	Duval
12	Harry Green	E	23	182	6-2	Gainesville
13	Willie DeHoff	E	22	170	6-0	Spring Hill, AL
14	Tommy Owens	B	22	146	5-11	Quincy
15	Justin Clemons	T	22	184	6-0	Plant City
16	Johnny Bryson	B	21	145	5-6	Duval
17	Clyde Crabtree	B	21	147	5-8	Morton-Cicero, IL
19	Elmer Ihrig	B	24	174	5-8	Fort Myers
20	Louis Bono	C	23	178	5-10	Duval
21	Dennis Stanley	E	22	181	5-8	Hillsborough
23	LeRoy Bethea	B	21	172	5-9	Riverside
24	Tom Perry	G	19	160	5-10	Daytona Beach
25	Frank Clark	C	19	170	6-1	Culver
26	Jimmy Steel	G	19	185	6-0	Hillsborough
27	Loyd Baldwin	C	20	180	5-11	Miami
28	Carl Brumbaugh	B	21	164	5-10	Ohio
29	Jimmy Nolan	E	20	170	5-10	Duval
30	Ed Sauls	B	20	185	5-11	Leon
31	Alex Reeves	C	22	184	5-8	Alabama
32	Mike Houser	G	22	170	5-7	Duval
33	Dashwood Hicks	T	21	176	6-2	Hillsborough

35	Wilbur James	G	19	186	5-11	Orlando
36	Ben Clemons	C	22	185	6-2	Leon
37	Lloyd Wilson	E	20	165	5-10	Hillsborough
38	Ernest Bowyer	B	24	170	5-10	Lakeland
39	Dale Vansickle	E	20	170	5-11	Gainesville
40	Rainey Cawthon	B	20	180	5-11	Leon
42	Royce Goodbread	B	20	190	6-0	St. Petersburg

Before the 1929 season began for Bachman, former quarterback Edgar Jones became athletic director and Joe Bedenk left. Van Fleet returned unexpectedly, awaiting another military assignment, and was around long enough to serve as assistant coach during 1929-30. Vansickle also stuck around to help out. Higgins, Owell, and Holsinger continued as the other aides.

Bachman's second season was almost as successful as his first. The Gators finished 8-2, losing 19-6 to Georgia Tech and 14-0 to Harvard at Cambridge, Massachusetts. The season saw another win over Georgia, 18-6, this time, and included a great closeout win over Oregon, 20-6, in Miami.

"The trip to Harvard has a great memory for me," said Bachman. "I recall we were changing trains in New York City in Grand Central Station, and were picking up Dr. Tigert and his friend, Grantland Rice, the great sportswriter who went to Vanderbilt with Dr. Tigert.

"In the station, newsboys were racing around with five-inch headlines declaring: 'Market Falls.' It was the beginning of the worst part of the depression, and with that all things later would go wrong in Florida. Not just football. Everything would go down the drain.

"I can remember Dr. Tigert on his knees in Tallahassee trying to get $500,000 to run the university. At Harvard we lost 14-0, but we played fine and would have won except for a fumble at the goal line on our first touchdown drive. I'll not forget that."

To Bachman the 1929 team "Was as good as the 1928 team and would have been better had we not lost (halfback) Carl Brumbaugh from the year before. He was our passer, and he was our thinker. He could get the ball to Vansickle. In those days the halfbacks passed more than the quarterback. And boy did we pass. In the flats a lot, like they do now.

102

"Brumbaugh went to the Bears where he played quarterback for about 15 years on the great teams with Red Grange, Bronko Nagurski, and those fellows."

But the very, very special win in that 1929 season was the last one, the finale of the great quarterback, Crabtree. It was a 20-6 win from Oregon, played in Miami in what may well have been the seed for the Orange Bowl extravaganza of the future.

The game was played in a place called Madison Square Garden Stadium, located behind the armory and developed through the use of wooden stands assembled for a Jack Sharkey heavyweight fight. It was about where the Miami baseball stadium stands today.

A crowd of 18,000 saw Florida win the game sensationally with Crabtree closing out his four great years with an 81-yard punt return for a touchdown, and two others coming on a

President John J. Tigert (1928-47) was his own man.

31-yard scamper by Ed Sauls and a 10-yard dash by Red McEwen.

The victory gave Florida and Bachman an 8-2 record and a 16-3 mark for two seasons. That combination has not yet been equalled. The 1965-66 Gators of Ray Graves and Steve Spurrier went 16-6, and the 1969-1970 Gators of Graves, Doug Dickey, and John Reaves went 16-5-1.

Florida football, 28 years old (23 at Gainesville), was at its zenith under Bachman during 1928-29. But in Bachman's last three years the Gators were also-rans. And after 1929 it was years and years before the Gators challenged anybody for any title.

Oh, they went 6-3-1 in 1930, losing 20-0 to Alabama, which went unbeaten, and 13-6 to Tennessee, which lost only to Alabama in ten games, and playing difficult Georgia (7-2-1) to a scoreless tie.

But the other loss was to Furman, 14-13, and that did not set well with alumni. And the Gators had gone 4-0-1 in their first five games, giving up just seven points, before crumbling.

The Gators smashed Georgia Tech 55-7 and went to Chicago and beat that school 19-0. Later, Chicago gave up football, and some wag cracked, "Florida did it. When Florida beat them, that was the last straw."

"It wasn't," said Bachman, "just that Florida football deteriorated. All of Florida deteriorated during the depression.

"All we gave by way of scholarships in those days were meals at Ma Ramsey's and room to the top players who could not afford it. If you were a star and could pay all of your way, you did. Like Rainey Cawthon, our great halfback from Tallahassee. His dad was state superintendent of schools.

"We got our money, what we had, from friends and alumni who would sponsor players. Without money we could not compete with the more established schools like Georgia Tech, Georgia, Vanderbilt, and Alabama which had such a head start on us."

Whatever the reason, Bachman's last three teams went 11-15-3. His 1931 and 1932 teams won five games in 19 played, beating North Carolina State, slumping Auburn, Sewanee, The Citadel, and one genuine goodie, a 12-2 upset of highly regarded UCLA in Bachman's last game at Florida. The handwriting was on the wall during that dismal 1931 season. The Gators lost five of their last six games, tying the other. During that streak the Florida offense—three years earlier the best in the country—managed only two touchdowns and a safety.

It was little better in 1932. The Gators opened with wins over Sewanee and The Citadel. In the 19-0 thrashing of Sewanee, Herb McAnly set a record that will be hard to erase. He took the ball from center five yards deep in his own end zone and raced 105 yards for a score. It went into the books as a 91-yard touchdown run from scrimmage.

But a 17-6 loss to North Carolina State started a six-game losing skein that sealed Bachman's fate. By the time for preparations for the UCLA game, the coach's last at Florida, things were truly unhappy. The Gators were losing, and their partisans were broke. It meant for a disapproving audience.

"I remember we prepared an odd way for that game," said sophomore quarterback Sam Davis, who was battling touted Million Dollar Monk Dorsett for the job. "There were some morale problems. Before the game they divided the squad by choosing up, just like you do on the sandlot. Coach Bachman would pick one player and Holsinger the other.

"All week long we'd heard nothing but the word 'Frankovich,' which was the name of the great UCLA runner. You know we called him something else, of course. We worked hard because we had some talent on that team.

"We won that game," recalled Davis. "We beat those guys. We blocked a punt, and old Herb McAnly passed to (Ernie) Schirmer for a touchdown. I know it made Bach feel good to end that way. I personally thought the man was a great coach."

As with Sebring, Bachman's departure was not protested by the school's adminstration.

"I had a five-year contract," said Bachman. "It was up after the 1932 season. I had been negotiating with Michigan State anyway. Jimmy Crawley had resigned there to go to Fordham, and he recommended me for the job there.

"Yes, there may have been some alumni who were unhappy. But I can say Dr. Tigert urged me to stay around. I decided to leave for the same money I was making, $7,500. I left because I thought the material would be better up there. Frankly, looking back, I am satisfied with what I achieved at Florida. I honestly believe I got all that was possible out of the material. That 1928 team, well, on a dry field, not a team in

Hub McAnly ran a school record 91 yards from scrimmage for a 1932 touchdown against Sewanee.

America could have beaten us."

It still gnawed—that critical 13-12 loss at Tennessee...in the mud.

A Rally Before The Fall

Perhaps the best reason for cherishing the memory of that 8-1, 1928 team was that no other Florida team would do as well for nearly a quarter of a century. After Bachman's second team built an 8-2 record in 1929, it was to be 1952 before a Gator club could win as many as seven games!

The beginning of the decade of the 1930s saw the start of a 19-year dry spell that included only 3 winning seasons, a 13-game losing string, and the departure of 5 head coaches under less than comfortable circumstances. Toward the end of the period it became traditional for Florida to play Auburn for sole ownership of the conference cellar each season.

The only years when victories outnumbered losses saw records of 6-3-1, 5-3-1, and 4-3. The latter included wins over two naval air stations during a World War II year, 1944. Like many other schools, the Gators did not field a team in 1943.

From 1933 through 1950 Florida produced but two first team all-SEC players, both backs, Walter Mayberry in 1937, and Charley Hunsinger in 1948 and 1949. They may be part of the reason that it was said for so long that natives of the state of Florida had speed and ability and were thus fine backs and pass receivers, but few big, strong linemen were produced in the Sunshine State. College scouts flocked to Florida in increasing numbers in the Thirties, Forties, Fifties, and early Sixties, saying that the state did indeed turn out excellent backs.

The theft of some of those speedy backfield men by colleges from other states may have aided in Florida's downfall, which was already under way by 1932 when Bachman left—by mutual consent—after a 3-7 season—to go to Michigan State. Bachman had been making $7,500 a year, but his successor would be offered a cut...to $3,900.

To follow him Bachman recommended one of his staff members, a former Gator end named D. J. (Dutch) Stanley, who got the job partly because the board of control had said it wanted a Florida alumnus as head coach, and wanted ex-Gators in as many positions on the staff as possible.

"They got the idea from a member of the board who was from Yale," said Bachman. "And he said they did that there so what they did at Yale was good enough for Florida."

The most surprised man in college football when Dutch Stanley was named head coach was Dutch Stanley. Nash Higgins, a graduate of Wabash, was older and had been recommended by the committee on athletics.

"I was over visiting a sick friend of mine," recalled Stanley, 67 years old when he thought back to that day in 1933.

"His name was Claude Lee, and he ran the theater in Gainesville. He was an important man in town. He was lying there in bed and said to me, 'I got news for you. You are going to be named head football coach at Florida.' I was stunned.

"I thought I was the least likely candidate. I was only 26, and had to be the youngest head coach in America."

They drafted that policy of hiring Florida alumni as coaches, so Stanley went and got them—ex-players Rainey Cawthon, Ernest Bowyer, Ben Clemons, and Pat Pattillo. The older, more experienced Bachman assistant, Higgins, left to start the football program at the University of Tampa. Ironically his two unpaid assistants were also ex-Gators, Joe Jenkins and Red McEwen.

The student newspaper and the *Seminole Yearbook* praised the idea of all-alumni coaches, and the athletic board found that it could pay less.

"We had to; there simply was no money," said Stanley. "And it would get worse."

The young coach and his staff managed a 5-3-1 first season and a better 6-3-1 the second year. But in 1935 the record slipped to 3-7-0, two of the wins coming over Stetson and

Gator Coaching Staff, middle 1930s: Josh Cody, Lewie Hardage, Carlos Proctor, Dutch Stanley, and Rand Dixon.

slumping Sewanee.

Stanley's three-year record was a winner, 14-13-2, "and no matter what, it was a winner, looking back," he said.

Six of the fourteen wins were over Stetson, Rollins, and Sewanee.

Stanley said he sensed growing disapproval in his second season, and it "got bad in the middle of the third," when he lost five in a row and seven out of eight.

"In the last game I would coach," said Stanley—the 1935 finale against South Carolina—"somebody gave me a paper before the game. A story by Ed Ray in the *Tampa Times* said I was going to be replaced. I knew the Jacksonville group was for it anyway, and it was the Jacksonville people who were helping us, mostly, with what financial help we got. Anyway, I read the story to the boys, and I think it helped us beat South Carolina in my final game."

Such a turn of events has become habit-forming at Florida. Virtually without exception Gator coaches on their way out won their last games. Many were well aware and bitter about the impending dismissal.

Stanley had few all-America types on his teams, though he had those who were big on effort.

Mayberry, he felt, "is as good a back as I ever saw. He was smart and he could pass and kick."

Stanley did have a fine back in Julius Brown, a couple of tough tackles in Bill Stark and Hal Starbuck, a fine center in Welcome Shearer, and a quick, good-passing halfback named Billy Chase. All received all-SEC nominations on second or third teams, but only Mayberry made the first.

Other solid Stanley performers of that time were guards Tommy and Julian Lane, Floyd Christian, guard Art Shouse, guard Drayton Bernhard, fullback Charley Stolz, end Chuck Rogers, end George Moye, and fullback Jimmy Hughes.

"Hughes was one of my best," said Stanley. "He never quit. He was a factor in our upset of Auburn, 14-7, in 1934.

Stanley is proudest of two back-to-back victories in 1934. After beating Auburn the Gators came from a halftime deficit to whip Georgia Tech, 13-12.

It was homecoming, on the four-year-old Florida Field, and more than 20,000 fans were there. Many were already campaigning for Stanley's scalp.

"Tech had us 12-0 in the third quarter when I saw one of the great sights of my life," Stanley recalls. "Alton Brown blocked a punt at the Tech one, and Bill Turner scored with it. Stolz got us another score later, then old Bill Stark kicked the point that won it for us.

"I had heard reliably that people in high places in Tallahassee were after me before those two games. When we won I got a wire from the governor saying 'All Florida is proud of you today.'

"It was an old story. I was Monday's bum and Saturday's hero."

Stanley tried hard. His salary was $3,600, so he laid bricks for the Works Progress Administration when not coaching.

Working with some of the other coaches and even some of the players, he laid many of the bricks on the Florida campus. To further supplement that paycheck he helped track coach Percy Beard take up tickets at the basketball games.

Finally, after the pain of the 3-7-0 season of 1935 had settled in, "I knew they wanted me out," said Stanley. "Some benefactors from Jacksonville actually came to me and said if I'd resign quietly, they'd see I was taken care of, kept on in

Versatile Billy Chase captained the 1935 Gators.

some capacity. I said I couldn't do it that way. If President Tigert and the board wanted me to quit, then okay.

"Well, in a few days, Dr. Tigert and his wife came by on a Sunday afternoon and said they wanted to take me and Nell for a ride. He finally told me there was pressure but he could handle it. If I wanted to stay, fine. If I wanted to quit, he'd understand. I said I'd resign if my staff could be taken care of and I could have a position of dignity. He agreed. I headed the intramural department and worked in phys ed and then became an assistant coach again for Florida and later for Duke."

Dutch Stanley, it turned out, wielded far more influence over Florida athletics out of the head coaching job than he could have in it. He returned in 1946 to become head of the department of physical education and had a direct hand in the hiring of three more Florida head coaches.

"I still say what's important is that we did wind up with a winning record," said Stanley of his 14-13-2 worksheet.

In a way he was right.

The worst was yet to come.

The Forgettable Years —
Part I

The noble experiment with alumni coaches lasted only the three years of Dutch Stanley. Frustrated, the Florida administrators turned northward for their next two coaches, and the two they got were of similar philosophies and comparable success. Both were defensive-minded and tried to ram the ball down the enemy's throat, and both tried to wear out the opposition.

"Sadly, as it turned out, usually it was us who were worn out first," said Julian Lane, guard, captain, and sometimes placekicker on the 1936 team.

Josh Cody, Stanley's successor, took over in 1936, lasted through 1939, and was asked not to come back. He compiled a record through those years of 17 wins, 24 losses, and 2 ties.

Cody was picked by Athletic Director Edgar Jones from Dan McGugin's Vanderbilt staff. Cody had played for the Commodores and coached a short time at Clemson.

His first year—1936—was a disappointment. A good freshman team—some said the best—had come along, and hopes were high. But the only wins came over Stetson, The Citadel, Sewanee, and Maryland.

In four years at Florida, Cody's records were painfully alike: 4-6-0, 4-7-0, 4-6-1, and 5-5-1. But the Cody years did produce some talent. Walter Mayberry, 1937 all-SEC back and the first all-SEC player Florida developed, trotted onto Florida Field for the first time, as did Forest Ferguson, a brilliant two-way end who became a Gator legend in his days at Florida,

Biggest member of the 1938 Gators, 6-2, 220-pound Clark Goff of Pittsburgh, only 19, participates in early cheesecake.

setting a school pass-receiving record. Both Mayberry and Ferguson rank on all-time Florida teams, and observers of Florida football over the years agree that they would be heroes today.

One of the brightest spots for that period was a punter named Bud Walton. Florida was a defensive team, and punting was needed. Walton filled the bill: he set a most-punts record that still stands, kicking 83 times in 1938. Against Georgia Tech that season Walton punted an incredible 23 times and helped the Gators to a scoreless tie.

For the last game of his career at Florida, Cody took his 5-5 team to Auburn. The Plainsmen had picked the Florida game for the dedication of its new football stadium, which would be called Cliff Hare Stadium. Just before the Florida game 7,500 permanent seats were finished in a complex that now holds 63,000.

With Charley Tate scoring the only touchdown for Florida, the Gators tied Auburn, 7-7, for the nearest thing Florida had to a victory in that stadium through 1972.

But that accomplishment was not the highlight of Cody's years at Florida. It was the fourth game of the 1939 season, at Boston's Fenway Park on Columbus Day. The Gators, losers to Texas and Mississippi State and winners over Stetson, were taking on undefeated Boston College under a new coach, a man named Frank Leahy.

Leahy lost only one regular season game in his two years at Boston, that to those underdog Gators from Florida, 7-0. Leahy even started his second string. It was a mistake. Halfway through the first period Walton passed twenty-five yards to Leo Cahill for the lone touchdown of the day, and Walton added the point-after.

Florida spent the rest of the afternoon fighting off Boston's offense, led by a sensational runner, Charlie O'Rourke. Once the hosts did score, but officials detected holding, and it was called back. Eight times Boston College was stopped inside the Gator fifteen-yard line, and six of those times Fergie Ferguson was responsible for the game-saving play.

His performance that day would have to rank with any in Florida history, for sheer single-handed, effective defensive heroics.

Gator John McCarty became governor of Florida.

Kocsis, Florida's Alternate Captain, Is a Student of Herpetology

Guard-captain Frank Kocsis of the 1938 team was a rare Gator indeed. He was a snake-handler on the side. He is not known to have smuggled one into combat on the football playing field.

Though it was a big victory, celebration was not to be. "I remember," said one lineman, "those assistants Cody imported from Pittsburgh yelling at us for hollering on the bus on the way back to the hotel after beating Boston College."

Leahy, despite the loss, carried the Eagles to a 9-1 season and the Cotton Bowl for a 6-3 loss to Clemson before going 10-0 the next year and picking up a 19-13 win over Tennessee in the Sugar Bowl. Not long after, he began building national championships at his alma mater, Notre Dame.

But Cody's fate was not as good. Even with the sensational

Captain-guard Julian Lane, 1936, later became mayor of Tampa and state senator.

victory over Boston College, the 5-5-1 record could not save Cody. The theory was simple: play defensive ball and win, okay. Play defensive ball and lose, and it is dull.

For the 11 games and a split-even record, Florida had averaged 7 points a game. Opponents had averaged 6.

The Forgettable Years —
Part II

Tom Lieb was an Olympic discus champion. He had also been a superb tackle at Notre Dame and was a promising head coach of record, running the show at Loyola of Los Angeles when Cody departed. Lieb had a brother, Joe Lieb, a noted Florida attorney who later became a federal judge. Perhaps here was the man to put some life into the Florida football program. Something had to be done for sure. The Gators had finished the 1939 season dead last in the conference.

In 1940 Tom Lieb took over and lasted through the war years, but his ledger of 20 victories, 26 defeats, and a tie was not good enough to earn him an invitation to return to the campus in 1946.

Lieb gained a reputation as a tough taskmaster.

"He'd never take you out of a game," said Benny Lane, Julian's brother, a center and tackle who played one season for Cody and then finished under Lieb.

"If you were dying, you'd just have to make it to the sidelines somehow and he'd send in a replacement," in those two-way days.

Lieb stayed through 1945. He did not simply inherit a program that at the time was unmoving. He came into a state that still had not recovered from the depression, a state that had not begun to feel the great population explosion that would soon come. And he arrived with war just around the corner.

The new head coach went north to recruit the big men he needed for his power offense. Names like Nick Klutka, Floyd

Head Coach Tom Lieb (center with ball) and his Gator staff of the early forties.

In the forties the Gator waterboy was Tootie Perry, who had been a Gator hero at center in the early twenties.

119

Konetsky, Bill Latsko, and Ziggy Sklowdoswki began appearing on the roster. Lieb blended with these a handful of Cody holdovers, and it began to look as if he might make life tolerable and reasonably exciting for Gator fans.

Tommy Harrison was a brilliant back who had career totals of 1,170 yards passing and 963 rushing to rank him among the top half dozen all-time yards producers for the Gators. Ferguson, Walton, and Tate were still around. With them were an angry lineman named Peanut Hull, ends John Piombo and Frank Smoak, a swift runner in Pat Reen, and one of the most aggressive Florida guards ever, Mush Battista. Along with these, Lieb inherited college football's most famous waterboy, a former Gator captain, Tootie Perry, whose mad dash to the huddle with the waterbucket became a highlight of game action.

At times, there was little else to cheer about. But the first year, though it was a 5-5 season, was not so bad because the 1940 team was the first to ever beat Georgia and Georgia Tech in the same year. The Gators whipped Tampa, 23-0; Maryland, 19-0; Miami 46-6; and the Georgia schools, Tech, 16-7, and the Bulldogs, 18-13.

The 1940 season was Butts' second at Georgia, and he was still having problems. He had put together a 5-6 win in 1939, including a vital 6-2 defeat of Florida. Losing to the Gators would contribute to a little-better 5-4-1 mark for 1940.

It was a pip of a game, in Jacksonville, with 20,000 people watching.

Georgia led 7-3 after a Paul Eller field goal for Florida. But Ferguson blocked a punt that John Piombo (who later became president of the Gator Bowl) turned into a touchdown, and later Walton threw 45 yards to Fondren Mitchell for another.

The win over Tech came the next weekend in Atlanta, with Piombo going 71 yards with an interception, Eller kicking a field goal, and Red Mack scoring to produce the 16-7 decision.

The 1941 season continued Lieb's losing trend at Florida and was not memorable, but 1942 produced an unforgettable game. The Bulldogs of 1942 beat Lieb's Gators, 75-0, for what remains the worst defeat in Florida history. It was sweet revenge for the Bulldogs of Coach Wally Butts who were on their way to beating Florida seven times in a row after losing to Florida in that 1940 game.

Mush Battista, great player who became an assistant coach.

To forge the lop-sided 1942 win, Butts used his great runner, Frank Sinkwich, only half of each of the first three quarters. Sinkwich scored twice and passed for two more in the shocking wipeout of the Gators.

The game was in Jacksonville, and Florida, 3-4 at that point in the season, dreamed of upset. The Gator student body had pajama-paraded all over Gainesville the night before. The theme was "Sink Sinkwich!"

The loss so appalled influential Gator partisans that they pledged that such a thing would never happen again, that they would find a coach who could beat Butts and Georgia.

That 1942 team of Butts, Sinkwich, and all-American end George Poschner went 10-1-0 for the year. The loss was to Auburn. The tenth win was over Texas Christian, 40-26, in the Orange Bowl. The next year, Georgia beat Florida, 38-12, and went to the Rose Bowl for a victory over UCLA.

A fascinating bit of irony about the 75-0 victory came

from later history. A standout lineman on the Georgia team that annihilated Florida was Gene Ellenson, who later became assistant head coach—and almost head coach—at Florida. Ellenson got his chance to feel the misery of agonizing defeat by Georgia several times as a Florida coach, once by the humbling, near-backbreaking score of 51-0 in 1968, and once to stop Florida's best shot at the SEC championship and run at an undefeated season.

In his five years of coaching at Florida (there was no team

Mobilized Gators of 1940—Bud Walton, Ted Taylor, and Tex Hanna, from left.

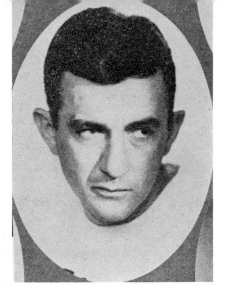

Red Sanders as assistant Gator freshman coach in 1939. He went on to head coaching success at Vanderbilt and UCLA.

in 1943), Lieb had only one other experience which rivaled that double-victory situation of 1940.

His 1944 team produced a 4-3 record, the only winning season for the Gators from 1934 through 1951. It included wins over Mayport Naval Air Station, 36-6; Jacksonville Naval Air Station, 26-20; Maryland, 13-6; and Miami, 13-0. Losses were to Mississippi, 26-6; Tennessee, 40-0; and Georgia, 38-21.

But it was a winner, produced with players straight out of high school—those who declined the opportunity to join the military.

Since it was the only winner in 18 years, its members should be noted: ends Joe Graham (captain) and Dewell Rushing, tackles Paul Mortellaro and Jack White, guards Fletcher Groves and Ken Hamilton, center Roger Adams, quarterback Buddy Carte, halfbacks Ken McLean and Bobby Forbes, fullback Jim Dyer, and a group of reserves that included Ottis Mooney, who later coached at Florida and Miami. Forbes was an all-Conference player and in later life became an all-World softball selection and recovered from cancer.

Lieb's time was up after the 1945 season, a 4-5-1 effort. His finale was a 12-0 loss to the United States Amphibs.

Two Who Gave Everything

In a time when Florida's roster was not top-heavy with superstars, two stood out. They were back Walter Mayberry and end Forest (Fergie) Ferguson. Both, observers declared, were superstars then and would be superstars today.

Mayberry finished in 1937. The Gators were 4-6 that year, but Mayberry captured the fancy of Florida followers and the admiration of the opposition. Tiger was his nickname and he looked anything but that. The label came from his unflinching, resolute play on the field. An extraordinarily handsome youth, but shy, he played high school ball at Daytona Beach. Incredibly he returned to the game after suffering a broken neck.

"It looked as if his career was ended for sure," said Benny Kahn, forever the sports editor of the *Daytona News-Journal* and observer of Gator football. "But somehow Tiger came back and played.

"As a collegian at Florida, he was fast and deceptive. He could punt as well as he could run, and he could run as well as he could pass. He was a genuine triple-threat man.

"Another thing. He could punt the ball out of bounds in the coffin corner, and believe me, those Gator teams in those days bad needed that kind of help. They had to punt often. Mayberry got a lot of practice."

Kahn declares that Mayberry could play for Florida today as a regular at "quarterback, runningback, or kicking specialist. I mean it. This is not one of those 'them were the good ole

Walter Mayberry—star halfback.

days' things with me. Tiger Mayberry was that good. And he was modest about it all, and handsome. He had everything going for him but the war."

Like the other Super Gator of those years, Tiger Mayberry went off to war and gave his life. He became a Marine pilot, went down in the Pacific, and died in a Japanese prison camp.

That other Super Gator, Forest Ferguson, was a big man, tall and rangy, a natural athlete, recalls his teammate of three years, Benny Lane. "Fergie took up boxing one year," Benny said. "He was undefeated. He wandered out to the track one day, picked up a 16-pound shot, and threw it 50 feet without knowing how. His last year he went out for baseball and was good at that, too."

In 1942 he set an AAU javelin throw record. "He had an odd build—a huge chest, and enormous shoulders. His arms were long, too. He had a tiny waist and skinny legs. He was a fast, powerful man who lived to compete in sports."

Ferguson would have been a premier tight end today. As it was, in 1941, when passing was hardly what it is today, Fergie caught 26 passes in 19 games, third best in the nation. His performance was tops in the SEC, and he made the all-Confer-

Fergie Ferguson, football hero, military hero.

ence team. Ferguson caught both of the Tommy Harrison touchdown passes that upset a good Miami team, 14-0, that year.

"Like the rest of us," said Lane, "he played both ways and was as good on defense as offense."

From Stuart, Florida, Fergie became a starter as a sophomore and started every game of his career. From ROTC he went on active duty and was a second lieutenant in the army's D-Day invasion of Normandy. There he won the nation's second highest medal for bravery under fire but was wounded critically. He never recovered and died of those wounds ten years later.

Ferguson's contributions to Florida and the United States prompted the Fergie Ferguson Award, given each year to the most valuable senior. The selection is made in the spring and presented annually at homecoming the following season.

Winners through 1973 were:

1954   Fullback Mal Hammack
1955   Center Steve DeLaTorre
1956   Tackle Larry Wesley
1957   Halfback Jim Rountree
1958   Quarterback Jimmy Dunn
1959   Guard Asa Cox

126

1960	End Pat Patchen
	Guard Vic Miranda
1961	Tackle Jim Beaver
1962	End Sam Holland
1963	Center Jimmy Morgan
	Back Hagoode Clark
1964	Back Larry Dupree
1965	End Charley Casey
1966	Quarterback Steve Spurrier
1967	Flanker Richard Trapp
1968	Guard Guy Dennis
	Back Larry Smith
1969	Back Steve Tannen
1970	Tackle-End Jack Youngblood
1971	Quarterback John Reaves
1972	Linebacker Fred Abbott
1973	Tackle David Hitchcock

Bear Wolf Brings The Golden Era

The very best teller of Gator tales is Red Mitchum, a sort of white Flip Wilson. The big, auburn-haired, velvet-voiced Alabamian was lucky when his high school football ended at Gadsden. Alabama chose not to offer him a scholarship, and he went south to Florida in 1949. At 6-3 and 185, he became an end. But more than that, he became part of a Gator period that has spawned more stories and was more immortalizing for its participants than any other time in Florida football history— ever.

Mitchum's days at Florida provided him with enough material to sustain him for a lifetime of after-dinner speaking. As a sales executive for a firm in Ocala, a convenient 35 miles from Gainesville, Mitchum is the Gators' wandering drumbeater. He fractures audiences with his true stories of Florida football tribulations of those days, adds some bonus Andy Griffith-Dave Gardner material, some Flip Wilson, and some country music singing accompanied by his strumming of an open book of matches, as if they were a miniature guitar.

Mitchum likes most to tell stories of a tackle named Curtis King, who according to Mitchum talked as if his mouth were filled to the teeth with mush, slow and deliberate in speech and less than sophisticated in outlook and comment. They played alongside each other in the Florida line, and King was fair game for Mitchum.

"It was against Kentucky," Mitchum begins this story. "It was when Bear Bryant was coaching, and they had the great teams of George Blanda, Bob Gain, and so on.

"We were getting killed, as usual, and I was getting murdered by Gain, who was opposite me. He was a huge man and mean as a snake, an all-American and later a great pro. In the game Gain had succeeded in breaking my nose, chipping my cheekbone, and knocking out a favorite molar of mine.

"When we went back into the huddle, and some of my teammates were sympathizing and wiping the blood and dirt off my face, Curtis looked at me from across the huddle and said, 'Red, you look kinda whupped.' I said, 'I am whupped, Curtis.' 'Well,' Curtis said, 'when we come out of the huddle, let's holler something at 'em even if we have to take it back.'"

The period of which Mitchum spins yarns and which King summed up with that thought has come to be known as the Golden Era of Florida Football. Or simply, the Golden Era. Because it was anything but that.

It was the coaching period of a good guy, a man still revered by his ex-players, a man whose job was saved once by a student demonstration before they were called that. It was the four years of Coach Ray (Bear) Wolf, 1946-1949.

In the Golden Era of Bear Wolf, the Gators won 13 of 39 games. Three of the victories came over Furman, one over Rollins, and one over Kansas State—the 25th straight loss of the Kansas Wildcats.

That Golden Era began when Florida convinced former player and head coach Dutch Stanley to return from Duke as dean of the college of physical education. No sooner had he arrived than he was told to find a new head football coach to replace Lieb.

"I'll be honest," Stanley said. "My first choice was the coach at Oklahoma State, an Indian fellow named Jim Lookabaugh."

In 1945 Lookabaugh had coached the Cowboys to an 8-0 season and victory over St. Mary's in the Sugar Bowl.

"I thought for a time I had Lookabaugh," Stanley said, "but at the last minute he changed his mind."

At the time, Florida was hardly a coach's dream and Stanley was not overwhelmed with applications. But he went to the NCAA meetings in New York to find his man.

First, he offered the job to Jess Neely, the scholarly man

Ray (Bear) Wolf made Florida Gator history. He coached the "Golden Era," a time vividly recalled whenever Gators gather.

who'd left Clemson for Rice. Neely said thanks but no thanks. "So then," Stanley said, "I began checking Wolf. He had applied for the job."

Wolf played at Texas Christian and as head coach at North Carolina from 1936 through 1941 had compiled a 38-17-3 record. He had beaten Wallace Wade's Duke once during that period.

Baseball had been his first love, and he even made it to the major leagues long enough for one appearance at bat. "I hit a screaming drive right back through the pitcher's box," Wolf recalls. "The only thing wrong was that it resulted in a double-play."

But baseball was not necessarily any more unlucky for him than football. He once missed a 20-yard straightaway place-kick against Southern Methodist when the three points would have brought the Southwest Conference title to TCU.

When World War II broke out, Wolf went into the Navy V-12 program and for a year coached a pre-flight team at the University of Georgia. When the war was over, he was job-hunting, and Florida had the vacancy.

"I decided to go with Wolf if the board would go along with it," said Stanley.

"I remember, Bear came into Gainesville on a Sunday. The next day he met with the board. I understand that in the meeting one of the members asked Wolf what his religious denomination was, and Wolf said, 'Why, I'm Catholic.' Then thinking about what they may or may not mean, Bear quickly added, 'But my wife's a Christian.'

"It broke up the meeting, and Wolf got the job."

The Golden Era had begun.

The Golden Era encompassed only two SEC wins and two ties. Its first 13 games—Bear's first 13—were all losses. That is by far the longest losing streak in Florida history, and yet it is the very nucleus of the strange heritage that is the so-called Golden Era. While TGE covers the entire Wolf career, its climax seems to have been the 13-game losing streak.

True, there were positive aspects under Wolf. For instance 1949 produced the first win over Georgia since 1940. In 1948 Florida beat Auburn and scared the daylights out of Alabama before losing, 34-28. Under Wolf the Gators flew their first chartered plane to a game—to New Orleans to play Tulane in 1947—although the Green Wave won that one, 35-0.

Other positive aspects involved a sensational punt and kickoff return scheme developed by Wolf and his Gators. And in those days the Gators played before the largest crowd ever to see a regular season game in Florida to that time. A total of 55,981 saw Miami beat Florida, 28-13, in the Orange Bowl in Wolf's next-to-last game in 1949.

The Golden Era was on the wane.

But They Never Quit Trying

It was an odd assortment of potential Gators who met with Bear Wolf and his new staff July 19, 1946. In spring training he had installed the double-wing, making the tailback the key to the offense rather than the quarterback. To fill the vital slot he moved his returning quarterback, Argus Williams, to tailback.

The new system would depend heavily on big, strong backs on offense; small, quick backs on defense. And on that hot summer day he had gathered "some mixture," according to Jimmy Kynes. A high school hero out of Marianna, Florida, Kynes was big for those days, standing 6-3 and weighing 204. He played end, halfback, and center-linebacker before his four years were up, and was captain and all-SEC in 1949.

But that day, "I was apprehensive," he said. "We had the players from Lieb and 1945, we had all those veterans returning from the war, and we must have had 105 freshmen."

Wolf and his assistants, Paul Severin, Buster Brannon, Ted Twomey, and Mush Battista, were bent on producing a winner—and they practiced that way.

"We began practicing July 19, and we practiced all summer, right up to the season," recalled Kynes. "Then we went into the season without a letup. There is a chance, looking back, that we may have been tired by the time the season came along."

Wolf found some talent but little depth. One true athlete was Charley Hunsinger, a fast-starting, hard runner from

Harrisburg, Illinois. Hunsinger had played for the Jacksonville Naval Air Station team the year before, and leading Jacksonville alumni had convinced him to enroll at Florida.

By September, Wolf had the New Gators ready for their opener against Mississippi. The squad had been narrowed to 65. A breakdown showed 55 from Florida, 34 former servicemen, and 22 freshmen. Somehow, though, the Gators were not ready enough and lost that opener to Mississippi, 13-7.

Walter Cobb's synopsis of that first game under Wolf went: "Season's hopes for a perfect Gator record were dashed by Ole Miss as Florida's inexperience was obvious. Bright spots in the Gator attack were the line plunging of Vic Vaccaro and the kicking and passing of Billy Parker. The Gators' lone score came on a bullet pass from Parker to Joe Chesser. Warren Tiller kicked the extra point."

Cobb was premature. Florida's first year under Wolf was a "perfect" 0-9-0. A couple of games were close, like the 20-13 loss to Miami, the 27-20 defeat by Villanova, and that opener. Depth was the problem. The 1946 Gators led the great 11-0 Georgia team 7-6 at the end of the first half in Jacksonville. But the final count was Georgia 33, Florida 14.

It would not be uncommon in 1946—and even in the next several years—for Florida to lead better teams—or play them even for two quarters—only to succumb to numbers. Other losses that first year were to Tulane, Vanderbilt, North Carolina State, Auburn, and North Carolina.

When Auburn beat Florida, 47-12, in Gainesville in the 1946 finale, it allowed the Plainsmen to move out of the SEC cellar and leave it for Florida's sole occupancy. And it marked the end of a six-game Auburn losing streak.

When the terrible disappointment was done, somebody asked Wolf about 1946 and he said, "It could be worse. We could have had ten games scheduled then."

Looking back, though, he said of 1946, "The thing is, we never went into a game we didn't think we'd win."

Kynes said the same thing, but "We didn't have enough players and of course we were still broke at Florida. We'd play in the same helmets and shoes we'd practice in."

Yet the 1946 season was not without its moments of excitement. Besides the double-wing, Wolf had installed a punt

The late-forties Gators ran for their lives, like Hal (Buggo) Griffin here.

and kickoff return scheme that was about the most exciting product of his career. With speedy backs like Bobby Forbes, Hal (Buggo) Griffin, and Loren Broadus, Wolf used a double safety. When one of those darting runners received the ball on a kick, he would turn and hand off or fake a handoff to the other back.

It worked plenty. In his career Griffin returned punts 87, 75, and 68 yards, and a 98-yard (officially 96) against Miami in one of the close losses of 1946. Arnold Finnebrock wrote of that particular play, "The 17-year-old Griffin faked to Buddy Carte and made a breath-taking 98-yard return to put the Gators ahead 13-7 before the homecoming crowd of 21,105."

Griffin stood 5-8 and weighed 158, and he could fly. He wound up playing in all 39 games during his four years on the squad.

"Griffin would always be ready on Saturday," Wolf remembers. "He got hurt. He had to as fast as he ran in traffic. But he was always ready to play."

That 1946 season saw some other interesting performers take their places on Florida Field. In time, Hunsinger became a two-time all-SEC choice and, "He'd have been all-American at a better-known school of the time," said Angus Williams.

Williams, quite a player in his own right, worked under three coaches at Florida, winding up as a defensive back under Bob Woodruff in 1950. Lieb and Wolf were fired with Williams on their teams. "Woodruff survived me," said Williams.

Wolf followed the lead of Lieb and Cody and came up with a master punter, Fred Montsdeoca. Later the Florida baseball coach and one of the university's most effective alumni, Montsdeoca had many great punting days in his year at Florida, but he hit a high point against Alabama in 1949 when he averaged 53 yards per kick, though Alabama won, 35-13.

Wolf also started the development of a fine pass receiving end in Broughton Williams, a good placement man in Laz Lewis, a promising quarterback-passer in Doug Belden, and some durable linemen such as Frank Dempsey, who went on to a distinguished pro career, Fletcher Groves, Paul Montellaro, Charlie Felds, Cliff Sutton, Bob Cummings, Bob Gilbert, Aaron Brown, Tommy Bishop, Dewell Rushing, Dick Lashley, Harry Hobbs, Joe Hawkins, Fal Johnson, Marcelino Huerta, Frank Lorenzo, Chesser, and Kynes.

They were a place to start, but they were not enough.

Despite a summer of hard work the 1947 Gators opened with a loss to a Charley Connerly-led Mississippi team, 14-6, then lost a game everyone in Florida thought they would win, to North Texas State, 20-12. Next the Gators went to Auburn and though they led 7-0 and 14-13, they blew the leads and the game, falling 20-14 for the 13th loss in a row over two seasons.

Florida was at its lowest of low points, having lost 13 straight and next facing a team it could not beat, North Carolina State on the Wolfpack's home ground. State was ranked 18th in the nation.

The Golden Era was at its very brightest.

Victory At Last

Former Tennessee star Beattie Feathers was the coach of the 1947 North Carolina State team, a good one built around holdovers from the 1946 club that went 8-2 and to the Gator Bowl. The Wolfpack of 1947 had begun with a disappointing 7-0 loss to arch-rival Duke, the lone touchdown coming on the return of an interception off a batted pass. But Feathers had brought his team back for a 14-0 win over Davidson and an 18-0 win over Clemson. Thus, State was a three-touchdown favorite as it looked toward the game with Florida in Raleigh's Riddick Stadium on the night of October 18, 1947.

The Gators headed north in a strained atmosphere. Already, there was "Fire Wolf" talk around the state, and nothing suggested that Florida could win the game.

Perhaps the only optimistic gesture about the game was made by the WRUF Radio broadcast team driving to Raleigh to report the play-by-play back to Gatorland. Their audience would be broad because almost no Florida fans were among the 18,000 attending the game.

Dick Crago, just 22 and a former student, was handling the play-by-play for the group Paul Acosta directed. Bill Rohan, now deceased, did the color, and Don Davidson was the spotter. Crago, who later owned his own station in Vero Beach, recalled the drive to North Carolina:

"As we were riding through Georgia, we kept seeing these little stands advertising fireworks," recalled Crago. "Wouldn't it be a great touch, somebody said, if we should beat North

Carolina State, to fire some Roman candles and sky rockets from the broadcast booth after the game. So we stopped and bought some.

"Yet," Crago sighed, "as the game approached, we grew less and less inclined to think Florida might win, so nobody bothered to take the fireworks to the booth. I have made many mistakes in my life, but few dismay me so much as the thought of the great touch it would have offered later that night, firing those rockets and candles out of the booth over those North Carolina State fans' heads."

Wolf, looking back, said, "I can only remember that I had coached harder in losing those 13 straight than at anytime in my career. I knew our chances were slim at North Carolina State, but we would simply go bow our necks and try again."

Florida received, did nothing, punted, and forced a punt from the obviously overconfident Wolfpack. State's punt gave the Gators a first down at their own 30 to start their second series of the game. As the Gators prepared to break huddle, the Right Half Sucker play was called.

"In it, well, it's a trap up the middle," said halfback Bobby Forbes in a look-back 25 years later. "Mostly they were keying on the other halfback, Chuck Hunsinger. I believe Doug Belden was the quarterback. As I recall, Doug faked to Chuck, then handed to me, and I broke straight over the middle.

"I remember their linebacker actually pushed me aside at the line of scrimmage trying to get to Chuck, not knowing I had the football. I shot through and nobody touched me the rest of the way."

The rest of the way for the Clearwater speedster was 70 yards for a touchdown. It was suddenly 6-0, Florida.

Wolf called on Laz Lewis to kick the point-after. He had missed his first three of the season, then hit two in the previous week's game against Auburn. This time, he was good for a 7-0 lead.

"We felt good, but I can't say we felt confident," said Fletcher Groves, the rugged little guard who had thrown a key block in the touchdown dash and was game captain.

The Gators, juiced up by the lead, checked State's powerful running game but was having trouble with the passing. In the second period the Wolfpack finally worked the ball down the field with its aerial attack, and Charley Richkus scored from the three.

Jim Byler, a 20-year-old sophomore kicking specialist from Chicago, kicked wide, and Florida made it through the half and then the third period still ahead 7-6.

It was that way with three minutes left, after a punishing clipping penalty stopped a Florida drive at the State ten and gave the Wolfpack another opportunity with plenty of time left.

On a first down at the Gator 45, Richkus threw toward end George Bloomquist at the Florida 10. Forbes stumbled and ran into Bloomquist before the ball got there, and the interference call gave State a first down at the 10.

When Florida became coed after World War II, unchanged was the Gator favorite song, "We Are The Boys From Old Florida," being sung here in 1948 by these unboys.

Things seemed then to turn Florida's way. A clipping penalty moved the ball back to the 25, and on the next play Loran Broadus intercepted a Richkus pass at the 20 and returned it to the 30. Time was running out, the game seemed safe, with the losing streak broken.

On the first play Florida fumbled and State recovered. Here was the pressure all over again, a 13-game loser against a team they could not beat.

Three tries got the ball to the Florida nine. But the Gators' front stiffened, surrendering four yards in three attempts. It was fourth and goal, thirty seconds left, and Feathers went to his placekicker, Byler, again.

The try was not even close.

"It was a shank," remembered Kynes.

"It was the prettiest sight I remember seeing in football," said Crago. "It shot right and low. As soon as he hit it, you knew it was no good."

Laz Lewis ran out the clock with quarterback sneaks, and Florida took it, 7-6.

It was done! Over! Victory was theirs. At last. The first ever for Wolf at Florida. The first for the Gators since beating Presbyterian in 1945.

"We were all a little stunned," said Groves. "Then we ran over and picked up Coach Wolf and carried him onto the field. He'd not had a ride like that at Florida."

Up in the broadcast booth, Crago wished for those Roman candles as he shouted the great news back to Florida.

In Gainesville, "a delirious, singing, shouting, rampaging crowd of University of Florida students took charge of University Avenue within 10 minutes after the final whistle blew in Raleigh, North Carolina," read Whitey McMullen's account on page one of the *Gainesville Sun* the next day.

"Surging mobs blocked traffic, horns blasted to the unleashed enthusiasm of thousands of the Gator rooters as the throng wafted their way from the campus through downtown Gainesville and back to the campus. While downtown, the roaring crowd mobbed in front of all three theaters demanding the 'free shows,' an ancient heritage of Florida students after a winning football effort.

"And there rose from some the shouts of 'Who wants to

fire Wolf now?'

"Added to the confusion was the constant tolling of the bell in the Chemistry Building which some enterprising student invaded to send peal after peal into the other celebration noises."

Florida had indeed done it. The spell had been broken. Victory had come even though the Gators managed only 8 first downs to 17 for State. The Wolfpack had passed for 9 completions and 117 yards. Florida had passed 7 times, completed 3, for 13 yards.

But the score was 7-6, Florida.

After it was done, Feathers was a gracious man.

"Florida deserved to win and while I hated to lose, it couldn't have been to a nicer guy than Ray Wolf," he said.

Lineman Frank Dempsey, on returning to Gainesville and seeing the welcoming party the next day at the gym, said:

"Isn't it swell to look up and find people smiling at us again?"

From the crowd of the well-wishers, the *Gainesville Sun* reported, "came cries of 'Bring on the Tarheels.'"

That would be the following weekend's homecoming opponent, the North Carolina Tarheels and a fellow named Charlie Justice.

Rally Round The Coach, Boys

The rapture that was so long in coming to Florida players and partisans was quickly gone. Despite whatever inspiration that upset victory and a full house at homecoming could provide, it was not nearly enough to handle Carl Snavely's undefeated Tarheels. Charlie (Choo-Choo) Justice and a side-kick named Jose Rodgers did more celebrating than anyone, destroying Florida, 40-14, with three first-quarter touchdowns.

The next week the Gators trampled Furman, 34-7, with Forbes, on three successive carries by him, scoring touchdowns of 88, 57, and 41 yards. The victory made Florida appear capable of giving arch-rival Georgia trouble in Jacksonville the following Saturday, but it was not to be. Johnny Rauch passed for 133 yards and two touchdowns and ran for two more in a 34-6 smash of Florida before a standing room only crowd of 23,000.

Suddenly the undercurrent against Wolf swept the state again, and the coach, who then had a year and a half left on his contract, would be under fire until the day he left.

After the Georgia game, Pete Norton, sports editor of the *Tampa Tribune,* had some familiar phrases and philosophies to offer his readers:

"Wolf took over a green, inexperienced football team, and after almost two years it is still one of the youngest squads playing a major schedule in the South. The fact that the Gators will lose only five men during the next two years is indication enough that the current team is composed, for the greater part, of freshmen and sophomores and should reach peak form in

1948 and 1949.

"This is not written to alibi for Wolf, but as a cold statement of fact, and proves beyond a shadow of a doubt that Florida material is not as good as that at rival SEC schools.

"Next year, and we hate to write those two words after so many 'next years,' the Gators will have a better balanced attack with Angus Williams, a fine quarterback during his freshman year in 1945, back at the helm."

And so on.

Wolf finished the year with a tie at Tulane and wins over Miami and Kansas State for a 4-5-1 record, and all predicted better things for 1948, the final year of his contract.

Things did get better—slightly. With Hunsinger reaching maturity, the season went 5-5. Against Auburn at Tampa, in the year's third game, Florida took a 16-9 victory for their first Southeastern conference win under Wolf, their first league win since 1945, and their first in 16 tries. It was a fact, however, some noted at season's end, that Auburn that year beat only Southern Mississippi and tied Louisiana Tech for a 1-8-1 record.

That year the Gators still could not handle Georgia, but played about their best game of the year in the finale against Alabama, even though they lost, 34-28.

Hunsinger's superb performance in that game—he scored on a 96-yard kickoff return, a 77-yard run, and a 5-yard pass reception—prompted *Birmingham News* Sports Editor Zipp Newman to write the lyrics for a song about him. Early Crumly wrote the music, and they called it the Hunsinger song. The song, sung "brightly," the authors cautioned, went:

Verse—
Hunsinger's a humdinger
Not ever will he linger
In ramming a ball
Thru the en-e-my's wall.
Chorus—
No player is torrider
Than this lad from Florida
Hun-sing-er the Hum-ding-er
You ought to see him go.
Verse—
I may be a bum-sing-er

143

But he's the goods
Is Hun-sing-er
No campus flirt
But an end he can skirt.
There is no record of the number of copies it sold, but Hunsinger is one of the few of the Florida football fraternity involved in song. Doug Dickey would be later, as coach.

Written for and dedicated to Gator halfback Chuck Hunsinger.

Despite Hunsinger's rave notices and despite the near win against Alabama, Wolf's three-year contract was up. His cumulative record was 9-19-1. Three of the wins were over Furman. Only one was a Southeastern Conference victory—that over Auburn, which was then in annual competition with Florida for last place. Wolf had not beaten Georgia.

It is likely that his time would have been up had not the students and football team come to his support with public demonstrations. A giant rally was held outside the old College Inn on campus. Speaking were student leaders, including captain-elect Jimmy Kynes, who with Hunsinger had made all-SEC in 1948. Wolf was given a one-year contract extension and told to produce.

"I felt we had made some progress and could have a decent season," Wolf said, looking back.

But it was not in the cards. The season went 4-5-1.

The year 1949 wound up with one great achievement and one very, very low point.

After beating The Citadel, Furman by a point, tying Auburn, 14-14, and smashing Tulsa (with Jim Finks at quarterback for the Hurricanes), Florida was 3-2-1, facing Georgia at Jacksonville with the wolves howling. The Bulldogs were having an uncommonly bad year and were 3-4. Florida had a chance, but Georgia was favored.

With 36,500 watching, the Gators had one day of the coveted "next year." Hunsinger and Kynes led the way as the Gators clubbed Georgia 28-7.

Norton's story went:

"The score was the biggest ever made against a Georgia team, and the margin of victory cracked the record made by the 'wonder team' of 1928 that licked Herdis McCrary and his Company 26-6 at Savannah.

"Chuck Hunsinger, who went into the game rated the best running back in the South, came out of the contest ranked among the top ball-luggers in the country.

"The fleet-footed Gator back gained 174 yards in 18 tries, more than the whole Georgia team, which moved the ball 141 in all. Hunsinger scored three of the four Gator touchdowns and placed the ball on the other with quarterback Angus Williams, who called his best game of the year, sneaking it across."

But as was the habit, the joy was but for the moment. The Gators lost their final three games, 35-0 to Kentucky, 28-13 to Miami with nearly 57,000 watching in the Orange Bowl, and finally 35-13 to Alabama.

Perhaps none of Wolf's defeats at Florida matched that applied by Kentucky in Tampa in November, 1949. Coach Paul (Bear) Bryant had a great, great team with Babe Parilli at quarterback.

Phillips Field was oversold. Some counterfeit tickets added to the problem, and people lined the sidelines, actually spilling onto the field.

Williams, the quarterback, would say later: "It was the most crushing defeat ever in my experience. It was a total beating, physically and on the scoreboard."

Hunsinger gained only 22 yards in 10 carries against the awesome Kentucky forwards, the lowest output of Chuck's career. Kentucky rushed for 310 yards, though Parilli played only a half, and the Gators suffered their only shutout of the year.

Florida never got beyond the Kentucky 30. Williams said he had trouble getting backs to take the football. "Why, I'd hand it off to them and they'd hand it back!" he said.

People on the sidelines said later that they occasionally heard from the Gator huddle, "Hell, no. Not me!"

Williams said that when he would fake to a back, the back immediately threw up his hands to show the onrushing Kentuckians he did not have the ball.

In the *Tampa Tribune* the next day, one observer wrote that, "The only clean tackle made by a Florida man all day was by the manager, Dick Stratton, who was tending to a wounded Gator on the sidelines, and when it appeared the injured man might be trampled by a Kentucky runner on an end sweep, Stratton brought down the back."

Stratton later became a top Jacksonville television personality, president of the Gator Bowl, and for years managed and narrated the Gator television playback series.

The losses to Miami and Alabama were academic.

Wolf had assembled a 13-24-2 record, a win percentage of .351, and had replaced Josh Cody as producer of the worst mark. He was gone.

Beleaguered Coach Wolf takes to public forum in his own behalf, with F Club's support.

"I don't remember the details. But I knew it was going to happen," said Wolf. "It had to. I still feel like we built more foundations and plenty of character. It was a great experience. Dr. Miller (J. Hillis, then president) called me in and said that was that." It was.

Wolf was gone, on to a few years as head coach at Tulane, then a deanship at his alma mater, TCU.

Florida was enveloped in a demand for a total change, a new looking, a winning program never before equalled.

The governor of the state got involved. Something was going to be done. This time.

Honor Roll Of The Golden Era

If it is true that full appreciation of things comes after departure, it is also true at Florida. After time dims the memory, the bad times are funny, but the good times are still good. Inevitably the school tie grows brighter, the knot tighter.

That crowd of Gators who performed and suffered the pains and pressures of The Golden Era have lived those truths to the fullest. Generally, The Golden Era was the full four years of Bear Wolf's coaching—1946 through 1949—though the guts of it was during that thirteen-game losing streak. Through the years it has become so fashionable to be associated with The Golden Era of Florida Football that there are those who proudly proclaim involvement but who really do not qualify.

For the last dozen years, players and families of The Golden Era have met annually at some spa for story-telling and getting reacquainted. For the last half-dozen years Crystal River has been the favorite spot.

As is the case with most organizations, it soon was not enough just to meet and talk. A purpose was sought. Eventually, TGE developed a scholarship system to aid children of its departed comrades. Recently they contributed to the medical school education of Doug Belden, Jr., son of their admired quarterback who fell before his time, the victim of an aneurysm.

Belden was many things to Florida and those with whom he associated, but mostly "he was a leader and a complete man," said Coach Wolf. He was Florida's last four-sport letterman (football, basketball, baseball, and track) and at the time of his death was a successful businessman, civil leader, and devoted father. Indeed Belden was a contributor to the idea that The Golden Era should have purpose beyond fun and feast.

Is it so strange that this group from a single football period should hang so close together after college?

"Why not?" asked Marcelino Huerta. "We learned it at Florida. We always hung together. It was a rule. The way we were playing, it was for our own safety."

Here then follows the Honor Roll of The Golden Era, those Gator Gallants who tried so, as Wolf said, many of whom meet regularly and call Wolf by phone to chat with him and perk him up, just as they did during their football losing days. Here is the Honor Roll of The Golden Era, those who were varsity players on the teams of 1946 (0-9-0), 1947 (4-5-1), 1948 (5-5-0), and 1949 (4-5-1):

Bill Adams, Milt Adkins, Billy Mims, Tommy Balikes, Tommy Bishop, Harold Branch, Buddy Carte, Joe Chesser, Frank Dempsey, Bobby Forbes, John Gilbert, Bob Gilbert, Charlie Fields, Jimmy Kynes, Harry Hobbs, Chuck Hunsinger, Walker Jamison, Charley Walker, Leslie Mier, Ottis Mooney, Paul Mortellaro, Frank Lorenzo, Jim Kehoe, Dick Pace, Billy Parker, Jim Robinson, Joe Pratt, George Hills, Julian Schamberg, George Sutherland, Warren Tiller, Bill Turner, Vic Vaccaro, Broughton Williams, Hal Griffin, Dick Wiggins, John Cox, Jack White, Joe Hawkins, Grant Hester, Dewell Rushing, Aaron Brown, Ray Gatch, Fal Johnson, John Natyshak, Brady Mitchell, Corlis Carver, Bob Cummings, Cliff Sutton, Louis Pirozzolo, Wilbur Force, Tommy Bray, Ben Ewing, Hugh Adams, Fletcher Groves, Dick Lashley, Sammy Ciccone, Dave Wood, Bam Webster, Glenn Cary, Harold Hazlewood, Bill Meares, Doug Belden, Laz Lewis, Danny Sliman, Loren Broadus, Joe Michael, Fred Montsdeoca, Leroy Poucher, Eldridge Beach, Jim Yancey, Earl Scarborough, Alex Gardiner, Bob Gruetzmacher, Freddy Rozelle, Sam Cole, Red Mitchum, Jack Wells, Fred Pratt, Pat Driggers, Joe Garcia, Cail Lee, Marvin Brice, Conrad Dutton, Denny Herndon, James Jackson, Elphia Harden, Angus Williams, Wiley Bratcher, Scotty Peek, Lumbus, Kourlos, Russ Godwin, Don Brown, Carl Calnero, Handford Knowles, Bob Horton, Bob Horvath, Carroll Mc-

Two all-SEC players, center-linebacker Jimmy Kynes (left) and premier runner Chuck Hunsinger.

Donald, Paul Wheely, Dan Hunter, Charlie LaPradd, Jim French, Jimmy Smith, John Patsy, Tom Sebring, Cliff Freeman, Ellis Hunt, Bubba McGowan, Herman Bunton, Robert Mohler, Myron Gerber, Claud David, Bob Hewlett, and John Martin.

A fascinating number of these men have sent sons into uniform at Florida, and a fascinating number have gone on to leadership in national, state, county, and city affairs, to fine careers in coaching and education and in politics and business.

Considered optional members of The Golden Era are those freshmen of the 1949 team, the last year of Wolf. They were not eligible for regular season play, but their association with those on the varsity was sufficient to qualify them for membership if they chose. Some have, some have not.

Those eligible as Golden Era members if they choose are:

Hubert Brooks, Jackie Pappas, Len Balas, Haywood Sullivan, Billy Morris, Jim Rauls, Bobby Flowers, Jack Nichols, Jimmy Reeves, Claude David, Papa Hall, Floyd Huggins, Dickie Rowe, Curtis King, Buford Long, Billy Reddell, Bobby Knight, Sam Oosterhoudt, Kent Stevens, Joe Wright, Mikey Kelly, Dan Howell, and Tommy Bray.

Nine Golden Era members played all four years of Wolf: Tommy Bishop, Frank Dempsey, Jim Kynes, Chuck Hunsinger, Frank Lorenzo, Billy Parker, Bill Turner, Hal Griffin, and John Cox. They are the most honored members and permanent members of the executive board. And Hal Griffin perhaps gave more than any. He played in every game the Wolf-Gators played in The Golden Era.

Golden Era chronicler and bard Red Mitchell says The Golden Era can best be described by a conversation tackle Curtis King had with Bob Woodruff, the man who would succeed Wolf, shortly after Woodruff arrived on the Florida scene.

"Woodruff had stopped the scrimmage and was lecturing on a coaching point," said Mitchum. "He had gotten specifically to the importance of the tackle position and had said that's where most games are won and lost. King was watching an airplane flying overhead, and when Woodruff spied him and recognized he was inattentive he shot the question at King: 'King, where are most football games lost?'

"King, without hesitating, shot back: 'Why, right here at Florida, coach.'"

He Wanted To Be A Chemist

In 1939, still relatively early in Florida's football depression period, Dan Riss took on a student assistant to broadcast Gator football games, live from Florida Field, reconstructed from Western Union when the Gators were on the road.

University radio station WRUF held its customary auditions for student announcers in the fall of 1938, and among those failing was a bright, young friendly-faced chemistry student named Otis Boggs. Boggs reapplied and got a job in the spring recreating a Mulberry-Green Cove Springs basketball game.

This time Riss liked what he heard and hired Boggs for $15 a month as a student announcer to work the 1939 Gator football games with him. Boggs did the color, Riss the action.

Young Boggs really wanted to be a chemist, with broadcasting as a hobby. But Riss left after 1939, and Otis Boggs took over play-by-play of Gator football games with the Mississippi State opener in 1940. Since then he has broadcast 311 Gator descriptions.

Otis has missed a few seasons, being gone for World War II during the 1944 and 1945 seasons, and in 1947 he went to Dallas for a year. He has even missed a couple of games, but for over 30 years he has been as much associated with Florida football as the nickname Gator.

"Sure, people blame me for some of the losses," he says, "but that's all right. I aim to associate with the Gators. After all, I am the voice of the Gators."

Otis Boggs and two of his early colleagues at WRUF, Sol Fleischman (right) and Ray Danzler (center).

He is cussed and discussed and gets mad at himself when he gives a number instead of a name, or when he uses one of his more common cliches, like "helmet high," or "booming spiral," or a kickoff that goes "end-over-end."

Boggs was born near the Clemson football field, but went through school in Florida, winding up high school at Auburndale where he was class valedictorian and a good basketball and baseball player. He graduated from Florida with a group major in history, German, English, and chemistry.

Teaming with Boggs in the booth are engineer-director Bob Leach and color man Ted Covington, a Lakeland insurance man who does the job just because "I like it."

So does Otis like it. That is clear from his broadcasts, his full attention to the game, his genuine excitement without losing coherency.

"I defy anyone to sit down and talk for two and a half hours and make no mistakes in reporting or grammar," said Otis. "And I defy anyone not to get caught up in the excitement going on. I'm sure I'm biased. This *is* the Florida network, and I've been looking at them a long time. But I hope I never belittle an opponent or fail to give credit. On the other hand, you can't escape letting people know who you are for."

His biggest moment?

"Being able to broadcast Florida's win over 'Orburn' (he also says 'Orburndale') in 1973. I broadcast the first game played at Cliff Hare Stadium with Florida, when Charlie Tate scored the touchdown that tied the game. It was the dedication. Finally winning there meant so much."

"My ambition is to broadcast the game that wins Florida the Southeastern Conference championship. I have my script ready. After 311 games, I should have."

His favorite criticism of himself?

"Well, I guess it was the Florida physics professor who kept hearing me describe 'end-over-end' kickoffs. He wrote and told me that on a kickoff, the ball does not go 'end-over-end,' but instead it goes 'end-under-end.' Now don't you know if I said that on an opening kickoff sometime, thousands of listeners would turn to another thousand and say, 'Did you hear that? Old Otis is off to a good start!'"

We Want A Winner!

Fuller Warren always was convinced that among his most popular promises in his successful 1948 campaign for governor was pledging a winning football team at the University of Florida.

"Next to my pledge to try to get the cows outlawed from public highways (which he achieved), my pledge to try to get that winning team at Florida seemed to get most applause," Warren recalled.

"The punch line, 'We'll bring the Rose Bowl to the Orange Bowl,' nearly always got an enthusiastic response," he said.

Specifically the governor indicated top executive support for such a campaign to upgrade football at Florida, and appointed some of his friends to help find a topnotch coach and assure that he could be paid enough money and get enough support to make changes he wanted.

He also backed a unique bill that would draw athletic scholarship money from pari-mutuel sports in the state.

"The idea of a night for football scholarships at pari-mutuel tracks was not my idea. It was that of William H. (Bill) Johnson of Jacksonville, and it is my recollection that the bill passed the legislature easily."

The bill called for setting aside a day or night from each meeting at the Florida tracks to turn profits directly to the University of Florida athletic association for football scholarships.

(Florida State was not included at that time because it was

just beginning its modern-times football program after being turned from a girls' school to co-educational. Later, funds from those days at tracks and jai alai frontons were pooled and divided among all the state's athletic departments, thus diluting it considerably. Furthermore it became permissible for a pari-mutuel plant to hold another day for a private institution in its area, as the Miami tracks would do for the University of Miami, the Tampa tracks for the University of Tampa. In time so many charity organizations sought the same considerations that the tracks began to back away and asked the legislature to strictly limit the number of "charity" and "scholarship" programs.)

But in the beginning, when Florida football was in desperate financial straits, the idea rescued the program.

"At the beginning of World War II and before the United States entered it, Churchill said, 'Give us the tools and we'll finish the job,'" said Warren. "Our administration gave some winning tools to the University of Florida, and it was a proud moment for me when that 1952 Gator team had its fine season (7-3) and then went to the first bowl game—which it won—ever. I regard it as a politician's promise kept, at times an all too rare thing indeed."

The coach-hunt committee went hard at it in seeking a top man to replace Bear Wolf, who resigned December 5, 1949. It is a fact that two coaches of great accomplishment came very close to taking the job.

Jim Tatum was one. He had gone to Maryland in 1947 and already produced two bowl teams, including the 8-1-0, 1949 team that beat Missouri in the Gator Bowl. Tatum was approached by Sam Butz of Jacksonville and expressed interest. But Dutch Stanley, still head of the physical education department, was in charge of the search.

"Tatum wanted too much," Stanley recalled. "He wanted too much control, as I recall. It wouldn't have worked. It didn't."

But even before Tatum—in fact, prior to Wolf's resignation—overtures had been made to Red Sanders, former Vanderbilt coach who had gone to UCLA the year before. Sanders was offered the job and shook hands that he would accept it but later changed his mind.

156

All the years of the Gators there also have been cheerleaders such as these. From left, back: Joe Evans, Bambi Goodman, Bernard Palmer, Pinky Leff, Doug Matranga, and Fred Wilson. From left, front: Gee Gee Gahr, Helen Kiekhaefer, Mary Lou DeNyse, Diana Ryan, Verena Fogel, and Patda Warren.

Freddie Russell, longtime sports editor of the *Nashville Banner* and a close friend of Sanders' remembers:

"Red had left Vanderbilt after the 1948 season to go to UCLA. At that time the UCLA job was not nearly as attractive as it would seem now. He was an instant success and, as it turned out, UCLA firmly resolved to hold him to his contract when Florida went after him.

"I was covering the minor league baseball convention at Baltimore in early December, 1949, when I got a telephone call from Sanders telling me confidentially that he was definitely going to Florida and he was going to meet with the members of the Florida Athletic Committee and Sam Butz in Atlanta within a few days. He wanted it to be super secret. I suggested that if he were seen in Atlanta it would arouse curiosity and that it would be much better for him to meet them in Nashville where, if necessary, he could say he was just back visiting his parents.

"They did meet in Nashville and a firm agreement was reached, but nothing signed. The committee urged Red to go ahead and sign, but he did not want to do that until he had returned to UCLA and informed them that he was going to Florida. He definitely was not trying to get more money from UCLA.

"Dutch Stanley can verify this for he was there. Red did shake hands with them and agreed to come to Florida. Sam Butz (veteran Jacksonville newsman) was a close friend of Red's and keenly disappointed when he changed his mind. I personally am convinced Sanders, with his tremendous recruiting and coaching ability, would have established a dynasty at Florida," said Russell.

It was so firm in Sanders' mind that he was taking the Florida job that he had decided on many of his assistants. But, at Los Angeles, a mighty student rally and pleadings of the administration forced Sanders to change his mind.

On December 8, a United Press dispatch read:

"Football Coach Henry R. (Red) Sanders cast his lot today with the West, deciding to remain at UCLA where he just finished his first season, rather than return to his native South and the University of Florida.

"It is believed UCLA matched Florida's financial offer, a rumored $15,000 a year on a long-term contract, and agreed to give Sanders more and better athletes to turn out a winning team."

Stanley and his committee resumed the search.

"I called Bernie Moore for a recommendation," said Stanley. Moore, longtime coach at Louisiana State, was the new commissioner of the Southeastern Conference. "Moore recom-

158

mended Bob Woodruff."

Woodruff, 34, head coach at Baylor since 1947, had improved the overall athletic plant and had rebuilt the slumping Bears to the point where they ran through an 8-2 season in the just-finished 1949 campaign.

A tough interior lineman, Woodruff was a hero for 1936-38 Tennessee teams that won 23 and lost 5 under Coach Bob Neyland. He graduated with an engineering degree and stayed for a couple of years to coach with Neyland before World War II. Woodruff spent enough time in the service to rise to the rank of major.

At one point in the military he had helped Earl Blaik coach those Glenn Davis and Doc Blanchard national championship teams at West Point, then on discharge went to work for Bobby Dodd at Georgia Tech.

Woodruff was handy when Florida went looking for him.

"I was in Miami," Woodruff recalled. "I knew about the Florida job. Some ole boy on the military staff at Florida called me and said I ought to get interested. I guess I was. I was in Miami coaching for Andy Gustafson in the North-South Shrine game.

"I got the call to come to Gainesville for an interview, if I could. I remember Margaret (his wife) and I flew to Jacksonville and were driven to Gainesville. I looked over the facilities, and we just talked.

"Later, I'd tell them the things I thought it would take to give Florida the overall program they wanted."

When he told "them," there was some balking and some flak, as Governor Warren said, but "they bought it."

Bob Woodruff was hired as head football coach and athletic director January 6, 1950.

He was hired in the most unlikely of places—at Florida State in Tallahassee, a school with whom he would do battle on and off the field in the future. The board of control was meeting there at the time.

His contract was for seven years and a staggering $17,000 a year.

159

The Choice: Burly Bob

"That meeting of Woodruff and the board was not a quickie," said Stanley. "He wanted so many changes. I believe it took about 12 hours, really."

Woodruff did want many things beyond the $17,000 salary and the seven-year contract.

"We had to have many things," said Woodruff, thinking back. "We weren't getting the players, didn't have the money or the authority to function. I needed some working room and some way to make that money.

"But, they agreed. They gave me just one order.

"They told me I had to beat Georgia."

Woodruff would do that. It would not be right away, but he would fulfill that most serious order. In his ten years of head coaching the Gators he would beat Georgia six times. Once he got rolling, he beat Georgia six of the last eight, an achievement of which he is most proud.

But, he said, "We needed many things, to get Florida on its feet.

"I proposed we go up with the West Stands at Florida Field to increase capacity to 40,000, and plan to enlarge more later. I needed to borrow $750,000 to do it, against future ticket sales. We did, and we paid it off 10 years ahead of time.

"I wanted the separate department of athletics to have working room, and the athletic director would answer only to the president.

"We needed to redevelop and reorganize the Booster

Club—the Gator Boosters—as the extra money raiser for scholarships for all our sports. I wanted Everett Yon to run it," and he did effectively until his death.

"I wanted to stop playing all over the state, keep the Georgia game in Jacksonville, but have the rest of our home games at Florida Field. We'd need to to pay off the enlarging of the stadium.

"I wanted to support the Florida High School Activities Association and Florida Coaches Association so we could work better in recruiting Florida athletes," and that happened with an annual clinic on campus and then the creation of the high school all-star games.

He also wanted, and got, money to hire more and better, in his judgment, assistant coaches.

Woodruff's plan was not just for football but for the overall athletic program which if improved would contribute to football's stability, he felt.

He also had that race track money and he had himself seven years, much longer than any coach before him, he had the governor behind him, and he was taking over a program on which it really would not take much to improve.

And while he took over a squad that had almost no veterans, he inherited a marvelously talented freshman team, one perhaps as talented as the one he would leave his successor 10 years later.

Woodruff quickly assembled a fine staff. In fact it was to his credit that he surrounded himself with good coaches, many of whom went on to important head jobs elsewhere.

Frank Broyles was one of the first men he hired. Broyles, a standout back at Georgia Tech, came as a backfield coach and later became head coach at Arkansas. It was Broyles who developed the man who would take over Florida's head coaching job in 1970—Doug Dickey, then a freshman on that first Woodruff-Broyles team. Later Broyles hired Dickey as an assistant, and still later Woodruff hired Dickey away from Broyles to become the head coach at Tennessee.

But, there in 1950, Woodruff also named to his first staff, John Sauer, who came from Earl Blaik's staff at Army and who also went on to important deeds in college and pro coaching; Tonto Coleman from Abilene Christian who wound up commissioner of the SEC; Eibner, Sam McAllister, Mush Battista, and of course, Dave Fuller, who stayed around longer than anybody.

Bob Woodruff took that staff, his projected program, and he indeed helped Fuller Warren keep his bond with the people of Florida. Woodruff fulfilled his seven-year contract, then received a three-year extension. He in his time returned respect to the Gator athletic program, football and other sports. He brought football to a level Florida had not before experienced in the SEC. He produced all-Americans and all-SEC players. He made the football program financially sound. He took the Gators to two third-place finishes. No seconds or firsts, but two thirds. Gators before him had not approached that plateau.

He beat Tennessee and Louisiana State, and he beat hated Georgia. He was involved in the origination (if grudging) of the series with Florida State University, and he won both of his games with that school. He produced several teams that were giants on defense. He produced Florida's first genuine bowl team, then a second.

He took the program far. But not quite all the way and that, and his own manner, and his passion for defense would in the long run be his undoing. Woodruff did not win the SEC. He took the Gators to no bowl other than the friendly Gator in Jacksonville. His teams lost, it seemed, so many, so very many, close ones.

In 1958 his Gators wound up 6-4-1, including the 7-3 Gator Bowl loss to Mississippi. The four losses were by a total of 15 points. Then there were the 6-6 tie and a 7-6 win over Georgia.

His overall SEC record was 54-41-6 against one of 13-24-2 by his predecessors.

It was, in the long run, Woodruff's own built-in inability to speak publicly, express himself, to state his position and make his point, and his own firm reluctance to try, that did him in. His press relations began poorly, became strained, and wound up terrible because he was what he says he was, "the oratorical equivalent of a blocked punt." He seemed to drift into his own thoughts in the midst of a conversation or press conference, totally oblivious to what was going on about him, to the questions asked. He simply did not answer questions at times.

Instead, he started a new conversation about whatever it was that had captured his thoughts. He did not intend to be evasive or rude, but to many it seemed that way. Toward the end he simply refused to discuss problem areas and offered no defense against complainers.

Among his good friends was the owner of Camp Mack, a fishing hideaway without phone and at the dead end of a road that led to the banks of the Kissimmee River, near Lake Wales. Woodruff often went there to avoid the world and to think. Woodruff was there for a day during the final, beleaguered 1959 season, and he noted that camp proprietor Leon Denton had put in 100 acres of watermelons on some of his property.

"He told me I ought to stick to what I know—that if I didn't get out of the watermelon business I'd lose my shirt,"

Burly Bob Woodruff (center) and his early fifties staff, from left: John Mauer, John Rauch, Dale Hall, Woodruff, Hobe Hooser, Hank Foldberg, and John Eibner.

said Denton. "I told him I would if he'd get out and answer some of those people talking about him and wanting some answers. I said if he didn't do that he was going to get fired.

"Well, he didn't and I didn't, and I lost $15,000 on the watermelons like he said I would and he lost his job like I said he would."

Woodruff got a great kick later when he was athletic director at Tennessee and had grown truly heavy, better then suiting the name Burly Bob some Florida writers gave him, and Bobby Dodd came up with the classic about him. Woodruff had been hospitalized with a wrenched knee. It was bandaged and he and his 290 pounds were lying up there in the bed, when he admitted that he had hurt it water-skiing. Hearing that, Dodd wondered:

"Water-skiing, eh? Woodruff? Who was pulling him—the Queen Mary?"

Yet his organization was superb, his people loyal, his administrative talents admired. But no, he made no impassioned half-time speeches.

He had one battle cry. It was "Oski Wow-Wow!" It was a sort of charge for the defense to go-get-'em. It was yelled when something big was achieved on defense, or there was a fumble forced, or a pass interception. At Florida it now is shortened to only "Oski!"

Charley LaPradd, the St. Augustine whiz who became Florida's first genuine all-American since Dale Vansickle in 1928, said of Woodruff's half-time speeches:

"He would come to the blackboard, with us about, stand there, go to a corner of it, and make about three notations, very small. Then he'd go over them one by one, returning after each to see what the next was. Coach had lots of reminders of things. He had a manager to remind him when to blow the whistle at practice. But, at those half times, each one, after the final point, he'd do the same each game. He'd turn to the board, take another look, turn around to us, give us that little grin of his and yell, 'and don't forget to OSKI WOW-WOW!' He'd do it everytime. And we'd leap up and yell, Oski Wow-Wow."

LaPradd was a magnificient football player. He, according to Dickey, "was a man before the rest of us." He was an iron man on defense and made the first team Associated Press

164

all-America for 1952, went on to pro ball, then to president of a junior college before returning to Gainesville to go into business.

"Woodruff," said LaPradd, in excellent description, "with his long periods of silence, would make you wonder if he was 30 minutes ahead of you or 30 minutes behind."

His achievements and his records demonstrate he probably was 30 minutes ahead of his listeners—who were convinced he was 30 minutes behind.

In his 10 years as the guiding hand of Florida as it blossomed to near (but not quite) full bloom, he ran into one severe setback that was not his doing and which he could not handle, but which seriously crippled his ability to win in the SEC. Just as the state had affected the results of the former coaches by the lingering depression, its sudden spurt in post-World War II growth and prosperity worked against the football program. Because the other major state universities and junior colleges had not yet been built, Florida and Florida State began to be swamped with applications for admission.

Until the mid-fifties, a high school diploma from a state high school with a decent average was the only requirement for admission. In the mid-fifties, because of the overcrowding, there was instituted a Florida state high school senior placement test. Even graduates of Florida high schools had to score certain grades on it to qualify for admission to Florida and Florida State, and the minimum kept rising as applications increased, rising through the sixties.

It was developing that students from Florida high schools, many of them promising athletes, could not qualify for Florida but could qualify for other SEC schools and returned to play against and help defeat their own state school. Florida did lead, with Dr. Phil Constans a prime mover, a fight for raised SEC academic minimums, but they still were not on par with Florida, and the high standards imposed by population growth. That harrassment, and that handicap, was not overcome until 1970.

"It was probably the biggest battle I lost," said Woodruff. "Many thought I lost another, that I was against the Florida State series. I was not. What I did lose was when they put in the testing. It affected us. It hurt the program. But that was later.

My first problem was the first season and the little school, The Citadel."

The Foundation Is Laid, But The Skyscraper Is Slow Rising

As the new athletic director, Bob Woodruff got things moving right away. He began in early 1950 enlarging Florida Field, stepping up recruiting and building a staff, and also cranked up the machinery needed to provide face-liftings for the athletic association and the Gator Boosters.

But as the new head football coach, Woodruff faced problems that meant considerably slower results.

"At my first spring drill in 1950 we looked around and found we had one letterman lineman, Carroll McDonald from Belle Glade," said Woodruff. "I mean the only one with real experience. This was after big John Natyshak decided he didn't want to go along with some changes we instituted, so he left," for the University of Tampa.

A crop of fine sophomores made the outlook brighter. Included among them was a super quarterbacking prospect named Haywood Sullivan, the best-looking passer who had ever been in a Gator uniform. Also among them was a shot-shot runner in Buford Long of Lake Wales, a speed-merchant named J. (Papa) Hall of Tallahassee, and some promising linemen such as Jackie Pappas, Mikey Kelly, Hubert Brooks, and a muscular walk-on, Charley LaPradd. A few of the men with experience under Wolf and promise for the future were halfback Jack Nichols, punter Fred Montsdeoca, tackles Red Mitchum and Curtis King, halfback Sam Oosterhoudt, ends Don Brown, Len Balas, and Bobby Flowers, and two backfield veterans in Angus Williams and Loran Broadus. Four-year Williams moved to

Halfback J. "Papa" Hall turns corner behind blocking of Rick Casares (20) and Sonny May (49) in Florida's 14-13 win over Tulsa in the 1953 Gator Bowl.

defense and became Woodruff's captain.

"One of my best moves was going to the junior colleges and finding a fullback ready to play. That was Floyd Huggins at Fort Scott, Kansas."

Coming in as a freshman that year was a brilliant blockbuster from Tampa named Rick Casares, who was destined for stardom in the years ahead.

"I guess I had no win at Florida that was any more important than my first," said Woodruff, looking back.

With the faithful gathered with predictable great expectations for a rout of The Citadel, it took a 78-yard punt return in the fourth period by Nichols to save the day, 7-3, after The Citadel had gone ahead in the third quarter. The Nichols run was "as beautiful as any I had at Florida, certainly as necessary," said Woodruff.

But there were some interesting sidelights. Sullivan passed for 11 completions in 23 attempts for a brilliant debut, and the Gators started 16 untried sophomores or newcomers in the 22 positions in those days of two-platooning.

"I would say," said Woodruff, "it was a colorful first year."

Though the record was only 5-5, which was not much of an improvement over Wolf's 4-5-1 of 1949, the Gators won three of their first four games, first The Citadel, then adding Duquesne and Auburn (27-7) after a field goal by Georgia Tech meant a 16-13 loss in the third game.

The biggie for 1950 came in the fifth game. Woodruff's youngsters were 3-1 and primed for a trip to Nashville to play unbeaten Vanderbilt, sparked by quarterback Bill Wade and end Bucky Curtis. The Commodores, having whipped Middle Tennessee 47-0, Auburn 40-0, Alabama 27-22, and Mississippi 20-14, were riding high.

"We had two plays," Woodruff said. "One was Sullivan to pass and the other was Huggins on the draw. We had to figure a way to stop Vandy.

"We were watching film of Vandy games the week of our game with them. In the back of the room Red Mitchum was calling out, just as each Vanderbilt play would begin, 'Run,' or 'Pass.' I stopped the movie and asked Red what he meant. He told me that they had a lineman who was telegraphing. He would make a move on his haunches when it was a run. We dropped our man off him all day so our linebacker could see what he was doing, especially on third down, and he'd call out the play in our code, whether it was run or pass. It worked. I know Mitchum has told the story a thousand times, but it is true, I must admit. Red Mitchum and Curtis King were good tackles for me."

Florida won the Vanderbilt game, 31-27.

"It was hard to win, even that way, that Vandy game," Woodruff said. "We got the ball with 30 seconds left. Broadus was smart. I sent him and told him to use the old drop-dead quarterback sneak twice. Just take the ball and fall on it, then sit on it until the ref makes you get up. He did it the first time, then the second, and a big Vanderbilt lineman said to Loran, 'Get off that ball or I'll kill you.' Broadus pointed to the clock, which showed zero, and said, 'You don't have time, fella.'"

On that flight to Nashville, Mitchum reported, one other thing happened:

"Everyone was really keyed up for the game, and while we were flying, everyone was up tight. Curtis was sitting near the back of the plane so I started taking him glasses of water. He asked me why I wanted him to drink so much water, and I told him the trainer said if he did, he wouldn't get airsick. I took him about ten cups, and he drank them. I knew eventually he'd have to go to the bathroom.

"Finally he did, toward the rear of the plane. There was a curtain separating the rear of the plane from the front. As he went through the rear, I waited until he had time to go to the bathroom, then I got on the inter-com. I had practiced a long time imitating Curtis' voice and had it down. I had never before used it on the team, but this time I did, over the public address

Frank Broyles, the singularly successful Arkansas head coach, when he was an assistant at Florida in the early fifties.

Three Bob Woodruff Gator assistant coaches at work: Dale Hall (left) who became head coach at Army; John Rauch, who became head coach of the Buffalo Bills; and Hank Foldberg, who became head coach of the Texas Aggies.

system. I said, 'I don't want anyone to get too excited, but the right wing just fell off the plane.' It came over sounding just like Curtis, but he came out of the men's room just after I said it and not in time to hear it. As he walked through the curtains, Coach Woodruff jumped up and hollered: 'Get your mind on the football game, King.' Frank Broyles jumped up and hollered: 'Get your mind on the football game, King.' Coach John Sauer got up and led Curtis to his seat and forced him down, also telling him to get his mind on the game.

"Curtis shook his head and said: 'Gosh, can't you even go to the bathroom without getting your mind off the football game?'"

There was not much to laugh about the rest of 1950. The Gators took a win over Furman, then fell consecutively to Kentucky 40-6, Georgia 6-0, Miami 20-14, and Alabama 41-13, meaning a 5-5 Woodruff inaugural.

Woodruff's second year was the same as the first, 5-5, with wins early and defeats toward the end. The Kentucky loss was much more respectable, 14-6, and two of the defeats were by single points only, 14-13 to Auburn, and 7-6 to Georgia.

The Gators were 4-2 after an important 40-7 romp over Loyola of Los Angeles and super passer Don Klosterman, but lost three in a row to Kentucky, Georgia, and Miami.

With a 4-5 record and only Alabama left, Florida prepared for the Tide's homecoming in Tuscaloosa, a 4-6 finish very much in prospect.

Alabama was a strong favorite, considering the Gators' three straight losses and total of eighteen points in the string. Woodruff's seven-year plan was falling behind. But things happened at Tuscaloosa.

A brief summary went:

"All the disappointment and frustration of one-point defeats, fumbles, and interceptions were turned on Alabama as the Gators stampeded the Red Elephants 30-21 in a wild and wooly homecoming upset. 'Bama led until the fourth quarter when Rick Casares kicked a 45-degree angle field goal from the four-yard line to climax a 96-yard drive. The clinch was applied later after Bill Wester intercepted a Tide pass and carried to the one where Sully scored. Haywood passed to Jim French for one TD, and Buford Long ran for two more. Sullivan had quite a day."

"Surely it was the highlight of a not-so-great year," said LaPradd, the star defender. "It was a great day. Casares, Sullivan, and Long, they were all brilliant. It then suggested to us we had a great future ahead in 1952. We talked of our 'next year' on the way home from Tuscaloosa."

172

Woodruff and his aides must have talked of it, too. They would return the entire backfield for 1952—Sullivan, Long, Casares, and Hall—plus LaPradd, new line sensation Joe D'Agostino, and a promising linebacker named Steve DeLaTorre, all to beef up the defense Woodruff was so insistent on having.

If ever there was to be a Year of the Gator, it looked for all the world like it would be 1952.

It was...in a way.

In fact, it might have been the best year of all if Florida's best quarterback up to that time had not also been Florida's best baseball catcher up to that time.

1952 — A Very Good Year

In Bear Wolf's last couple of years and continuing into Woodruff's time, with Governor Warren elected and the all-out effort for that winning Florida team underway, Gator recruiters went everywhere. Players were in great, great numbers, and many of them were quarterbacks.

That sweep of recruiters in late 1948 and early 1949 included concentration on the undefeated high school team in Dothan, Alabama. One back from that team, Bubba McGowan, had come to Florida. Now, assistant Mush Battista, the former fine Gator guard and a likeable, sincere sort, was back at Dothan trying to persuade a flashy, T-formation quarterback who could really throw the ball (football and baseball) to come to Gatorland. He could play right away as a sophomore in 1950, and Florida was then using the T-formation.

Up at Alabama the T-formation still was not it, and at Auburn not that much attention had been paid to Dothan's sensational quarterback named Haywood Sullivan. When he played in the first high school all-America game at Corpus Christi, Auburn went after him too, but "I think I decided on Florida for three reasons," said Sullivan, reaching into his memory to separate time and sports. "First, Florida was using the T, and I wanted to pass. Second, Bubba was there, a guard friend of mine, Billy Morris liked it and wanted to go, and Mush Battista worked so hard on me. He wanted us before anyone else did. Third, if I'd have gone to either Alabama or Auburn I'd have made one of the alumni groups in my town bitterly mad.

174

So, I picked Florida," said Sullivan.

Florida also said it would be okay to play baseball in the spring. Sullivan was a hard-hitting catcher. He spent his summers playing baseball in West Florida and South Alabama. He excelled in both at Florida those sophomore and junior years of 1950 and 1951.

"I guess I did get the biggest kick out of that last game in Tuscaloosa, in 1951, when I figured some in the win over Alabama. The game I hated the most was in 1950 at Lexington when Kentucky beat us 40-6 in the snow. It really snowed and the ice...I remember Bob Woodruff bought us all long-handle underwear, but that didn't work. They didn't last long. They didn't help at all. He spent $150 on them.

"And, after the 1951 season, well, then I had no real thought of doing anything but playing football at Florida in 1952, and baseball, of course. I was going to finish college and then probably play baseball. But I WAS going to play in 1952 with Long, Casares, Hall, and don't forget Sammy Oosterhoudt of Lake City. He was fine. We really thought we'd have a great team in 1952, and I wanted to be a part of it."

Then a couple of things happened.

First, major league baseball announced it was going to change its bonus rule. After 1952 anyone signing for more than a $6,000 bonus would have to stay on that team's major league roster for two years, whether he played or not. It was designed as a leveling rule to keep the rich from getting richer, and halt big bonuses.

Second, the Korean War was going strong, and Sullivan was in advanced ROTC. If he completed his senior year, he would then have a two-year obligation in the service. He could not play his baseball, and he would lose a ton of dough.

"I remember in the 1952 regional playoffs for a spot in the nationals, we lost to Duke but I had a great series. Hit some home runs and played well."

He impressed the baseball scouts. They began to put the heat on him. He was reminded of the bonus rule coming in, of the military obligation, and "I didn't need reminding we didn't have any money," he said.

Sullivan went to talk to Woodruff.

"He was nice, of course," said Sullivan. "I really didn't

Coach Bob Woodruff gets victory ride after his fine 1952 team won Gator Bowl over Tulsa.

know what to do."

He had been offered a $75,000 bonus by the Boston Red Sox. But he had to sign then.

"I remember Bob drove me to Jacksonville where we talked with Bill Terry," the Hall of Famer of the New York Giants who was in the automobile business there. He also was a Florida booster.

"We laid it out. Bill—and I'll not forget it—told Woodruff if what 'this boy says is true, it's a chance of a lifetime. I couldn't advise him not to sign.'

"We then drove to Dothan and talked with my parents.

176

Well, you know I signed with Boston."

And he went on to an impressive major league playing career, then one in management and administration. He is now the director of player personnel for the Red Sox.

He did go back to Florida for that final 1952 season but was ineligible to play, of course. Instead he helped coach the B-team and scouted.

"Yes, I got a little grief, but I understood. It was painful for me to watch those games and not be able to play.

"I didn't regret the decision. As it turned out the bonus rule did go into effect in November, 1952, so the truth is if I had not done what I did, I would have lost the $75,000. I needed minor league work and got it. I'd never have been signed for that amount and kept on the big league roster.

"As for Woodruff, he was a fine man about it, and I appreciate it."

Sullivan was missed. While 1952 became Woodruff's winningest year, and at that time the third winningest in all the years of the Gators, it gnawed at all involved that with Sullivan in the backfield it could have been the utopian fall. Instead it was a 7-3 regular season and worthy of the first true post-season bowl bid for Florida.

"When Sullivan left, it really did offer some problems," confessed Woodruff, who had brought in two more fine offensive coaches in John Rauch and Dale Hall. Hall would become head coach at West Point and Rauch a head coach in the pros.

First, he gambled. He moved Rick Casares to quarterback. Casares could kick, place-kick, and pass, some.

"But I felt out of place," said Casares. "I never really adjusted to it. I am a runner, and a blocker."

Over on defense was Doug Dickey, himself a quarterback from P. K. Yonge in Gainesville. It was a last-minute thought of freshman (and baseball) coach Dave Fuller that got Dickey to Florida. This was back in 1950. Dickey had hoped to play basketball at Florida, but not football. He was cutting grass as part of a job on campus as a freshman when Fuller rushed over to him and persuaded him to come out for the Gators that fall.

He did, and as a sophomore "I guess I got in three or four games at quarterback," said Dickey. "Haywood was the quarterback then, in 1951, and Rick backed him up a bit.

"In 1952 I was the safetyman. Casares was the quarterback. Fred Robinson and I were around as quarterbacks if needed."

Dickey ran a punt return 43 yards for one of the touchdowns, and Casares passed for two in the 1952 opener, a 33-6 win over Stetson.

The second game of 1952 was at Grant Field, in Atlanta, against a great Georgia Tech team. The year before, this Bobby Dodd club had gone 10-0-1 and beaten Baylor in the Orange Bowl 17-14 on a last-second field goal by a nerveless sophomore quarterback named Pepper Rodgers. Now the 1952 team had everybody back. Everybody included backs Leon Hardeman, and Glenn Turner, both Larry and George Morris on defense. That 1952 Tech team later put seven men on the 22-man first all-SEC team and gave up a total of only 52 points in 10 regular season games. Only one opponent scored 14 points.

Florida had beaten Stetson and Tech had crunched The Citadel 54-6.

It was a big one, and 32,000 came to see it. It was worth their time.

Florida moved ahead 7-0 on a 53-yard drive and three-yard run by Long, plus Dave Hurse's extra point. A 12-yard Bill Brigman pass to Buck Martin and Rodgers' conversion tied it at 7-7 through the half.

In the third quarter Papa Hall took a handoff from Casares, after the fake to Long, and broke into the clear for a 64-yard scoring run. Hurse's kick made it 14-7, Florida. But Brigman passed 24 yards to Jeff Knox, Rodgers kicked that point, and it was 14-14, not much time left.

"It was a tough game," remembered guard Hubert Brooks. "I remember Bobby Knight got his jaw dislocated and face smashed, and we left him in Atlanta after the game in the hospital.

"I remember Red Mitchum got knocked senseless but not out on a third down play, and as we lined up for a punt he said to me, 'I forgot what I do on a play like this.' I told him to stay right there and I'd be right back. I went down with the punt, then ran back and took Red by the arm. He was still there in his stance, and I led him off the field.

"But mostly I remember that little guy Rodgers because he was going off the field. He'd hurt his shoulder and it was fourth down, and Dodd sent him back into the game without his shoulder pads on."

He kicked a 17-yard field goal with only a couple of minutes left to give Tech the 17-14 victory over the Gators.

Georgia Tech went on to an 11-0-0 season then beat Mississippi in the Sugar Bowl 24-7. Only Florida scored two touchdowns in a game on Tech in 1952.

But the loss was there for Florida, an SEC loss, for Tech was still in the league then, and the offense had not clicked as Woodruff had hoped. Casares was not at home at quarterback and was missed as a runningback.

"I went to quarterback full time as soon as we got back from Tech," said Dickey. "It wasn't hard. There were those great backs and extra ones too. It was some kind of running attack. Rick was back at fullback. Fred Robinson and I would do most of the quarterbacking. He could throw. I couldn't.

Quarterback Haywood Sullivan fakes to Rick Casares and prepares to pitch to Papa Hall while Buford Long leads interference.

Wally Butts called me a knuckle-ball passer. On obvious passing downs Fred would come in. Otherwise I threw a few jump passes. We really didn't need to pass much."

The new combination bowled over The Citadel 33-0, then destroyed Clemson 54-13.

The Gators were rolling—and next was a poor Vanderbilt (0-2-1) in Nashville. It came to be the capsule opinion of Florida teams of the Fifties and Woodruff that they most certainly would lose one game they should not each season. Vanderbilt was that game for 1952. The Gators were lousy, falling behind 20-13 before managing to pull up to the respectable but academic seven point deficit. Vandy was an SEC member too. Florida was 3-2 but 0-2 in the SEC. Emotions were mixed. Talk of Sullivan's treachery was revived.

Georgia was next, at Jacksonville.

Woodruff still had not beaten Georgia in two tries, and the defeat by Vandy suggested that he was not going to in 1952 either. Georgia was 3-1 going against Florida and had taken a 19-7 win over the same Vanderbilt team that had beaten Florida.

The Gators wiped out Georgia 30-0. And it was a Georgia team that would finish 7-4.

"Casares was brilliant," confessed Georgia Coach Wally Butts later. "He could carry a 190-pound tackler 10 more yards."

It was the game of Casares' career. He carried 27 times for 108 yards and one touchdown, kicked all the points and a field goal of 24 yards. Long ran 77 yards for a score, and Robinson passed 12 yards to Len Balas for another.

"I think," said Dickey, "an interesting play was on the first play. Our Arlen Jumper and their great end, Harry Babcock, got in a fight, and both were thrown out."

Next the Gators beat Auburn 31-21, but lost to Tennessee 26-12, then downed Miami 43-6 and Kentucky 27-0.

They were only 6-3 and 2-3 in the SEC when the Gator Bowl offered them a bid to play Tulsa in the post-season game.

Many clubs let down after a bowl bid is received, but those Gators on December 6, bid in hand, shut out Paul Bryant's Kentucky team 27-0. Again Casares was great as was a defense that held Bryant's team scoreless for the only time that season.

180

Kentucky fumbled five times.

The summary was 7-3 overall, 3-3 in the SEC, an all-American for LaPradd, first team all-SEC for LaPradd and D'Agostino, second and third team all-SEC for Casares and Hall. Casares would go on to become one of pro football's super players with the Chicago Bears, after a final 1953 season at Florida.

The Gators finished 8-3 with a 14-13 Gator Bowl win over a Tulsa team that entered the game 8-1-1.

In the end Florida won the bowl game by the grace of a Tulsa offsides. It gave Casares the shot at another extra point try after he had missed the first. He made it the second time.

Florida shot ahead of Tulsa 14-0 on a one-yard Casares plunge and a 37-yard Robinson pass to Hall, plus Rick's kicks. Tulsa rallied, led by J. C. Roberts and Howard Waugh, to pull to 13-14 when Tom Miner's kick at the tying point was wide. Later, following another drive, another Miner kick at a field goal was no good, and Hall emerged the game's most valuable player.

It was a top team, that one on offense led by those great backs, plus linemen Curtis King, Jack O'Brien, DeWayne Douglas, Claude David, John Hammock, Sonny May, Hubert Brooks, Red Mitchum, Martin Cartlon and usual defensive starters LaPradd and D'Agostino, Bob Horton, Mikey Kelly, Howard Chapman, Jimmy Hatch, Art Wright, Arlen Jumper, co-captain Bubba Ware, Larry Scott, Harry Wing, Bob Davis and Jack Nichols.

"Statistically, overall," said Woodruff, "it was our best, because it was 8-3, but it was not our best in the SEC. We beat Georgia and maybe, I thought, things were on their way."

So thought plenty.

So they also thought how it may have been—with Haywood Sullivan.

"I wouldn't flatter myself to think it would have been better," said Sullivan. "But, yes, I have thought of what it might have been. Naturally."

181

Mid-Contract Blues

Bob Woodruff's middle years were neither distinguished nor undistinguished. They sort of happened and passed on into history without, on the surface, counting for much. Yet there were bright individual performers, and when it was over came the realization that his 1954 team had finished third in the Southeastern Conference, the highest place yet for a Florida team.

"In fact," said Woodruff, "as I look back, we came close to winning the SEC."

His 1952 season of 8-3 and bowl triumph had ended with more grand hopes for the 1953 season, but rules were changing and colleges had to convert from the one-way players of offense and defense to teams which played both ways.

"We weren't deep enough for that yet," he confessed.

Those 1953 Gators, with Casares and Dickey and many of those heroes of 1952 still around, finished a dismal 3-5-2 with only a victory over Georgia 21-7 worth reporting.

"It meant a lot to me," said Dickey, "because it was my best individual performance as a player in which I threw my only touchdown pass of my career. It went to Jack O'Brien and went 30 yards. Coach Johnny Mauer said when it left my hand he thought it was going out of the stadium, I threw it so high—but not that long."

In 1954, with a new key assistant named Hank Foldberg, the Gators had some new line hopes like John Barrow and Vel Heckman and veteran center-linebacker Steve DeLaTorre, a

182

punter named Don Chandler, a bruising fullback named Joe
Brodsky, and a platoon of quarterbacks—like Bobby Lance,

*Tonto Coleman, Florida freshman coach in the fifties who
became Commissioner of the Southeastern Conference.*

Dick Allen, and John May, and a broken-field whiz in and out of uniform named Jackie Simpson.

Florida finished 5-5 overall, but all five wins were over Southeastern Conference teams—Georgia Tech 13-12, Auburn 19-13, Kentucky 21-7, Mississippi State 7-0, and Tennessee in the finale, 14-0. It was Florida's first win ever, in eleven tries, over Tennessee. But, there were two SEC losses, 20-7 to Louisiana State at a time when Florida was 3-0 in the conference, and later a hated, critical, 13-14 loss to Georgia.

The loss to Georgia cost the Gators the title. Georgia had only a 3-2-1 record, and LSU, the other SEC winner over Florida, only 2-5. Florida had beaten challengers of that year, Georgia Tech, Kentucky, and Auburn. Alabama and Tennessee were slumping.

Mississippi won it with a 5-1-0 record and easy schedule. Georgia Tech finished second with a 6-2-0 record and Florida third at 5-2-0. Kentucky also was 5-2-0. A win over LSU early, or Georgia late, would have meant 6-1-0 and the Gators' first Southeastern Conference title.

In that bitter Georgia defeat of 13-14, the Gators fumbled seven times, both Georgia scores resulting from such errors. The week before, in the 7-0 win over Mississippi State, Florida fumbled nine times.

Dick Allen, generally alternating with Lance at quarterback, was knocked out in that Georgia game and "I believe that cost us the title," said Woodruff.

The non-league losses that year were 34-14 to Rice, 14-7 to Clemson, and a windup disappointment of 14-0 to Miami.

During his ten years Woodruff teams lost to Miami four of six times.

The season of 1955 was Woodruff's second loser, a 4-6-0 standard that included three finishing losses in a row to Tennessee, Vanderbilt, and Miami, and again only a win over Georgia (19-13) worth cheering about.

Woodruff in those middle years of 1953-54-55 had demonstrated defense as his coaching forte, and in those times quarterbacking was a primary problem, as was winning the close ones. He started to gain a reputation for losing the big ones close.

Bob Woodruff approached the seventh and final year of his

John Barrow, all-America Gator guard in 1956, who went on to become all-time, all-Canadian professional player.

contract in 1956 with a cumulative record of 30-29-3, almost dead-even. But the football program was respected, individuals were gaining all-star honors, financing was sound, and while hope still sprang eternal, the natives were a bit restless.

Woodruff's insistence on conservation on offense (which very nearly drove offensive aide Foldberg insane at times) was extraordinarily unpopular in defeat. Punting on third down is acceptable in victory but not in defeat, the old axiom reminded.

The So-Close Years

Among the wisest of Bob Woodruff's decisions was one not made on the sideline but in the Florida Field stands during the Florida High School all-Star game in August, 1955. As he watched, a slender quarterback from the South passed for two touchdowns in the 14-0 Rebel win.

The quarterback had written him the previous spring asking for consideration for a scholarship and he had heard from interested friends in Tampa suggesting a grant for that young man who had led Hillsborough High to great achievements, despite his 140 pounds. He was cool, could pass, and could punt out of bounds inside the 10 with surprising accuracy.

Tom Nugent, then the flamboyant coach of the pesky, uprising Florida State Seminoles, and Marcelino Huerta, coach at Tampa, had already offered the young man a scholarship. Nugent's offer was a one-year, make-good deal.

The night when Woodruff watched quarterback Jimmy Dunn perform so well for the South prep all-Stars, he had already signed that one-year contract with FSU, but he and his mom, Molly Dunn, had wanted a grant for four years.

At that time Florida and Florida State had no hands-off policy involving athletes who had signed grants. They were fair game until they enrolled. Later they would sign such a grant, but none was in effect when Woodruff sent Hank Foldberg down to see Dunn after the game.

He told Jimmy and his mom Coach Woodruff surely would

186

like to see them after the game, in the office. As this was going on, Nugent was congratulating Dunn and talking about scholarship.

Woodruff that night offered Jimmy Dunn a four-year scholarship to Florida. It was what Dunn wanted and sought from the start.

"I ask you," said his mother afterwards, "would you have taken four years over one if they were offered your boy?"

She and Jimmy took it, and later Nugent publicly suggested that the scholarship he had offered was for four (it was for one, the Dunn copy showed) and that "we still believe that in addition to football ability, moral fiber is important to every man."

Dunn never forgot that challenge, remembering it for a special purpose on a Saturday in late November, 1958.

Jimmy Dunn became in the seasons of 1956, 1957, and 1958, the heartbeat of Bob Woodruff's so-close years. In those three years Woodruff's teams went 6-3-1, 6-2-1, and 6-4-1 for an all-right 18-9-3 total. Twice they threatened the SEC title-chasers, once they went to the Gator Bowl again, and so many times they lost by the narrowest of margins in key, critical games.

Those years also began the series with Florida State, with a victory, and during those years little Jimmy Dunn would start all but four of the games. His starting-game record was 17-7-2. He played offense and defense. He made no all-SEC teams.

"Jimmy Dunn," said Woodruff later, "is pound-for-pound the best football player I ever coached."

That was the way Woodruff said things.

"I really don't remember having that much to do with Coach Woodruff as a player," said Dunn, now a Florida assistant in charge of the offense. "The assistants did most of the coaching, he the organization. Hank Foldberg and Harvey Robinson worked more with us."

They were working with the Gators of 1956 when it became apparent they had quarterback troubles.

"Dick Allen was back and to be number one," Dunn recalls. "They also had Jon May and had summoned Harry Spears from the army to come back and play some more. Mickey Ellenburg was around. I saw myself as number four.

The 1958 Gators at Disneyland before UCLA game. This was first modern Gator team to play UCLA.

"Then, Allen had some summer school book problems and left for the service. I moved to No. 3."

The Gators won that first game of Woodruff's so-close three years 26-0 over Mississippi State when Joe Brodsky made history by intercepting three passes, running a hundred yards with one for a score, and passing out in the end zone. He also was the top offensive ground gainer. Dunn punted superbly.

Clemson was tied 20-20, and Kentucky beat Florida 17-8, with its unsettled offense, though there were some brilliant runners, Rountree and Bernie Parrish, John Smyank, Don Deal, Brodsky.

In the Kentucky game Woodruff sent Dunn in as quarterback. He passed to Parrish for a score, and though that game was lost he was the starting quarterback.

Under the lithe Dunn, Florida set out on a great win streak. They beat Rice in Dunn's starting debut and in which "all I can say of my performance is I made no mistakes," he said. The Gators beat Rice 7-0, then Vanderbilt 21-7, LSU 21-6, Auburn 20-0, and Georgia 28-0. It was an impressive five game win streak—four of them in the SEC!

Florida then was an exciting 6-1-1 overall, built to a 5-1 standard within the SEC and had Georgia Tech and Miami left. Tech was the last SEC game. A win could mean a shot at the SEC title if Tennessee lost one of its three remaining games with Mississippi, Vanderbilt, and Kentucky.

The state was poised for something big again. Inexplicably Florida chose to start the senior quarterback, Spears, not Dunn. Fumbles were lost on the 25, 17, and 13, and there were short punts. Florida was thrashed 28-0, dropped to 5-2 in the SEC, and out of the race. Then Miami, led by Don Bossler, beat the Gators 20-7, and the flurry had frittered away to 6-3-1.

With much the same team in 1957 as in 1956 the Gators had an almost identical season. The 1957 result was 6-2-1 and 4-2-1. The nine-game schedule developed unexpectedly when the opener with UCLA had to be cancelled as Asian flu swept and decked the Gators.

However, even if the 1957 Gators had finished 9-0-0, they were not going anywhere. For the only time in the school's history, Florida was put on probation by the National Collegiate Athletic Association. They could not have gone to a bowl under any circumstance. The penalty had nothing to do with a football violation but with the transporting and feeding of baseball and basketball prospects. It was not serious and wound up meaning nothing, considering the record.

The big win in 1957 was a 22-14 upset of tough Louisiana State in Gainesville when all-American Billy Cannon was stopped cold. Rountree, Dunn, and Parrish were the offensive standouts, about the same ones to figure in a 22-0 victory over Georgia later on, another gratifying afternoon of that year.

The tie that season was a scoreless disappointment with Georgia Tech. Florida dominated the game and apparently scored on a Parrish to Rountree pass—but an illegal receiver was noted downfield. There was also the season-ending 14-0 win over Miami. The Hurricanes had had Woodruff's number until then, winning the first four.

The stage was set for a really big year in 1958. Sanctions would be off. Rountree was gone, but Parrish was returning with plenty of other heroes along with a defensive gang of muscle and one of the nation's best punters, Bobby Joe Green, now a Chicago Bear.

Then Bernie Parrish followed the lead of Haywood Sullivan in 1952, signing a contract to play pro baseball with the Cincinnati Reds. Parrish went on to an undistinguished baseball career and then tried pro football where he became a notable defensive back and then a politician.

As the years went on, there would be the thought that Woodruff, had he had more persuasive powers, might have been able to keep both Sullivan and Parrish.

But Parrish was gone for 1958, and "we were left with an interesting team," said quarterback Dunn. "We had a great punter in Bobby Joe and a great defense and a pony backfield. I stood 5-10, and I was the tallest. Don Deal, Doug Partin, and Jon Macbeth were all 5-8. Macbeth weighed 172, Deal and Partin 165, me 143. We also may have been the lightest major college backfield in the country. But we were geared to defense anyway."

The season, 1958, was one of the most unusual in Florida's impressive lineup of unusual seasons.

It went:

Florida   34   Tulane   14

Florida	7	Mississippi State	14	
Florida	21	UCLA	14	
Florida	6	Vanderbilt	6	
Florida	7	LSU	10	
Florida	5	Auburn	6	
Florida	51	Arkansas State	7	
Florida	21	Florida State	7	
Florida	12	Miami	9	
Florida	3	Mississippi	7	(Gator Bowl)

Within the SEC the finish was 2-3-1, worth a tie for eighth. Yet LSU managed to beat Florida only 10-7, and LSU went on to a 10-0-0 record and the national championship with Cannon that year winning the Heisman Trophy. LSU also won the SEC title. LSU beat Florida with a 12-yard field goal by Tommy Davis with three minutes left.

That season there was a classic 6-5 loss to muscular, menacing Auburn. The Tigers of that year finished 9-0-1, second in the SEC and fourth nationally. Auburn had won the national title the year before, when they beat Florida 13-0.

In that 6-5 affair Auburn showed such confidence in its defense that on its first series of downs it went for a first down on fourth with a yard to go on its own 38. And did not make it. Florida took over and went nowhere.

But after the scoreless first half, Florida took a lead on Billy Booker's field goal of 17 yards. It was 3-0 only until substitute quarterback Richard Wood passed Auburn ahead 6-3.

Then the Gators headed towards the upset of the year in football, a Mickey Ellenburg pass to Don Hudson giving first down on the Auburn 3. One play later a fumble gave the ball up. The Tigers made three rushes at the line, anchored by all-American Vel Heckman, got nowhere, and then Coach Shug Jordan pulled a grand strategy. He had quarterback Lloyd Nix take the ball behind the goal and kneel. Auburn gave up two points, a safety, but had a free kick and could punt away without harrassment. Even so, the score was narrowed to 6-5.

The pent-up, opportunish Gators came roaring back inside the five where at a critical point, third and short, there was an offsides. Ground was lost and Joe Hergert wound up trying a field goal from the thirty and it was not close.

There was no embarrassment, nor shame in defeat, as there

had been none the week before against LSU. But there were, in fact, defeats both weeks. The Gators were 2-3-1—surely the best 2-3-1 team in America—with Georgia next.

It was a rainy Jacksonville day, and Georgia pushed Florida all over the field. It was still 0-0 though, in the third quarter when Dunn called a routine option play to his left, starting at his own 24—nothing new or exciting.

Vel Heckman, all-America tackle, 1958.

His mother may have figured that it would be routine. She had ridden on the train all the way to watch the game, and at that moment she was powdering her nose in the ladies room.

"I went to the left," said Dunn, looking back on one of his two most vivid college memories. "The end came on in, so I cut inside him and back to the right. Then I cut the other way and scored."

Billy Booker kicked the point, and Florida won that pip, 7-6.

"I thought I had made a great run," said Dunn, "until I saw the movies. Then I saw Dave Hudson blocked three people. The only guys chasing me were big linemen, and it was raining."

Arkansas State was 51-7 and nothing the next week, and there ahead, with Florida only 4-3-1, lay the new great adventure—the first game ever against Florida State.

Florida's late great end Don Fleming hangs onto a wet ball in the 1958 Gator Bowl 7-3 loss to Mississippi.

Florida won it 21-7 after a nervous start, then beat Miami 12-9, and with that 6-3-1 record was invited to play the 8-2-0 Mississippi Rebels in the Gator Bowl.

One of the state's sportswriters predicted in advance, "Knowing the conservatism of Florida, or knowing its offensive capabilities, I predict Ole Miss will win 3-2."

The final score: Ole Miss 7, Florida 3.

Ole Miss scored on its first offensive maneuver with Bobby Franklin leading the way, and then Dunn led the Gators to a point from which Brooker kicked a 17-yard field goal. That was that—except for Florida fumbles at the Ole Miss 5 and 15, a Florida drive stopped at the Ole Miss 3, and some absolutely spectacular punting by Bobby Joe Green. One of Green's kicks, with a high snap from center, went 77 yards from the line of scrimmage!

It was done. The so-close years of Woodruff-Dunn. A new bucket of worms had been opened—the Florida State series—but the hue and the cry for Woodruff to win some of the big close ones went up louder and more often. For him, time was growing short.

But in his wake he had left the seed of the angriest of the Florida football series yet.

F - S - U

A problem that hit Bob Woodruff a year or so into his new job at Florida—other than that of increased academic entrance requirement—arose from suggestions from the northwestern part of the state that he ought to think about starting football relations with Florida State University, nee Florida State College for Women.

Until World War II the only problems Florida State posed for all-male Florida were (1) how students could get to FSCW, where the girls were, or, (2) how to get the girls to Florida, where the boys were.

Coeducation by decree followed World War II. With it Florida State University began a football team under a busy coach named Don Veller, and in almost no time voices from hither and yon began suggesting that the two schools meet in athletic competition in general but football in particular, and hurry about it.

Woodruff paid absolutely no attention at first. But, he says in a look-back:

"FSU started their political campaign for a game in 1951. At the time there was a board of control ruling against athletic participation between the two schools. I went to J. Hillis Miller, president of Florida then, and said, 'Let's go ahead and play.' He said 'No, the real issue is Florida State wants the medical school and a lot of other duplications in education.' He said it was the intention of the board of control when they made both coeducational not to permit competition between them. In the meantime our schedule had been completed to 1958. So, that was that for a time."

It was not for long. In fact former FSU president Doak Campbell reported that the subject of intercollegiate athletics between the two schools actually came before the board in 1949, but nothing was done. He said that talk increased in official circles as talk increased in unofficial circles in the early fifties.

FSU's first coach, Veller, was an eager but quiet man, ambitious but not pushy.

FSU's second coach came in 1953. He was Tom Nugent, a firebrand. He enjoyed talk and enjoyed controversy. He began an all-out effort to force the FSU-Florida series.

He began talking to the press, which did not just report his thoughts but began wondering why the two should not meet. The seed was planted by Veller, fertilized by Nugent.

Clearly, Florida did not need FSU. A win would mean little, a loss plenty. Financially, Florida thought that it was just an FSU plot to get a big money game. Anyway, Florida State was a girls' school.

Woodruff pretty much ignored the idea and was quoted once as saying as long as he was athletic director, there would be no games with FSU. The board of control in February, 1955, said that intercollegiate athletics should start between the two schools "upon terms to which the institutions mutually agree." And, "the details of scheduling athletic events will be handled by the agencies within the universities having responsibilities." And, "the director of athletics in each university has been instructed to proceed with the details of scheduling," quietly and without progress reports to the press. Woodruff said okay, he would play in a few years, soon as it was possible, in Gainesville, by SEC rules.

Nugent kept making noise. The FSU student body did too. So did some members of the press, and a couple of legislators.

In April, 1955, Senator James Connor of Brooksville introduced a bill into the Florida legislature urging the two schools to begin athletic competition, with amendments that it would not require existing contracts to be cancelled, that the games would be played under SEC rules, including existing guarantees to FSU from other SEC schools.

197

The instant bitter rivalry between Florida and Florida State begin November 22, 1958. FSU began with a burst but succumbed to the older school 21-7, quarterback Jimmy Dunn (No. 14) running and passing Florida to the win. In the bottom two pictures Dunn is shown in action, left, and receiving the MVP award, right. In the top picture star end Dave Hudson is shown intercepting an FSU pass in the days players played both offense and defense. Coach Bob Woodruff called Dunn (142) the best football player, pound-for-pound, he had ever seen.

The bill failed 15-19, but there was enough support for it for Coach Woodruff to know he needed to start moving. Later, the common story was that Governor LeRoy Collins ordered the game played to avoid further legislative involvement, but he says that is not so.

"My only involvement," said ex-Governor Collins, "really was a rather passive one. As governor I felt that in a situation like this I should take a neutral stance, leaving the solution to be found by those in direct authority, so I looked the other way. But when it got to a point of having bills introduced in the legislature and lines being sharply drawn there, I felt that the matter should be settled quickly by those in authority at the two universities rather than through legislative mandates and ultimatums.

"On one occasion, while the legislature was in session, and bills of this nature were pending, Dr. Wayne Reitz of the University of Florida (who in 1955 succeeded acting president John Allen as Florida president) was attending a board of control meeting in Tallahassee and came by to visit with me at the mansion. After we had discussed a number of matters, I casually, but still rather firmly, expressed the view that a game should be scheduled and that the decision should be made by the respective presidents and the board of control, and not by the legislature or by the governor. I don't recall that he made any special response to this, and I did not ask him to say anything. However it was just a short time after that that an amicable understanding was reached and I have always felt that Dr. Reitz was very cooperative in helping work this out," said Governor Collins.

"We had an opening in 1958 and 1959, so we agreed to play," said Woodruff, both games in Gainesville. Florida Field could handle considerably more people than Doak Campbell Stadium in Tallahassee, and, after all, money was one of the names of that game.

And almost as if he had had it planned all along, FSU coach Nugent had himself a fine team by 1958. The Seminoles were 7-2 going into the historic first game of the series with Florida. Two of the seven victories were impressive, over Miami and Tennessee. The other wins were over Tampa, Wake Forrest, Tennessee Tech, Furman, and Virginia Tech. The losses were to

Georgia Tech 17-3 and Georgia 28-14.

Nugent would face that hard-nosed 1958 Florida team, the one that had fought Auburn 6-5 and national champ LSU 10-7, losing both. This was the Florida team—the one Nugent would open against—whose quarterback was named Jimmy Dunn.

This was the quarterback whose "moral fiber" Nugent had questioned when Dunn gave back his one-year scholarship to Nugent and FSU for one of four years to Woodruff and Florida.

"Florida State had fought hard for the right to play the bigger university," wrote Julian Clarkson in his detailed history of the two-school rivalry called *Let No Man Put Asunder.* "The rest of the battles would be settled on the football field. The stage was set for the first meeting of the two state schools. Florida State had good material. So did Florida."

Against FSU's 7-2 mark, Florida was 4-3-1, but better than that. The Gator House was full that day, the mood expectant. Quickly it was not just another football game. Florida had to win. FSU surely would like to. It was as Woodruff had thought it would be. And Nugent.

"Sure I remembered what Nugent had said about me," said Dunn. "Moral fiber, those were the two words describing what he suggested I lacked."

The Florida kickoff was taken in by Jack Espenship. He handed it off to the late Bobby Renn who struck out southward down the left sidelines, fooling most everybody. Quickly it was apparent that only Dunn was between him and the goal.

High in the press box, looking through his glasses, Bill Beck of the *St. Petersburg Times* shouted: "Ain't nobody gonna stop him?"

It was poetic that Jimmy Dunn stopped him.

It did not matter. FSU scored soon after because the return had been for 78 yards to the 15. Quarterback Vic Prinzi handed off to Fred Pickard who scored for FSU. When the placement was good, FSU had a 7-0 lead.

Florida partisans were ruffled. The Florida players were not. In a matter of minutes all-SEC end Dave Hudson of Pensacola blocked a Renn punt, picked it up, and ran it in for a score, the conversion tying it 7-7. It seemed to deflate the FSU bubble.

"I have to remember the game after the things Nugent

201

said," said Dunn. "It was a highlight for me," and for Florida's football history.

Dunn scored two more touchdowns for the Gators who won the inaugural of the great series 21-7. After Hudson blocked the punt, it was, as it should have been. All Florida.

And Dunn was voted the game's most valuable player.

He accepted the trophy right about where he had accepted the most valuable trophy after the 1955 Florida High School game, the time when Coach Nugent came up and congratulated him and said he would see him in the fall for that one year scholarship. Dunn accepted the MVP trophy for the first Florida win over FSU right there about where Coach Hank Foldberg told him Coach Woodruff sure would like to see him in a few minutes so he could offer him a four-year football scholarship.

"Do I have to tell anybody how I felt?" asked Dunn.

No, and neither did Woodruff, a relieved man. The last thing he needed was to be beaten by the "girls' school." He was about to begin his final coaching year at Florida, and it was a fact, not all was well.

Woodruff Bows Out

With the heat turned up in the summer of 1959 Coach Woodruff felt the need to improve his quarterbacking corps. He desperately needed to have a good season in the fall ahead.

This was the time of odd-ball substitution rules. All clubs had a pair of two-way teams, and some had three, the third usually a group of offensive specialists.

Woodruff and aide Dick Jones, who recruited the Atlanta area, recalled that Dick Allen, the quarterback three years before, had another year's eligibility, and was out of the service then. They found him, and he enrolled and was, it turned out, eligible to play.

"The mood among the players going into the season was one of great confidence," recalled quarterback Wayne Williamson. "We had fine speed, some top players back like Dave Hudson and Pat Patchen, Ronnie Slack, Floyd Dean, L. E. Hicks, Don Deal, Doug Partin, Perry McGriff, Danny Royal, Bob Milby, Don Goodman, Dan Edington, Jim Beaver, Lawrin Giannamore, with Jack Jones and I and then Allen as quarterbacks. I know about 15 of us stayed up in summer school and worked hard. We thought we'd have a fine year, and we knew Coach Woodruff needed to have one."

Offensive line coach Hank Foldberg, probably the staff's foremost exponent of a more wide open offense, recalled, "Allen came to mind because we wanted to roll out and pitch and pass and run more." Williamson and Jones were, really, throwers.

Woodruff truly approached the season pretty confidently. He had a good team, and the year before he had been made a dean. He now had tenure.

That fateful season began well, a 30-0 mop-up of Tulane, but then came a luck-out over Mississippi State 14-13 at Gainesville. It was won only when Danny Royal blocked a punt late in the game and Dan Edington picked it up and ran it in to close the score to 12-13 and give Allen a chance to pass to the speedster McGriff for the two-point conversion.

Slight grumbles began. They quieted with a 55-10 wipeout of Virginia, and Florida was 3-0.

"But," Woodruff said, "already I was being attacked by some members of the press."

He was not really until the next game. It was at Rice.

Florida went ahead 7-0 on Jack Westbrook's run following a 75-yard pass interception return by Partin. Rice caught up 7-7, but early in the final period Williamson passed to Deal for the go-ahead points. Allen missed that try, and it was 13-7, Florida.

It seemed a safe situation when a very unlikely thing happened. A punt attempt went awry despite Bobby Joe Green's usual reliability. Rice got the ball, scored, and missed the point too.

It was 13-13 with some time left, and there Woodruff's deep-rooted teachings of Bob Neyland and Bobby Dodd took over. He did not try to score. He had the Gators run out the clock. He settled for the tie.

"I only recall," said Foldberg, "that we were unnerved by the bad punting situation before. It was a nervous situation. I know today you'd come out passing off your own goal-line. But not then, not Bob."

The players, most of them, were disappointed.

"We wanted to do something to try to score," said Williamson. "Remote as the chance was, we wanted to try."

Afterwards Woodruff offered an explanation that still boggles the mind.

"I will gamble to win," he said, "but I'll never gamble to lose."

It became his best remembered quote of the 10 years of coaching.

Now the furor rose across the state over the idea of agreeing to a tie. It seemed to epitomize Woodruff's thinking, and to some, indeed his career. Alumni beefed, newsmen wrote.

At Nashville the next week Florida was upset 13-6 by a Vanderbilt team that went into the game 0-2-1 to Florida's 3-0-1. A fullback named Tom Moore did them in, Moore and the Gators' own errors and listless play.

"We were awful," recalled Williamson. "We were down. I know I remember it because I threw two interceptions inside their 15 on plays sent in. I know for the first time they began calling my plays when we got close, leaving it to me the rest of the time. I began to resent it. We were not a happy team any more."

And Florida was not a happy state any more.

LSU beat the Gators 9-0 at homecoming, though Florida played well. That became a 9-1 LSU team. Next Auburn beat Florida but 6-0 at Cliff Hare in Auburn, and that would be a 7-3 Auburn team. The Gators were losing close to the best teams, still.

Georgia beat 'em 21-10 next. Georgia had a crack team, a 9-1 club and eventual Orange Bowl champ.

Those three losses to LSU, Auburn, and Georgia, all were to fine clubs—but they were losses and they followed that go-for-a-tie at Rice and the upset by Vanderbilt.

The 1959 Gators were 3-4-1 after starting 3-0-1. Only Florida State—the second of that series—and the arch-rival of that time, Miami, lay ahead. Miami had a fine team and was talking Orange Bowl.

Now while the Gators were faring poorly, so had been Florida State under its new, enigmatic coach, Perry Moss. FSU was 3-5, had been zapped by Georgia 42-0, and beaten ingloriously by William and Mary 9-0.

The second meeting between the two state schools was as dull as advertised. Moss tried some pre-game psychology which was worth nothing. He did not bring his team onto the field until just before kickoff.

Florida won easily, 18-8, after taking an 18-0 lead. Westbrook scored twice and was the MVP.

But it did not help Woodruff's plight. At that point probably nothing could, not even what happened in Jacksonville the final Saturday of Florida's fitful 1959 season.

After a slow start, the Miami Hurricanes had come like a storm. Behind a talented quarterback named Fran Curci the good Andy Gustafson team had beaten North Carolina, South Carolina, and Michigan State (18-14) in a row. The 'Canes stood 6-3 and were awaiting Florida and an Orange Bowl bid.

The 'Canes had been told they could have the Orange Bowl spot, in the ole hometown, with victory over 4-4-1 Florida the final Saturday at Jacksonville. Gustafson led Woodruff 6-3 in the Florida-Miami series, but the Gators had won the last two.

The howls were out for Woodruff on game-day, a day neither he, nor Dick Allen, nor Fran Curci, nor Andy Gustafson would ever forget.

Dickie Allen, the late-arriving, aging quarterback, played better than he could for his old coach that day. He passed, he ran, he place-kicked the Gators to a convincing 23-14 victory that knocked Miami out of the Orange Bowl, and earned Allen National Back of the Week honors.

But it did not save Woodruff's job. There is the story that after the cold, consolation afternoon for Burly Bob, he gestured in the direction of the high-paid seats and muttered some take-that suggestion, but that is not like him.

Even as he was beating Miami so severely, and helping his pride, a poll of sportswriters covering the game was overwhelming in the belief Woodruff should step out. The prevailing attitude of veteran sportswriters was that Woodruff had made great contribution, brought the program a giant-step, but it was unlikely the pinnacle could be reached under his coaching techniques. The prevailing attitude was that Florida was beyond, thanks largely to him, the go-for-a-tie posture.

Woodruff explained:

"Certain members of the board of control asked our president, Wayne Reitz, if he could persuade me to resign my position with Florida. I told him I could consider resigning as coach, but if I remained at Florida it would depend on what kind of a job I had and asked him if I could continue in the position of athletic director, and if I didn't have the combined job what kind of duty and salary adjustment could be made."

Many thought Woodruff should stay on as athletic director, for his administrative talents were proven. The overall

206

Dick Allen, who had two terms as a Gator quarterback.

Florida intercollegiate program was peaking.

"But no arrangement could be made," said Woodruff, "for me to stay as athletic director, and rather than cause the president a lot of trouble I decided to give my resignation as requested, although it was with great reluctance because I thought we had a bowl team in school since we had one of our finest freshmen teams there and Larry Libertore, a quarterback, was not eligible my last season and was redshirted due to academic problems.

"All that turned out true, of course. Florida's 1960 team, then under Ray Graves, but left by me, went to the Gator Bowl and had a fine year."

Foldberg, who went on to become head coach at Wichita and Texas A&M before entering the real estate business in Arkansas and sending a fine tight end son back to the Gators, said that the last year was "a troubled one. We knew things were happening, but really Bob didn't keep the rest of the staff that informed on how he stood, even to the end."

The rest of the staff was Hobe Hooser, John Mauer, Harvey Robinson, MacCara, Dave Fuller, John Eibner, Dick Jones, Earl Scarborough, and Jim Powell.

"Sure, I know part of Bob's problems was his devotion to defense and conservatism. But it was deep. I once pleaded so from the press box over the phones with the bench to send in a pass play I knew would work...well, they wouldn't answer me. I finally ran out of the press box, around the stadium, and in through the end zone to the sidelines and pleaded with Woodruff and Hooser to do it. Woodruff finally said he'd take it under consideration.

"Nothing happened so I got mad I guess, wrote down the play on a piece of paper, and sent a kid in with it. I think it was Don Deal. I don't remember. I know I watched and almost fainted as he ran into the game, and when he reported to the referee he handed the ref the play and went on into the huddle. They never did call it. I guess we lost. I don't remember. Toward the end of the game the ref came over and handed the note with the play on it to Bob, saying he might want it for his file.

"But, there when the trouble started, we were all very loyal to Woodruff. We didn't think he deserved to go. When he did, well, I guess I was considered only briefly for the job." Though Foldberg had support in some quarters around the state, "I think they wanted a whole new ball game."

"I did not want to resign at Florida. I loved it, and I still do," said Woodruff, speaking then as athletic director of the admired University of Tennessee program.

"I'll say that that Richard Allen and the rest of my Gators gave them a game to remember us by in that final win over Miami, which I might add meant we also finished with a winning season, 5-4-1. There hadn't been many of those before I got here. I'm proud of my years, my players, my staffs, my achievements at Florida."

His overall record: 54-41-6.

"And by the way, we beat Georgia six times in ten. I kept that promise."

His record simply was not strong enough to overcome his lack of communication, his reputation for conservatism no matter what, the general public conviction that he was best summed up by his own quote after that 13-13 tie at Rice, the one that went:

"I'll gamble to win, but I'll never gamble to lose."

In brief, the estimate of most was that the program had reached the highest point to which Bob Woodruff could take it. Maybe somebody else could take it another step upwards, closer to the coveted Year of the Gator, the SEC championship, the cherished Next Year.

One of his three-year players said it this way: "I really think Coach Woodruff was more concerned with not losing than with winning, if there's a distinction. I think there is. Once, I remember, we were leading a tough team at the half 14-13, and Coach Woodruff said to us, so help me: 'Don't you boys get your dobbers down now. You're not out of it yet.'"

The Best Of Bob

In his ten years as head football coach Bob Woodruff produced three genuine all-Americans, and a heavy lineup of all-SEC players, giving the Gators their best-yet national attention and recognition. He also was proud that he attracted to Florida assistant coaches who went on to major positions, players who became top professionals, and some themselves coaches—such as Doug Dickey now the head coach of Florida.

Woodruff is reluctant to name his personal all-Fifties team, even to pick his very best team, but he would list some superlatives. The 1952 club had the best overall record, with 8-3, but 1954 and 1956 had the best SEC standards ever, 5-2, worth third place. His 1958 team which went 6-4-1 may have been the dearest to him because it was the best defensively. The first win, 7-0 over The Citadel, the first win over Georgia, 30-0 in 1952, the inaugural win over Florida State in 1958, and that final take-that win over Miami, he said, meant the most to him in thinking back.

Woodruff also listed these opinions:

BEST LINEMEN—Charles LaPradd, Joe D'Agostino, Carroll McDonald, Asa Cox, Vel Heckman, John Barrow, Charley Mitchell, Steve DeLaTorre, and Arlen Jumper.

BEST BACKS—Haywood Sullivan, Rick Casares, Buford Long, Jackie Simpson, Mal Hammack, Jimmy Rountree, Jimmy Dunn, Ed Sears, Doug Partin, John Symank, Bernie Parrish.

BEST ENDS—Don Fleming, Dave Hudson, Bob Flowers, Ray Brown, and Jack O'Brien.

210

Jackie Simpson, runningback hero of the fifties.

BEST DEFENSIVE BACKS—Jackie Simpson, Jim Rountree, Jack Westbrook, Doug Partin, John Symank.

BEST ALL-AROUND BACKS, in order—1, Rick Casares; 2, Jimmy Dunn; 3, Jackie Simpson; 4, Jim Rountree; 5, Dickie Allen.

SMARTEST QUARTERBACK—Doug Dickey.

BEST RUNNER—1, Rick Casares; 2, Jim Rountree; 3, Jackie Simpson.

BEST PASSER—1, Haywood Sullivan; 2, Jimmy Dunn; 3, Dickie Allen; 4, Jackie Simpson; 5, Fred Robinson; 6, Jim Rountree.

BEST KICKER—1, Don Chandler and Bobby Joe Green; 3, Casares; 4, Fred Montsdeoca.

The Man From Inskip

Dr. J. Wayne Reitz became president of the University of Florida in 1955, halfway through the Bob Woodruff period. Though no athlete himself, save "some track in Colorado," Reitz believed in a strong intercollegiate athletic program, including football, and wanted winners, but not winners above all.

Woodruff's resignation was not pleasant for Reitz, and "I sought to have him stay on as athletic director," he recalls now. "It was not an easy time for us all, but we had to do what we had to do. Coach Woodruff, I must say, brought us a long way."

Many of those of influence in the state wanted Woodruff to remain as athletic director, for his premier qualities were organization and administration. Those strong points were demonstrated even further later when he returned to his alma mater, Tennessee, to become athletic director of the Volunteers' highly successful overall program, and Woodruff also found a role as an influential administrator with the Olympic Games in Munich.

But Woodruff was hurt and angry, and he turned down the athletic director's job.

Dr. Reitz appointed Dutch Stanley, Phil Constans, and Jim Richardson as the committee to select the successor to Woodruff. Applications poured in, the list including many favorite sons who were turned down quickly, infuriating some. Names like Marcelino Huerta, Hank Foldberg, and Charley Tate were tossed around in the press for a time.

Florida's ever-aggressive sportswriting corps took out on lead after lead in the death race for the first story of the final selection. Though the committee sought to act secretly, it was impossible as the state's leading papers had writers, photographers, and correspondents stationed everywhere after THE Gator story of the time. Joe Halberstein, of the *Gainesville Sun* then, Jack Hairston of the *Jacksonville Journal*, Bill Kastelz of the *Florida Times-Union*, Bob Hudson of the *Tampa Tribune*, Bill Beck of the *St. Petersburg Times*, Edwin Pope of the *Miami Herald*, Bill McGrotha of the *Tallahassee Democrat*, Benny Kahn of the *Daytona News-Journal*, Bob Balfe of the *West Palm Beach Post-Times*, Bob Bassine of the *Orlando Sentinel*, and I, then of the *Tampa Times*, pressed all sources seeking the major news beat.

The name which cropped up as the leading candidate was Ara Parseghian, then the head coach at Northwestern. Parseghian would have had the job if some poor communications had not gotten in the way.

"Our committee scouted around and decided to call two men to Gainesville for interviews. First Davey Nelson of Delaware came, then Ara Parseghian of Northwestern," said Dr. Reitz.

Nelson was an innovative man, a perennial coaches' association official, and had a marvelous record at Delaware. He spent the Christmas holidays each year declining jobs at bigger schools. But he kept the date for the interview and said he would think about it.

Then Parseghian was invited.

"I'll tell you the thing I remember most about all of it," said Parseghian in 1974, after his Notre Dame had beaten Alabama in the Sugar Bowl to become national champions for the second time under his guidance. "I remember the DC-7 that I flew to Florida had engine trouble from Atlanta to Jacksonville going down and that scared me. Then on the way back from Atlanta to Chicago, there was more trouble. I guess that should have been an omen of what the job might have been.

"In any case, I liked what I saw. I went back home and decided to take the Florida job if it were offered to me. I told my athletic director, Stu Holcomb, that. But nothing happened. I got no calls. The coaches' meetings were coming up in New

213

York, and Stu was pressing me. If I were leaving, he needed to know before going to the meetings so he could find a replacement. But he wanted me to stay. He pressed me some more, and I told him I would stay. I too had to go to New York.

"I understand I got a call and an offer of the job after I had told Northwestern I would stay."

Dr. Reitz says the details are hazy, but he remembers that the decision had been made to hire Nelson if he wanted the job, and there was a waiting period. "Dutch Stanley tells me we did then decide on Parseghian, but after he had decided to stay at Northwestern."

In Atlanta another phase of the hunt was taking place. Dr. Reitz had called a man he greatly admired, Coach Bobby Dodd of Georgia Tech, for some suggestions.

Dodd's assistant head coach was a hard-working, former Tennessee and Philadelphia Eagles end named Ray Graves. Graves was much admired among coaches. He was a good coach, a gracious man, and surely the heir apparent to Dodd. Graves was in comfortable circumstances, and he knew it and liked it.

"I think it was soon after our last game and in December, 1959, while we were practicing for the Gator Bowl game with Arkansas that Coach Dodd called me into his office," Graves remembers. "He said Dr. Reitz of Florida had called him for some recommendations for a successor to Bob Woodruff. He called, he said, because he admired Coach Dodd's work and because Coach Dodd's son, Bobby Jr., had been a Gator freshman in 1959.

"Coach Dodd and I agreed that the best two men for them to talk about were Davey Nelson and Ara Parseghian," said Graves. "Dodd asked me if I was interested in the job at all. I said no. I had some things I was working on at Tech that were unfinished. Now as the days went on, we heard Nelson had declined the job and Parseghian had decided to stay at Northwestern, and we were in Jacksonville practicing for the bowl. Frank Broyles asked me if I had considered the job. I said not really, and he said I should.

"Next pertinent thing I remember, I left the Gator Bowl banquet to answer a phone call, and met Dick Stratton and Van Fletcher, big Jacksonville alumni, and they were encouraging

214

me to take it. By now Coach Dodd was encouraging me to take the job, and I was bringing it up with my wife, Opal. Now we go to New York for the NCAA coaches meetings, and sure enough I am invited to an interview with Dr. Constans, Dutch Stanley, and the others.

"We met once, then again, and they made me an offer. I more or less accepted the offer right there," said Graves, and it was instantly headlines in Florida, largely on some New York sleuthing by Furman Bisher, *Atlanta Journal* sports editor who knew Graves well and chanced to meet him in the company of the Florida coach-seeking committeemen. Graves confirmed to Bisher what was happening, and Bisher reported it.

The offer was $19,000 a year. "I guess it represented a little pay cut for me then," said Graves, "because we had so many things going in Atlanta." Tech coaches traditionally have had the opportunity to supplement their salaries off the field in Atlanta as effectively as any major college in America. The search was over.

Ray Graves was coming to Florida and bringing, among other things, a different personality than Woodruff's.

Graves, like Woodruff, had been a University of Tennessee lineman. From Inskip, Tennessee, a Knoxville suburb, Graves was an outgoing man, a lover of country music, bass fishing, and defense-first on the football field.

It became formal when he signed a five-year contract at the Holiday Inn in Gainesville. He had sneaked in under instructions to cloak-and-dagger it to the motel, even changing cars. A formal press conference was to be called later.

"The photographers and writers were there waiting for me," Graves laughed.

That day began a career of good relations with the Florida press, not a docile, unquestioning group. Graves always appreciated the value of good press, and he had the knack so many lack to spot and make known an off-beat story or a human interest angle.

Too, Graves would demonstrate in the years ahead an unshaking ability to stand straight in defeat, to take the blame himself for whatever happened, though he faced some bitter times with the good times in the next ten football seasons with the Gators.

215

Ray Graves' 1963 staff, from left, front: Jimmy Dunn, Pepper Rodgers, Ottis Mooney, Gene Ellenson, and John Donaldson. Back row: Sterling Dupree, Don Brown, Graves, John Eibner, and Dave Fuller.

According to some, the personality characteristic that would cause him and others pain in the years ahead was his determination to please everyone with whom he was in contact at the time, a need to say or react precisely as he thought the present audience would have him. According to this version, the word "no" Coach Graves found difficult to command.

In New York in January, 1960, Graves began assembling a fine staff. The first man he hired was Gene Ellenson of Miami, a former all-American guard at Georgia. Ellenson had left the business to sell real estate in Miami. Then Graves got Jack Green to head the defense, the uncontainable Pepper Rodgers the offense. The staff was rounded out with John Eibner, John

Donaldson, John Mauer, Jim Powell, Dave Fuller, Earl Scarbrough, and young Jimmy Dunn, not long out of Florida uniform.

In their first policy meeting, Reitz told Graves that his priorities were:

(1) For Graves to function within the academic standards of the school; (2) for him to avoid conflict with the academic family and to maintain a gentlemanly environment for players; (3) to, with those concerns in mind, put the best possible teams on the field.

Reitz added that he would especially appreciate it if the new head coach and athletic director would earn his $19,000 salary (plus TV money) by beating Florida State, Georgia, and Miami every single year, the rest of the opponents as often as practicable.

Graves, like Woodruff before him, knew that the high in-state entrance requirements would hurt him for they were stiffer than most teams he faced, and he was to be proven right. He predicted, and it came to pass at times, that he would lose Florida high school standouts who preferred Florida but who could not qualify, though they would not always understand this. As a consequence no small number of players in that category went on to a rival school and returned to Gainesville with eyes flashing in anger at being passed over, and contributed to some Gator defeat.

That would be later. Right then it was a new day for Florida football. There was a new coach, and another Year of the Gator had begun. The Man From Inskip who promised wide-open football had arrived, and he would very quickly get everyone's attention with his first season's product.

The Flying Start, 1960

Before the 1960 season Ray Graves toured Florida for a series of get-acquainted sessions with supporters and fans. Everywhere he promised to play no-holds-barred offensive football—this above all. To run such a show he had hired as his offensive chief Pepper Rodgers, a fiery, gambling young ex-quarterback at Georgia Tech. And to carry out the plan, Graves and Rodgers had a pair of sophomore quarterbacks of special talents.

First, there was his old boss' son, Bobby Dodd, Jr., primarily a thrower and somewhat slow afoot. More geared to the running game was a Miami product, a wiry, will-o'-the-wisp named Larry Libertore. He could run with deception and handle the football with deftness. He looked fragile and out of place, but he was not.

It was the option that caused Libertore to choose Florida for his football. "I had a burning desire to play football," said Libertore. "I was never concerned about my size or weight (5-10 and a vulnerable 138 pounds). I was fortunate to play in tough high school competition for a Miami team that won the Big Ten Conference championship.

"The University of Miami was interested in me, perhaps because Fran Curci was their quarterback and the option play was part of their game. They offered me a scholarship. So did Florida State, but the University of Florida expressed to me its desire to go to the option-oriented football program.

"I wanted to help introduce the option at the University

of Florida," recalls Libertore. "The possibility of being a starter as a sophomore appealed to me, and I knew that wouldn't be possible at Miami because Curci would be a senior at the time. I also considered the possibility that the option would be over-exposed by the time I would be eligible to play at Miami." So Libertore signed with Florida.

Everything seemed to be falling into place for the two quarterbacks, the exciting runner and the intelligent thrower, and for Graves, who found the quarterbacks to operate a more wide-open style of play, and for the fans, who were starved for it. Woodruff had left Graves some sound material, and the crop of sophomores looked exciting even beyond Libertore and Dodd.

As it turned out, fate would play into the hands of the two ambitious, so-different quarterbacks.

Graves arrived in a state where the followers of Gator football were longing for the so-called and nebulous "wide-open" brand of football. Graves knew this well. He knew of Woodruff's total conservatism, third-down punts, and pass only at last resort philosophy. Graves toured Florida before his first season on a get-acquainted barnstorm. Everywhere he went he repeated that he would play no-holds-barred offensive football. This above all.

And he had recruited from the Air Force Academy just the man for executing that philosophy. He was offensive brain Pepper Rodgers, a fast-talking, gambling, cocky quarterback at Georgia Tech who thrived on pressure. His personal history included last-second field goals kicked to win bowl games. Rodgers would be a primary contributor to the Graves success so long as he was at Florida, but because not all gambles win, Rodgers eventually would be the unjust object of criticism for the risk the fans had wanted so, and he would leave unhappy but become head coach at Kansas, then UCLA, then Georgia Tech and develop into one of the finest, most imaginative head coaches in college football. But he and Graves did not part the great friends they had been, Rodgers feeling when he was under fire for carrying out orders he had deserved more support from the top. He feels that way today.

Yet that first year, in 1960, working as Ray Graves' new offensive coordinator, and with the pass-run punch of Dodd-

Libertore, Rodgers got something going that was magnetic for victory-starved, thrill-starved Florida fans. The Gators actually were on the offensive, while Ellenson and Green were building a stout defense. That defense would shut out three and allow three others only two touchdowns.

That first year of Ray Graves, 1960, is one of the half-dozen best remembered in Gator history, and not just because it was the baptismal year of the Graves Decade and the regularly reassembling lettermen, The Silver Sixties. It is remembered because Ray Graves took that first Florida team of his and moved the Gators from mediocrity to an attention-getting 9-2 season. Only the 8-1 record of 1928 averaged out better percentage-wise.

It is best remembered, perhaps, because of three mighty victories—the pivotal early 18-17 win over Georgia Tech, the 10-7 upset of Louisiana State at Tiger Stadium in Baton Rouge, and the final 13-12 Gator Bowl victory over Baylor that made the season 9-2. It is best remembered too because only a 10-7 loss to Auburn prevented Florida from winning the elusive Southeastern Conference championship. In that first year under Graves the Gators emerged 5-1 in the SEC and finished undisputed possessor of second place. Mississippi won the title with a barely-better 5-0-1. Alabama was third at 5-1-1. The truth is, the second place finish right off the bat would be the highest finish of the 10 Graves teams, in the SEC, though there would be another 5-1-0 standard worth then third position.

The turnaround of Florida football came in the third game of that first Graves year, in the game against Georgia Tech. Tech was still a member of the SEC at the time. But first, before Tech, and all that drama to come, Graves' new Gators had to play George Washington and FSU.

"I must say we didn't look too good in practice," Graves said. "We decided to go with Libertore as No. 1, because he gave us the triple-look. But frankly, I didn't know what to expect. We were going to open with George Washington, and our only scouting report was one offered by alumnus Red Mitchum who was stationed in Washington and watched them from a bridge."

The opener, it turned out, was a 30-7 snap over George Washington and did little to establish Graves' coaching philoso-

The 1960 Gators—they went 9-2.

phy for the 14,000 who attended the game at the Gator Bowl in Jacksonville.

Neither did excitement reign the following week after an undistinguished 3-0 win over still struggling Florida State. The win came on a field goal of 37 yards by Bill Cash, a native of Florida State's own Tallahassee.

But the third game of the 1960 season gave Gator fans what they had been crying for. It was early October, and the opponent was Georgia Tech. Both teams were 2-0, but Tech was a solid pick for the Gainesville game, which was the subject of terrific press buildup. It was ex-boss against pupil, father against son, family vs. family, with Mrs. Dodd in the stands, her loyalties divided.

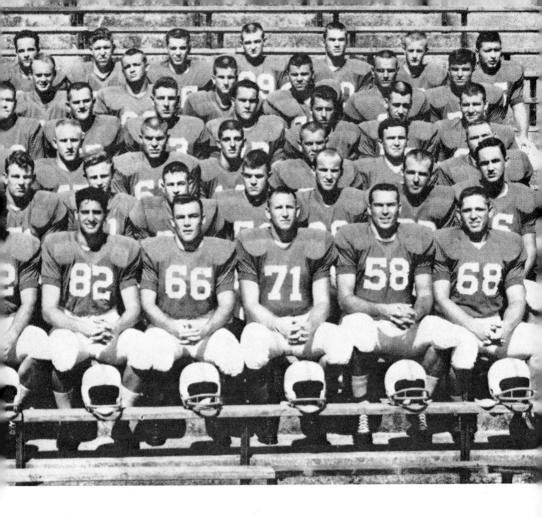

The game was even better than the buildup. It was a see-saw afternoon, with one team taking the upper hand, then the other. Finally, with five minutes left and Tech leading 17-10, Florida had the ball with a first down at its own 10. The Gators managed two first downs, and Bobby Dodd, Jr., went in to replace Libertore. He was promptly thrown for an 18-yard loss. On third down Dodd went straight back, found halfback Don Deal in the clear, spun the ball to him, and Deal made it to the Tech 25, a 32-yard gain and a first down when the need was critical. Bob Hoover and Don Goodman battered their way to the Tech two in three plays, but two more slams at the line got the ball only to the one-foot line, and a fumbled ball recovered by Dodd at the three wasted another play.

A football Saturday at Florida.

It was fourth down there, with 32 seconds left. Libertore remembers:

"Faced with this situation, we ran the option play where I was very much aware that there would be no plays remaining after that one. I was fortunate in being able to find Lindy Infante at the perfect angle for a pitchout, and he was able to thread the sidelines, just missing stepping out of bounds. He scored."

It was 17-16, Tech, with seconds left.

Graves said it never occurred to him not to go for the two-point conversion and victory—or defeat. Cash surely would have kicked the tying point, and 17-17 with Tech would not look bad in the records and across the nation. But Graves knew full well it would not satisfy the long-suffering Florida fans he had preached to all summer about being offensive, a go-for-broker.

Almost with the Infante score, Graves' left hand shot straight up, then out toward the playing field and his players.

He held up two fingers. Then, so did all the players standing around him, and they were photographed that way in the most famous still photograph of his career.

On the field, "It never occurred to me to go for the extra point as we had already decided to go for two points," said Libertore later.

"We had devised a 'hurry-up' play in which I would fake to the fullback, Jon MacBeth, as if we were running the option like

Halfback Lindy Infante cuts just in time to score Gator TD in great comeback against Tech. Note scoreboard has 33 seconds left, Tech leading 17-10. The two-point conversion, a Larry Libertore pass to Jon MacBeth, followed to initiate the Silver Sixties of Ray Graves.

Ray Graves, and everybody else, signals go-for-two, and the Gators did and beat Georgia Tech in 1960, 18-17.

on the previous play. Jon was the only receiver-target. So I had two chances: If I saw an opening, I would run; or I could pass to MacBeth. Infante was the halfback again.

"The play began, again to the right, Infante the pitchman faking after MacBeth had faked. At the very last second—I had almost decided to run—a Tech defender, a big fellow, appeared in my path, and I saw I had no way of making it. At that instant I saw MacBeth break into the clear at about one o'clock. Everyone knows what happened."

Libertore lofted a pass to MacBeth who, Graves said later, "juggled the ball. He almost lost his scholarship right there, maybe his life."

But he did not drop it, and the Gators had beaten Georgia Tech 18-17. Florida had turned it around, and Graves had his two feet on the ground as firmly as he had his two fingers in the air a minute before.

"There was never a question," agreed Graves. "There was no decision to make. We were going for the win. I wish that had been the toughest decision I ever had to make at Florida."

Graves, who loves, appreciates, and enjoys being involved in high drama, was ecstatic.

"I know, I know," he said in later years. "I do like things like that...the family tie...me being from Tech, and Bobby Jr., on the team, and Pepper Rodgers, and things like that.

"It was a must, you know. Dodd had recommended me for the job. I had to prove he was right.

"What is the truth is that I think some games you are meant to win and some you are meant to lose. It was our destiny that day at Florida Field to beat Georgia Tech. When I see the drive to that last touchdown on film now, I keep wondering how Bobby Dodd Jr., is going to get the ball to Don Deal, if MacBeth will catch the pass.

"Sure, that win set me off on my career and Larry Libertore on his way to a place in my heart. Libertore, with larger hands so he could pass more accurately, would have been a great triple-option quarterback. As he was he helped us to a great starting season."

But as so often happens a great defeat followed a great win. Florida went to Miami the next week to lose to Rice 19-0 before only 19,000 in the Orange Bowl. Libertore was booed in

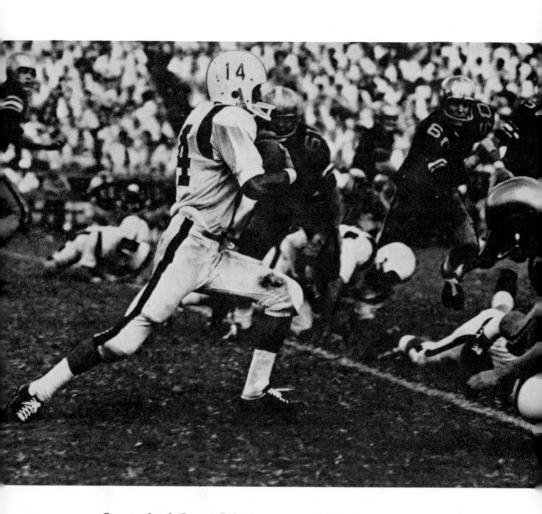

Quarterback Larry Libertore gains 10 yards to set mood for the great Gator upset of Georgia Tech, 18-17, at Florida Field.

his own home town despite his performance the week before. The Gators have never since taken a game to Miami other than the Miami home end of the Florida-Miami series.

The Gators got back to work then and beat Vanderbilt with little problem and thus took an impressive, if not overwhelming, 4-1 record to Tiger Stadium in Baton Rouge. LSU, though not that good that year, was favored because of where the game was going to be played.

Libertore recollects: "I felt good going into the game. I

remember saying to Pepper Rodgers' wife Judy that the entire team felt like we were going to have a good game.

"We received and began our first possession at our own 34. The first play of the game was designed to look like an option, but there was no halfback to pitch to. He was blocking. I took three or four steps to the left side of the line, saw a small opening, cut into the hole, and realized I was in the secondary. A halfback was coming over, but I cut back on him, was in the clear, and scored.

"If I had any thought at the time, it was that I was as surprised as the people in the stands. I can still recall the silence that fell over all those people. I was aware that somebody was chasing me and gaining but that I outlasted him.

"If I remember correctly, at the end of the first half, we had 69 total yards rushing and 66 came on that first play."

Later, Billy Cash kicked two crucial field goals, one for 47 yards, and Florida won that game at Baton Rouge, 13-10.

The first Graves Gators had jumped to 5-1 overall and 3-0 in the SEC.

Then Auburn jumped up and whipped the Gators, as Auburn had so often done and would continue to do. This one was Florida homecoming before 40,000, and the final score was 10-7.

Each team drove for a long first half score, and the count was 7-7 at intermission. But in the third period Ed Dyas kicked a 31-yard field goal that cost the Gators the elusive SEC title. Even a 7-7 deadlock would have resulted in a tie with Mississippi for the championship. Florida finished 5-1, Ole Miss 5-0-1.

But the season was not quite over. Florida handled Georgia 22-14 before the largest Gator Bowl crowd ever, 48,622; thumped Tulane 21-6; and crushed Miami 18-0 before 61,000 in the Orange Bowl.

With the 8-2 finish came the invitation to play Baylor in the Gator Bowl. More seats were put in, so nearly 51,000 saw Florida score twice in the first half and win it 13-12. Libertore was voted the game's most valuable, but linemen Ronnie Slack and Larry Travis recovered a Baylor fumble in the end zone for the pivotal second touchdown, and Cash kicked the marginal point.

229

Florida had gone 9-2 in Graves' first year. The state was his oyster. Though the more exciting offense got most of the credit, the defense actually played an equally important role. Ellenson and Green did a job that helped the Gators shut out three opponents and allow only three as many as two touchdowns.

The second place finish in the SEC seemed great at the time. As it turned out, it was Graves' best conference standing in his ten years, though another 5-1 record would be worth third place.

In Dodd He Trusted

The personal and public life and times of Robert Lee Dodd have been interwoven with the history of University of Florida football from his sophomore year as a Tennessee quarterback until his windup years as one of the few head coaches at Georgia Tech. And most of the memories have been fond. All of them, he says, have been intriguing.

It began with the pass he threw in Knoxville in the final game of the 1928 season to beat the unbeaten Gators 13-12, and it ended in 1963 when Tech beat favored Florida in the rain at Grant Field 9-0 in the season opener. Playing relations were broken off after that indefinitely, but in between there was a Florida Field 0-0 tie in a hurricane which swirled around the players and the 41,000 brave patrons.

And, in between, there was the counsel Dodd gave his key assistant, Ray Graves, to take the head job at Florida in 1960, even though Dodd's son was a quarterback there and the two schools had four games to go on a contract. From that came Graves' career-making 18-17 Florida win over Tech, head coached by his ex-chief. And there was Pepper Rodgers, who had been a Tech quarterback and place-kicker under Dodd and who joined Graves at Florida. And there was Bobby, Jr.

"I did not want Bobby, Jr., to go to any school where he would play against Georgia Tech," Coach Dodd recalls. "However, since I told him he could choose any college, other than Georgia Tech—the school he wanted to attend to play under me—he chose Florida because he knew Bob Woodruff and

231

Harvey Robinson (assistant coach), who were the coaches at the time he accepted. I think Bobby, Jr., wanted to go to a Southeastern Conference school to see if he would be good enough to play the so-called 'big-time football.'"

Though it is not an everyday conversation topic, some strained relations did develop between Coaches Dodd and Graves when young Dodd never became the No. 1 quarterback in his three years at Florida.

"About that 18-17 Florida-Tech game," said Coach Dodd, "I think it was one of the most exciting games I have ever witnessed. The buildup, of course, was so great, with the family involvement, and unlike so many times when games like that turn out dull, this one didn't. The result probably was a great thing for everyone concerned, particularly Coach Graves and his new staff. It meant a great deal to them getting started at Florida, and gaining the confidence of the Florida people. As for us, I guess we could stand another loss, and as you know, we evened things up the next couple of years." Tech did, winning the last three under the contract, and all by shutouts, 20-0 in 1961, 17-0 in 1962, and 9-0 in 1963. Those results were of special consolation to one Charley Tate. Tate was the former Florida Gator fullback out of Jacksonville, and former Florida assistant who had sought the head job Graves won. He was chief of the Dodd defense that blanked the Gators three in a row, before he became the head coach at the University of Miami.

"I'd be lying," said Tate in recollection, "if I didn't say that as much as I love my old school Florida, not many things have pleased me more than shutting out the Gators I wanted to head coach, not many things until later on when we at Miami beat Florida after they'd been invited to the Sugar Bowl (1965)."

The Florida-Tech series, a popular one, was broken off because Coach Dodd wanted the games played in Atlanta and Jacksonville, not Atlanta and Gainesville, site of the 18-17 Gator upset. Tech, at the time, was an eagerly-sought, big payday opponent.

"The series was broken off because I discussed with Bob Woodruff the difficulty of playing in Gainesville, due to the lack of motel/hotel service for our team and our followers, and asked him to play the Florida home game at Jacksonville, rather

Bobby Dodd

than Gainesville. He agreed to this, and then later told me that he had so much pressure put on him by Gainesville people that he could not change the game. I told him he had given his word to play in Jacksonville and Atlanta, and he should live up to that commitment even though he had not signed a contract. Anyway, here is where the series was broken off. Of course later the Gainesville accommodations improved, and 1978 was set as the resumption date of the old series."

In another belated revelation, Dodd said:

"I have had wonderful experiences with Florida football and started to accept the head coaching job at Florida, way back when I was an assistant coach at Georgia Tech, and Dr. John Tigert offered me the head job at Florida. I did not take it because my boss, Coach Alexander, told me to stay at Georgia Tech."

Finally, Coach Dodd confessed that the 18-17 upset of his team was not the only damage done to him by the Gators.

"My last football game in college at Tennessee was playing Florida in Jacksonville, and I had the only punt blocked in my college or high school career. And the Gators did that."

All's Well That Ends That Way

Florida's second year under Ray Graves was more like the days before he came, with a 4-5-1 finish. That second year, said Graves, "was my poorest team." It was his only losing season, including even a humiliating—some Gators folks say—3-3 tie with Florida State, a 15-6 loss to Miami, and one lone bright moment.

That came against Georgia in the Gator Bowl in Jacksonville. With the record at 3-3-1, the Gators had scored only seven points in three games including successive shutouts by LSU and Georgia Tech, and the quarterbacking was suddenly uncertain. Graves and Rodgers decided to go with a gangly signal-caller named Tom Batten.

Batten had the hour all who play in the arena dream of. He threw three touchdown passes—to Lindy Infante, Bob Hoover, and Ron Stoner—and connected for a total of 194 yards in directing the Gators to a 21-14 defeat of the Bulldogs. The day earned him honors as the Southeastern Conference back of the week. Batten later distinguished himself again in a different uniform, that of Air Force pilot in the war in the Far East.

In 1962 bright additions came up from the Gator freshmen: a strong-legged quick starter named Larry Dupree, a cocky Irish quarterback from Miami named Tom Shannon, plus some muscular linemen. Infante, Hoover, and Richard Skelly and talented defensive back Hagoode Clark had returned, along with some top linesmen in Larry Travis, Jack Thompson, Anton Peters, Bill Richbourgh, Jimmy Morgan, Dennis Murphy, Floyd

Dean, Bobby Lyle, Russ Brown, Roger Pettee, and Frank Laskey.

"It was our strangest season," said Graves about 1962. "It was the only time ever at Florida that I cried."

The Gators of 1962 beat Mississippi State 19-9 in the opener, then were soundly beaten by Georgia Tech 17-0.

Next they played Duke, and Shannon had emerged as the No. 1 quarterback, the sensational Dupree the No. 1 runner. In the second quarter Dupree went 70 yards for a touchdown, Shannon passed to Sam Holland for one, and Jim O'Donnell jammed through for another.

It was 21-0 at the half and in the bag.

Duke won the game 28-21. In Florida it was judged the biggest giveaway, the biggest letdown, in Florida history. In North Carolina it was considered the greatest comeback, the greatest show of resolution in Blue Devil history.

After the game, in the privacy of Jacksonville's Roosevelt Hotel, Ray Graves cried. It was the only time he failed to appear at a press event.

"But," said Graves, reflecting on it, "history shows we had a way of coming back after a big defeat for a big victory."

It was surely so, for in one of the most important games, the Gators pulled up their socks and slammed a pretty good Texas A&M team, coached by ex-Florida aide Hank Foldberg, 42-0, then ripped up Vanderbilt 42-7. Shannon was the guiding light in both lopsiders.

Next came a heartbreaking 23-0 loss to LSU, followed by a rewarding 22-3 win over an Auburn team that arrived in Florida 5-0 and ranked nationally. A 23-15 whipping of Georgia followed, and then it was to be Florida vs. the best-yet Florida State team at Gainesville.

The erratic Gators were 5-3. FSU had just tied Georgia Tech, which had beaten Florida. Emotions were running high on both sides.

The year before, fighting had broken out after the game and lasted for some time. During those fights *Tampa Tribune* photographer Vernon Barchard captured a photo of a one-legged fan, clinging to a single crutch and with the other crutch lying on the ground, flailing away at an enemy with his free arm.

Those things—and other ghosts from the past—were remembered on both sides as the 1962 game approached.

Bill Peterson, the Seminoles' coach, had his team in overnight retreat at Silver Springs. Some Seminole turned on an educational TV channel out of Gainesville in time to catch the start of the Pepper Rodgers show. Shannon and O'Donnell were the guests, and Shannon was having a field day.

"I have no friends at FSU," he said of the school which also sought to recruit him. "Seems to me that they get all the Florida rejects."

No matter what subjects Rodgers broached, Shannon found a way to bad-mouth Florida State. Rodgers squirmed all the more in the studio with each bullet. Forty-five miles away in Silver Springs, the Seminoles were unbelieving at first, then furious. They would show him the next day.

When the players got off the buses the next day at noon near the Florida gym, they were like mummies, they were so angry. "I never saw a team so mad and so ready to play," Peterson said.

They were too ready. They jumped offsides repeatedly. Shannon continued to taunt them from his side of the line, and the Florida defense confused the offense with signal calls similar to those used by FSU.

Though FSU went ahead 7-0 and led at the half 7-6, the Gators won it 20-7. The breaking point was a 63-yard punt return for a touchdown by Clark, a walk-on player who went on to a fine career with the Buffalo Bills.

Then as suddenly as the Gators were up for FSU, they were down for Miami, and the Hurricanes upset them 17-15.

The Gator Bowl invited them back anyway, with their 6-4 record, to play Penn State, Lambert Trophy winner as champion of the East, loser of one game in 1962, and winner of three straight post-season bowl games.

Penn State was a big, big favorite on that overcast December afternoon.

Gene Ellenson had moved to head the defense and changed Florida's operation for this game, creating the "monster" defense. To agitate the visitors from the North, the Gators pasted Confederate flag decals on their helmets.

Then they went out and beat the Nittany Lions 17-7.

Bobby Lyle kicked a 43-yard field goal, and Shannon passed to Dupree seven yards to make it 10-0 at the half. It stayed that way until Shannon passed to Clark 19 yards for another score on the final quarter's first play. Penn State reached Florida territory only twice, scoring on one of those drives.

Florida was 7-4 after a topsy-turvey, turbulent season and twice a bowl winner in the first three Graves years.

Colonel Everett Yon, player, coach, effective Gator Booster head, and for whom Gator player dorm Yon Hall was named.

The Letter

It was Thursday night October 11, 1962, late in the evening and suddenly late in the young season for the Gators. They had beaten Mississippi State soundly, 19-9, been badly beaten by Georgia Tech, 17-0, and on the previous Saturday jumped ahead of a good Duke team 21-0, only to lose it 28-21. No previous Florida team had given up such a lead to lose. The Gators were down, the fans mad, the coaches puzzled because they thought they had the nucleus of a good club.

The team coming to Gainesville the next Saturday was a fast Texas A&M team coached by Hank Foldberg. Foldberg had been an assistant at Florida under Bob Woodruff and wanted to succeed Woodruff. He sought the job, but was turned down. Foldberg had something to tell his team to rile them as he was riled.

So it was at that late hour that defensive assistant Gene Ellenson, a profound man, an ex-Rose Bowl participant and all-American, and a journalism graduate, wondered how he could help give extra purpose to the Gator players.

He sat there in his office in the stadium and by 2 a.m. had written a letter he would have distributed to each Gator, with Coach Graves' permission. Graves could not get it copied fast enough once he read it.

If you had been a member of the 1962 Gators you would have, late Friday night before the Texas A&M game, in your motel room, had this letter from Ellenson slipped secretly to you:

"Dear Wade Entzminger (let's say):

"It's late at night. The offices are all quiet and everyone has finally gone home. Once again my thoughts turn to you all.

"The reason I feel I have something to say to you is because what you need now more than anything else is a little guidance and maybe a little starch for your backbone. You are still very young, and unknowingly you have not steeled yourselves for the demanding task of 60 full minutes of exertion required to master a determined opponent. This sort of exertion takes two kinds of hardness. Physical, which is why you are pushed hard in practice, and Mental, which comes from having to meet adversity and whipping it. Now all of us have adversity— different kinds maybe—but adversity. Just how we meet these troubles determines how solid a foundation we are building our life on; and just how many of you stand together to face our team adversity will determine how solid the foundation our team has built for the rest of the season.

"No one cruises along without problems. It isn't easy to earn your way through college on football scholarships. It isn't easy to do what is expected of you by the academic and athletic. It isn't easy to remain fighting when others are curling around you or when your opponent seems to be getting stronger while you are getting weaker. It isn't easy to continue good work when what you're doing isn't appreciated by others. It isn't easy to go hard when bedeviled by aches and pains and muscle sprains. It isn't easy to rise up when you are down. The pure facts of life are that nothing is easy. You only get what you earn and there isn't such a thing as something for nothing. When you truly realize this—then and only then will you begin to whip your adversities.

"If you'll bear with a little story, I'll try to prove my point.

"On midnight, January 14, 1945, six pitiful American soldiers were hanging onto a small piece of high ground in a forest somewhere near Bastogne, Belgium. This high

240

ground had been the objective of an attack launched by 1,000 men that morning. Only these six made it to the objective. All the others had been turned back, or killed, or were lost. This grimy, crudy group of six men were all that was left of a magnificent thrust of 1,000 men. They hadn't had any sleep other than catnaps for 72 hours. The weather was cold enough to freeze the water in their canteens. They had no entrenching tools, no radio, no food. They had only ammunition and adversity.

"Two times a good-sized counterattack had been launched and been beaten back by the six largely because of the dark and some determined hand-grenade throwing. The rest of the time there were mortars falling everywhere, the dreaded above-ground bursts scattering shrapnel like buckshot. The Germans were beginning to sense the location of the six.

"Then things began to happen. First, a sergeant had a chunk of shrapnel tear into his hip. Next a corporal went into shock and began sobbing. After more than six hours of the mortar barrage and two counterattacks beaten off, no food in two days, well those fellows there were involved in some blue ribbon adversity.

"Another counterattack began and succeeded in making it to the position. Hand-to-hand fighting is a routine military expression. I have not the imagination to tell you what this is really like. A man standing up to fight with a shattered hipbone, saliva frothing at his mouth, still him gouging at the enemy with his bayonet, then strangling with his bare hands.

"It went on, that fighting in the confusing dark, by the five (the corporal was out of his mind), until the attackers backed away.

"Now the mortars began again, and nothing had changed what was available from the start. The retreat route was clear and open, but nobody left the hill, until at dawn airborne troopers arrived in relief. It still wasn't quite light. The lieutenant in the group picked up the sergeant with the broken hip and carried him like a baby. Another led the babbling corporal like a dog on a leash. The other two of the original six lay dead after the night

241

in-fighting. It took four hours for the four to make it, only two of them by their own efforts. They were as ghosts.

"After a meal and 10 hours of sleep, the lieutenant and surviving sergeant were sent on a mission 12 miles behind German lines and made a link-up that closed the Bulge.

"Today, two of the final six lie in Belgium graves. One is a career army man. One is a permanent resident of an army hospital in Texas for the insane. One is a stiff-legged repair man in Ohio. And one is an assistant coach of football at the University of Florida.

"Now, this is no documentary, or experience in self-indulgence. It was told to you to show you that whatever you find adverse now, others before you have had it as bad or worse, yet hung in there to do the job. Many of you are made of exactly the same stuff as the six men in the story, yet you haven't pooled your collective guts to present a united fight for a full 60 minutes. Your egoes are a little shook. So what? Nothing good can come from moping about it. Cheer up and stand up. Fight an honest fight, square off in front of your particular adversary, or adversity, and whip it. You'll be a better man for it, and the next time it won't be so tough. Breaking training now is complete failure to meet your problems. Quitting the first time is the hardest—it gets easier the second, and even easier after that.

"I'd like to see a glint in your eye Saturday about 2 p.m. with some real depth in it—not just a little lip service—not just a couple of weak hurrahs and down the drain again, but some real steel—some real backbone and 60 full fighting minutes. Then, and only then, will you be on the road to becoming a real man. The kind you like to see when you shave every morning.

"As in most letters, I'd like to close by wishing you well and leaving you with this one thought. 'Self-pity is the roommate with cowardice.' Stay away from feeling sorry for yourself. The wins and losses aren't nearly as important as what kind of a man you become. I hope I have given you something to think about—and remember, somebody up there still loves you."

The next afternoon the recipients of that letter written by Lt. Gene Ellenson counterattacked and drove A&M back to Texas, 42-0. That was the first victory in the campaign that would wind up with triumph in the Gator Bowl with a win over Penn State.

The Miracle From Macclenny

Of the sophomore discoveries of 1962's 7-4 season, none seemed more promising than the brash southpaw quarterback from Miami, Tom Shannon, or halfback-fullback Larry Dupree from Macclenny, a north Florida town five miles south of the Georgia border.

Dupree flashed onto the Southeastern Conference scene with such sudden success that he was voted consensus all-SEC as a sophomore. In his three varsity years—1962-64—he did not miss playing a single game, though a painful knee, injured early in his first year, throbbed for two and half seasons. He ran his way into a permanent place in Gator history and into the hearts of those privileged to see his quick bursts upfield so often on long touchdown runs.

Larry Dupree was involved in matchless high drama in his junior year when he made the difference in Florida's win over Georgia, though at the time his young wife was lying dangerously ill and his first child was in a day-old grave. And he closed out his touchdown scoring poetically with an 11-yard run that beat arch-rival Miami just as all seemed lost. Yet, Larry Dupree came within a last minute decision of going to Georgia.

Spec Townes, Georgia recruiter, had been the first to pay much attention to Dupree during Larry's senior year for Macclenny's Baker High and Coach Tom Covington. Larry had already been up to Athens to see a game or two, and both his parents were from Georgia.

Then Dave Fuller showed up with his sincere manner and

gentle persuasion, and Larry went down to watch Florida beat Tulane in 1960. That was Graves' first year, and it was an exciting time in Gainesville.

"Coach Graves impressed me, and I guess I'd followed Florida more than anybody else," said Dupree, now a contractor in Macclenny and a former city manager of the town that he says "is growing by leaps and bounds."

He called Townes and told him the night before scholarship signing time that he was going to Florida, "a decision I made, I think, because I figured I was going to live here, so I should play ball here. The truth is, it didn't occur to me to go to college until Coach Townes and the others started paying me some mind when I was at Macclenny my senior year. It was such a small place, and all I ever did was carry the football on just about every play."

Florida then had a rash of good backs—Bob Hoover, Dick Skelly, Lindy Infante, Allen Poe, Jim O'Donnell, Sam Mack, Bruce Starling, Dick Kirk, Allen Trammell, Ron Sonter, Jerry Newcomber, and Shannon, Libertore, Batten, and Dodd Jr., as quarterbacks. Dupree thought he could break into the lineup, but he knew he would have to learn to block and convince the coaches he was as capable as he thought he was. Dupree was anything but cocky. He was confident. He said little. But he performed.

His sophomore year, 1962, was a time of three teams, one offense, one defense, and the one that went two ways, the first or Big Blue team. Dupree at first was on the Go or offensive unit. He moved to the Blue unit for the third game, the Jacksonville battle with Duke. That was the one Florida lost 28-21 in the big Duke comeback. In it Dupree ran 70 yards for a score and figured strong in the 21-0 lead, but did not play in the second half after that first lick to his knee.

Dupree was not big at 6 feet, 190 pounds, nor fast for 100 yards, but "I felt I could hold my own with anybody in 40 yards," he said, "and I don't know why, but I was taught to believe—and I believed—that I could score each time the football touched my hands.

"When I got to Florida—not before—I kept hearing there was some politics about playing. Me, I never saw any. I just worked hard to make the team. And that first year showed me that I could play. The last game, the Gator Bowl, the win over Penn State, that was the highlight.

"I hurt my knee in the spring again but worked all summer to make it strong for the 1963 season. We went only 6-3-1 in 1963, but I figured we had a better team than that. What we did do that we all remember the most was beat Alabama up there in Tuscaloosa 10-6 and beat a good Florida State team 7-0."

The 1963 season started in a disappointing way. Tech beat the Gators 9-0 in the rain at Atlanta when a Florida gamble failed early. Then came a 9-9 tie with Mississippi State remembered most because of bench calls for repeated quarterback sneaks by Shannon and a late pass which Randy Jackson dropped when it would have meant the winning touchdown. Jackson was a tackle and the tackle-option play was then legal.

The Gators next were unimpressive beating Richmond 35-28 and headed to Tuscaloosa as a decided underdog to Alabama. Paul Bryant-coached teams had never lost in Denny Stadium, and the Tide had a quarterback named Joe Namath.

The Crimsons lost that afternoon because Bobby (Grubby) Lyle of Haines City kicked a 42-yard first quarter field goal, and in the early part of the last period Dick Kirk of Fort Lauderdale, not very big and not that fast, broke through off tackle and shot 42 yards for a touchdown, with end Charley Casey making a big block. Jimmy Hall kicked the 10th point, and though Alabama scored later on Namath's dive these Gators had knocked off a giant 10-6 in one of the school's proudest moments.

"I'm emotional," said Dupree, "and I always grew silent in the locker rooms before the game. But all teams have loud people, and I must say I often wondered if everybody on the team cared as much as I did. I was wrong. They just did it differently. I saw it that day in Tuscaloosa.

"Fred Pearson was a big, old, good-natured tackle from Ocala. Just before the game I looked over there and saw him crying. Everybody saw it. Then we went out and beat Alabama." Dupree did not score, but he carried the ball all afternoon, gained nearly 100 yards, and had two long runs called back.

A 21-0 victory over Vanderbilt followed with Shannon and Poe starring, but the next week Florida's homecoming crowd

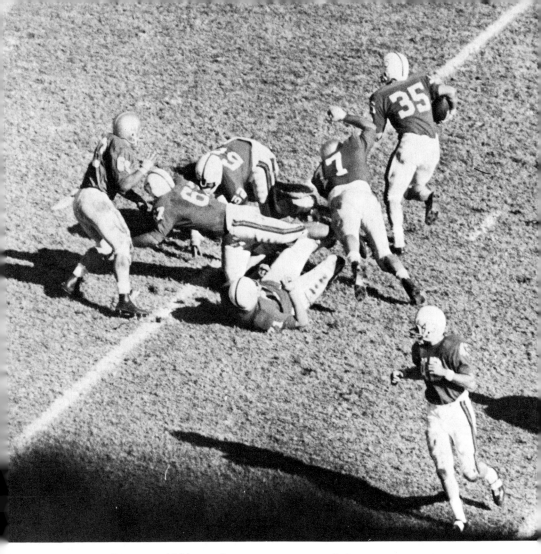

Larry Dupree (35) strikes out on touchdown run against Georgia.

witnessed an embarrassing 14-0 defeat by Louisiana State "just when I thought we had it going and when the Gator fans were so hungry for the win."

That did not end the humiliation, for next came the bi-annual trip to Auburn and the bi-annual defeat. This one was 19-0, and the Gators suddenly were down again, 3-3-1 on the record, but down.

The Georgia game was coming up, and a win was badly needed. That Thursday night, with Dupree's wife Denise expecting a child at any minute, Larry and friend Allen

247

Trammell were passing the time at the Dupree apartment, discussing the game against favored, 4-2-1 Georgia.

"Denise went into labor suddenly, so Allen and I took her to the Alachua General Hospital," said Larry, thinking back to that fateful, terrible November Thursday night in 1963.

"We waited and waited at the hospital, and Allen finally went home at midnight. Things seemed all right then. But from one to three, nobody said anything to me. About three they came out and told me there had been complications. They told me our baby was dead—stillborn. They told me Denise was in pretty bad shape herself."

Larry Dupree was 20 years old. The parents of both had come to town and were not far away.

"It was all so confusing," Larry recalled. "But the family got together early Friday morning, and we decided the best thing was to go ahead with the funeral as soon as possible."

He called a preacher friend, Robert Dunaway, and late that afternoon the family took the Dupree baby to the Macclenny cemetary 50 miles away and buried the child, the small confused group silent through Reverend Dunaway's brief graveside service.

Larry returned to spend time with Denise, who seemed better, and when he left the hospital that night—sleepless for so long—the route to the apartment carried him by the Florida Field meeting rooms. He saw the team was there and went in. When he entered, wise Coach Gene Ellenson walked out, leaving the time to the boys.

"I hadn't known what to do," Larry remembered. "I didn't know if I should play the game or not. I was so concerned about what was right. And I didn't know what people would think. I didn't want to let the team down, but then...Anyway, after I talked with the team, I had decided if Denise wanted it, too, and she were better in the morning I'd play. I figured what the team wanted was what was important."

He slept a few hours, went back to the hospital, and Denise was better. She told him to play.

That was 8 a.m. Saturday, six hours before kickoff in Jacksonville, 70 miles away. Larry's father-in-law was Eldridge Beach, head of the Gainesville district of the Florida Highway Patrol, a former Gator halfback, and soon to become head of the State Highway Patrol. The troopers delivered Dupree to the Roosevelt Hotel in Jacksonville at 10 a.m.

There were no hurrahs at his arrival. "Not any comment much at all," he recalled. "I wondered again if I was right, if it was right. The newpapers had stories about my child's stillbirth. I worried until we were on the field, and then I began to see that the players were silent because they were sympathizing and determined to win the game for me. And how they blocked. And tackled."

Early in the game Dupree's uncertainty about the crowd ended. He shot through the right side, cut out, then in, and went some 65 yards for an apparent score. The officials said he stepped out.

"I knew then the crowd accepted me," said Dupree, "with the great cheer for my run, the boos at the call, and the cheers later on for me. I have never been aware of crowds that much. That day I was."

It was a tough game. Dupree scored once, Bruce Bennett scored once on an intercepted Larry Rakestraw pass, Ken Russell fell on a key onsides kickoff ball, and when Dupree burst through the line for the winning score and the ball shot clear, good friend Matthews fell on it for him to preserve the 21-14 final.

At game's end, "my teammates picked me up and carried me from the field," remembers Dupree, "and Jimmy Morgan grabbed the ball from the official and pushed it into my arms. I have it still and always will."

But the season was not done.

President Kennedy was assassinated the following Friday, but Florida played anyway and beat Miami 27-21 in the Orange Bowl. All over the nation, college adminstrators faced the decision of whether to play. As in most cases the decision that night was to play, though the game very nearly was cancelled just before kickoff when Miami President Henry King Stanford tried to reach the announcer's booth but was blocked by the *Miami Herald's* sports editor, the late Jimmy Burns, long enough for the game to start for the 57,000 present.

The win put the Gators at 5-3-1, and Florida stopped Florida State 7-0 with Dupree setting a ball-carrying record that stands to this day. He carried the football thirty-one times, two more than Rick Casares in a game in 1952. Dupree scored the game's only touchdown and again made all-SEC.

He had carried the ball 189 times in 1963, then a season high for Florida backs, and had rushed for 745 yards. Thought was given to surgery on Dupree's knee in the summer, 1964, and he made a trip to the Duke medical center where it was discovered that he had a torn ligament, but nothing was ever done.

He played his senior year in 1964 never at full speed, but was a vital part of the talent-rich Gators who went 7-3 in that season.

"We were better than 7-3 in 1964," said Larry Dupree, who beat Miami that year with the last touchdown run of his career. "But I have no words to describe the feeling of always having had the move to get away from a tackler, and then, as I did often in 1964, finding that I could not make that move again."

Son Of A Preachin' Man

Steve Orr Spurrier was born April 20, 1945, at Miami Beach, the son of a preaching man, and while it is not recorded whether the proud father, the Reverend Graham Spurrier, put a Bible, baby bottle, or football in the new son's hand first, it is a fact that they all got there quickly and had excellent results. Young Steve grew into manhood a Christian, a splendid, well-coordinated physical specimen, and a football player beyond even the most ambitious dreams of his dad, a former guard at Erskine College.

The happening was at Miami Beach because that was where the Reverend Spurrier then pastored. Soon after that the Presbyterian assembly sent him to Athens, Tennessee, then to Newport, and finally to Johnson City, when Steve was 12 and just then busting out all over.

The Reverend Spurrier worked with him from the start, and Steve was one of those rare ones indeed. Give him a baseball and he could pitch it, a bat and he could hit the ball, a basketball and he could dunk it, a football and he could pass it better than anybody around. Later in life he developed into a scratch golfer, playing that difficult game as effortlessly as if he were completing a third and twenty, fourth quarter pass to Charley Casey for the winning touchdown. Nothing to it. Spurrier was a natural athlete. And to go with it he had a dead-even disposition, an active brain, and functioned best in had-to circumstances as his initials—SOS—suggest. Thing is, Steve always seemed to answer the emergencies in which he was

251

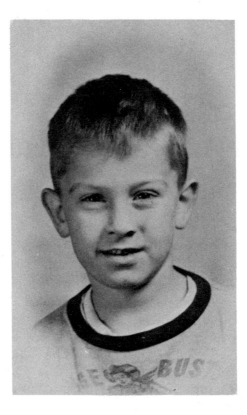

Little Stevie Spurrier, Son of a Preaching Man.

involved.

As a sixth grade basketball player, his team was undefeated. In Little League he pitched and shortstopped his team to an 18-1 record.

When he moved into high school, he never pitched a losing game for Science High. His baseball team won two straight state championships. His basketball team lost in the regional finals his last two years. His football team went 6-4, then 5-5 and finally 7-4. Kermit Tipton was his coach, and he gave Spurrier the chance to do what he liked most—pass the ball.

Spurrier's dad saw to it that the sports appetite never went wanting. While he lived in the Presbyterian manse, directly behind was the Scout House gym. When it snowed, Spurrier worked out in the gym. The preacher had a set of keys. They even built a protection for the windows so they could practice batting indoors when it was cold.

All that was except on Sundays. Spurrier had a perfect 13-year Sunday School attendance record of which he is extremely proud.

Steve Spurrier, Johnson City, had scholarship offers for baseball, basketball, and football. He decided that it would be football and baseball, and that the football he would play would be at a Southeastern Conference school that was pass-oriented. Early in 1963 he visited Mississippi and Alabama and liked them both, but it was basketball season at Science High, and he had to turn his attention to that.

He struck off the list the state school he ordinarily would have attended, the University of Tennessee, because the single-wing, the old run-oriented offense of the late General Neyland, still was in vogue on the Knoxville Hill.

Down at the University of Florida, Head Coach Ray Graves kept getting nuisance calls from his brother in Knoxville, reporting on Spurrier and how Graves should get on the ball and try to land the sandy-haired hotshot. Graves got on the ball and invited Spurrier to Florida in early March for the annual spring, Orange-Blue game. Spurrier came. He had been told to bring along his golf clubs, even though it was still ungolfy weather in Tennessee—or Tuscaloosa, or Oxford, Mississippi, for that matter.

He saw the campus, the beauties, and talked passing offense with Pepper Rodgers and Graves. A former Gator punter turned student assistant while studying law, David Bludworth, took him to play golf on the university-owned golf course.

"That impressed me," said Spurrier later. "Golf in March and in the sun meant a lot. And Graves was honest with me. He was nice, and he didn't say I would start as a sophomore as others had. He said I'd have to earn it.

"Then Coach Graves visited us in Knoxville several times. He made no wild promises. But he did say it was a pass-oriented offense Coach Rodgers had, and I could see that. Also I think it helped that his dad was a minister and so was mine. I chose Florida because of the passing, the SEC, the weather, and Coach Graves," said Spurrier.

Steve Spurrier being acclaimed by Florida legislature.

Steve Spurrier, in the years of his eligibility, brought a new dimension to Florida football. Before he left for a professional football career he became the most achieving Gator in history. He took the Gators to back-to-back major bowls, the Sugar in 1965 and the Orange his senior year in 1966. He took the Gators to within one punishing defeat by Georgia of the Southeastern Conference championship.

He beat Florida State in the final minutes when all seemed lost. Indeed, eight times in three years he produced Florida victories though the Gators were trailing in the fourth quarter.

He passed, ran, handed off, punted, and kicked field goals beyond his range. In his three years at Florida Steve Spurrier broke every school record for game, season, and career in passing and total offense. He produced two-out-of-three wins

over Auburn.

He led Florida to three-out-of-three wins over Louisiana State, two of them in Baton Rouge. He beat Ole Miss twice, once at the Rebel homecoming, a total embarrassment.

He set in 1966 Southeastern Conference season records for most pass attempts (291), completions (179), and passing yardage (2,012). While he was quarterbacking, Florida scored a minimum of one touchdown in all thirty-two games in which he played, averaging twenty points per contest.

He became the all-SEC sophomore of the year, the SEC's most valuable player in 1966. He led Florida to records in 1964, 1965, and 1966 of 7-3, 7-4, and 9-2 and led the Gators to total national respectability.

He became the only player in Sugar Bowl history to be

judged the most valuable in the game while on the losing side. He was voted all-SEC quarterback his junior and senior years.

He was never actually injured. He was knocked out once at Auburn. He left the field for two plays, returned, and threw a touchdown pass.

He won the Heisman Trophy, symbolic of college football's most outstanding player, in 1966 by a landslide. A Southern player had not won since Billy Cannon of LSU in 1959. Spurrier beat out Bob Griese of Purdue in the one-two Heisman balloting.

And through it all he remained largely unchanged in personality and outlook. He remained a team man, unpretentious, and unaffected. A grateful university retired his playing number, 11.

Georgia Coach Vince Dooley said of him: "Sometimes the word 'winner' is over-used, but when I think of Steve Spurrier, I truly think of a 'winner.' He was capable of finding so many ways to win."

Heisman Trophy winner Steve Spurrier at work.

Anxious moment for Jeri Spurrier, wife of quarterback Spurrier.

Charley McClendon of LSU, who never could beat Spurrier, said of him: "He had a sixth sense that all great athletes have when they get crowded. In a couple of very clutch situations we put enough pass rush on him to force him to run, and he would start to run and get to the line of scrimmage and throw. When you get that type of performance with the pressure on you, you usually win the game." Spurrier usually won the games.

Spurrier took Florida believers to their highest plateau of achievement that December night in 1966 when he stood on the dais at the Downtown Athletic Club in New York City and accepted the Heisman Trophy for himself, his parents, his good

257

wife Jeri there watching, and his coaches, his teammates, and his school.

Many accompanied him to New York for the ceremony, including good friends Norm and Petie Carlson (he was the proud sports information director), and alumnus Bill Watson of Tampa. Spurrier told Watson, the Carlsons, and a few others later, "I know this is something, and in later life I'll begin to appreciate it more I'm sure. But right now the wins we had over FSU, LSU, and Auburn, and the one we hope to have over Georgia Tech (Orange Bowl, and they had it) mean much more."

It was the way he was, and still is, for on departure for the San Francisco 49ers of the National Football League, Spurrier became an instant, active Gator alumnus.

While he was in uniform Spurrier gave Florida partisans something unique to that point, and that was a total confidence in his ability to win that game being played down there. Gator fans knew Spurrier could pull it out in the fourth quarter. They believed.

Take that Saturday in late October, in his senior year, 1966...

The Good Times: 64 - 65 - 66

The opponent was Auburn, and for a change Florida was favored. The Gators were undefeated through six games in 1966 and had been memorable in wins over Northwestern, Mississippi State, Vanderbilt, FSU, North Carolina State, and LSU.

Now it was time for the seventh win, there at Gainesville with a record crowd exceeding 60,000 watching. The offensive heroes, like Steve Spurrier, sophomore running back Larry Smith, fullback Graham McKeel, wide receiver Richard Trapp, split end Paul Ewaldsen, tight end Jim Yarbrough.

But Auburn with two long plays, an 89-yard kickoff return by Larry Ellis and a 91-yard run by linebacker Gusty Yearout with a free ball fumbled into the air as Florida was about to score, had made it an absolutely sensational afternoon of scoring competition.

This was Spurrier's senior year now, and he was high in the running for the Heisman. The Gators were in the middle of the go for the SEC title and a major bowl bid. They had to beat Auburn.

Statistically there was no comparison. Smith was bursting loose repeatedly, and Spurrier was hitting everything in sight. But it was 7-7 after a quarter, then Auburn led at the half 17-13. Florida was out front 21-20 after three periods. Then it was 27-27, and less than four minutes were left in the hand-wringer.

At breakfast that morning Spurrier had mentioned to Wayne McCall that he felt like kicking a field goal that afternoon. He had kicked just one during the season, one of 41 yards in the opener in Evanston against Northwestern, but he had missed a shorter one against North Carolina State two games back. Wayne (Shade Tree) Barfield kicked the field goals, the shorter ones.

"You see, we didn't kick many," Spurrier explained. "We always scored a touchdown."

"I remember the game at Florida well," remembers Coach Ralph (Shug) Jordan of Auburn. "It was something. I know it was hot, and it was 27-27, and Florida got the ball at its own 12. I knew Spurrier's capabilities very well, and I knew the game was not over."

Less than four minutes remained when the Gators began what had to be a fateful drive. The Gators worked it masterfully to the Auburn 30 where it was fourth down and a lot, and time and Florida's perfect season were waning.

"It was a long field goal," Spurier recalls. "It was out of Wayne's range. I pointed to my chest, looking at Coach Graves, indicating I wanted to kick it, and he nodded go ahead."

On the other side of the field Coach Jordan was suspicious.

"We sort of anticipated a pass in place-kicking formation. We knew Spurrier hadn't been kicking field goals much.

"I watched him kick it," said Jordan. "It was wobbly, and the trajectory was low. In other words it was not a good place-kick, but it went through, and it was worth three points, and it won the ball game," and the stands erupted with the faithful who knew all the time he could do it.

Forrest Blue, the big Auburn center, who later became Spurrier's teammate on the San Francisco 49ers, said of that remarkable Spurrier achievement:

"I think if there had been no goalposts and the official had said, Steve, you'll have to kick it through my upraised arms, Steve would have done that."

It was the way he was. It was the way he began and the way he ended, and thus he was the focal point for the Good Times in Florida football in the Silver Sixties, the years 1964, 1965, and 1966.

In fact the Good Times began good with a 24-8 opening win over Southern Methodist, in September, 1964. Tom Shannon was the senior quarterback, and Jack Harper, Larry

Steve Spurrier kicks impossible 40-yard field goal with 2:12 left to beat Auburn 30-27 in 1966. Larry Rentz held the ball for the historic kick.

Dupree, and Alan Poe were there in the backfield, with sophomore Spurrier backing up. He came into the game in the second period and on his first pass hit Harper on a connection that covered 56 yards. Marquis Baeszler scored on the next play. It was Spurrier's first touchdown drive. It was the beginning of a 1964 season of peaks and valleys.

The peaks in the 7-3 finish were the wins over SMU, Mississippi State 16-13, Mississippi 30-14, South Carolina 37-0, Auburn 14-0, Miami 12-10, and finally the postponed smash of LSU at Baton Rouge 20-6 on a freezing night.

There was even a peak in defeat. One of the losses was a 17-14 edge-out by Alabama in Tuscaloosa, in one of the South's all-time premier football struggles. It was clean (one five yard penalty). It was close, and it matched two undefeated teams.

Steve Sloan engineered the close win over Florida at quarterback when Joe Namath went out with a knee injury. Randy Jackson and John Fieber scored for Florida, Jackson on a tackle-option pass from Spurrier.

The game was 17-14, Alabama, after a David Ray field goal with 3:06 left in the game. But here came the Gators, Spurrier passing to Casey and then to Dupree and Don Knapp. In the rush Spurrier, a sophomore then..."well, I made a mistake," he said later. "I misjudged the 7 yard line for the 2," and called the wrong play. No timeouts remained.

A field goal was attempted, but Jimmy Hall missed it and with good reason. Florida had only 10 men to block. Jimmy Jordan had come on with a message, had been unable to deliver it, and had left the field with the man he replaced.

"But it is the way a game is supposed to be played," said Coach Paul Bryant of Alabama afterwards. "Hard, and clean."

"When you hit as hard as those Alabama people do, you don't have to be dirty," said a bruised Dupree.

That was not the only disappointment in 1964. There were two more.

At Jacksonville, with the Gators still a nifty 5-1, Georgia beat Florida when little field-goal kicker Bobby Etter picked up the ball he was supposed to kick—it had gone awry on the centersnap—and ran it for the winning touchdown, 14-7.

Then the final indignity came at Tallahassee the following Saturday. The Seminoles of Bill Peterson in 1964 had a splendid team. In fact they went on to rap Oklahoma in the Gator Bowl with quarterback Steve Tensi and incomparable Fred Biletnikoff the passing combination.

Some psychologist on the Florida staff thought the Gators should print on their helmets for the FSU game, "Go For Seven," for the seventh straight win over the Seminoles.

It backfired. FSU won it 17-6. The game turned in FSU's favor early. Florida, with senior Shannon quarterbacking, appeared headed for a first score when down deep there, FSU's angry noseman, Jack Shinholser, timed his move perfectly. He jumped precisely with the snap and slammed Florida center Bill Carr on the head and hands. The ball never got to Shannon. He never touched it. It hit Carr on the leg and bounced high and ripe for the fumble recovery by FSU end George D'Allesandro at the Seminole 2. Shannon took much criticism that day and later, but films proved it was not his fault.

"I saw it. I had the best view. It was not Tommy's fault,"

said Dupree.

Even so Florida was in the game with nine minutes remaining. Les Murdock, the FSU place-kicker who later was determined to have been ineligible, had kicked two field goals, and a Tensi to Biletnikoff touchdown pass had helped produce thirteen FSU points. But Spurrier took over and got the Gators going and with passes to Harper and Casey worked the ball to the six where Harper ran it in. Hall's placement made it 13-7. FSU was still ahead with 9:03 left.

Down through the years Florida Gator coaching nerve centers have yielded decisions worthy of discussion at the moment of decision, as well as later. The famed Sugar Bowl calls after the 1965 season rank at the very top of the Top Ten Dubious Decision List.

High too is the decision made there at Tallahassee that afternoon. Spurrier said the players disagreed, but the decision was made. Remember 9:03 was left, the score was 13-7, and Florida had built the reputation for rallies late to win and had just moved effectively 66 yards in 7 plays to close it from 13-0.

Instead of kicking off deep and leaving it to the defense, an assistant coach persuaded Graves to call for an onsides kick. The kickoff man would kick the ball easy and to the side, have it travel the minimum 10 yards, and hope a Gator fell on it for Florida's possession.

It did not work. FSU recovered near the 50, and an aggressive Tensi passed the Seminoles to within Murdock's kicking range. His 40-yard beauty upped the score to 16-7, upped it out of sight, and FSU had broken through and beaten the old school.

Florida State fans went mad. It had been a long wait. Seven years. And Bill McGrotha, the devoted and expressive chronicler of FSU football deeds as sports editor of the *Tallahassee Democrat,* reveled as he wrote:

"The Girls' School Did It!"

Jim Selman of the *Tampa Tribune,* assigned to FSU, was there in the press box trying to decide how to describe the feat he had so long wanted to report. Bill Kastelz of the *Florida Times-Union* of Jacksonville, a wag, asked:

"How can you type with all that saliva dropping into your keys?"

The win earned the Gator Bowl bid which the winner was to be awarded and the Seminoles did their duty well, trouncing Oklahoma, 36-19.

The Gators had lost two in a row and were dropped from the bowl picture, but came back after a slow first half in the next game to beat a determined Miami 12-10 in the Gainesville rain and only when Dupree scored the last touchdown of his career to settle the issue.

Finally the Gators went to Baton Rouge where they surprised many by destroying Sugar Bowl-bound LSU 20-6 in sub-freezing weather. Halfback Jack Harper, an underrated contributor to Gator football, a floating-type runner and super receiver who "never caught a pass or made a gain or a block in practice, but never missed a pass, missed a block, or failed to gain in a game," as Shannon described him, was brilliant against LSU. He scored twice on passes from Spurrier and Trammell, and the talented, philosophical Shannon ended his Florida career by scoring one of the Florida TDs.

The Gators were said to be the best 7-3 team in the country. But all the bowl spots were taken by then.

Interest, confidence, and enthusiasm was at its highest ever in Florida after the 1964 season. The Gators touched, involved, and excited more people. Dupree and Shannon were gone, with others, but Spurrier was back, as were Casey, Harper, Ewaldsen, Barry Brown, Poe, Feiber, and a bright young receiving talent named Richard Trapp, from Bradenton, a pale and all-but skinny fellow who looked too frail to play ball. Trapp played only five-and-a-half games of high school ball, but he was vital to some of those comeback wins of the next two seasons.

There also was Bruce Bennett at safety to captain the defense, voluntarily giving up a shot at offensive quarterback for the defensive future he carried into professional ball in Canada later. And Larry Beckman at guard captained the offense.

The season of 1965 was a gripping one, a commander of constant attention. There had been a few coaching changes. Rodgers had left for UCLA and Ed Kensler had become chief of offense. Don Brown had joined up two years before. Fred Pancoast had arrived the year before when a Tampa sportswriter recommended him, and Graves hired him away from the head job at the University of Tampa. Tampa was struggling then, its future in football in doubt. Billy Kinard and Bubba McGowan also were on that Graves staff of 1965.

The campaign began in the heat of Dyche's Stadium in Evanston, Illinois, where Spurrier, then a junior, passed Northwestern silly, 24-14. But it lagged the next week when Mississippi State upset Florida at home 18-13, a dropped pass with a minute to play surrendering the victory to the Bulldogs.

Next Florida outslugged LSU 14-7, annihilated Ole Miss at Oxford, 17-0, and clubbed North Carolina State 28-6.

After victory over NC State, the record was 4-1, and Florida headed for Cliff Hare at Auburn where no Florida team had ever won. This Florida team seemed to have the best chance in a long, long time, and this team was on its way to victory—until near the game's end. The Gators had led 10-0,

Offensive chief Pepper Rodgers and his two star QBs, Steve Spurrier (left) and Tom Shannon.

then trailed 10-14, the first Auburn TD scored on an interception by Bill Cody, an Auburn linebacker from Orlando. Spurrier took the Gators to a 17-14 lead midway in the final period when he hit Casey on an 11-yard scoring pass. The game seemed safe until wideout Freddie Hyatt got behind defender George Grandy and a substitute quarterback named Alex Bowden lofted a pip into Hyatt's hands and Hyatt scored. The play covered 69 yards. Later a fumble recovery by Cody in the end zone stretched it to 28-17, and the Ghost of Cliff Hare ruled again.

Graves calls victory in the next game—after the wretched defeat at Auburn—one of his most important, and most exciting, a 14-10 win over Georgia. Vince Dooley had become the Georgia coach. It was a win characteristic of the Florida wins with Spurrier. Down 10-7 with 4:06 left Florida took the ball at its own 22 and a half yard line. SOS first hit Casey across the middle, and the great receiver managed to keep going until caught at the Georgia 19. Now Harper, the senior from Lakeland who had fumbled away an apparent score earlier, went down the Gator Bowl's west sidelines, heading south. Spurrier lofted one Harper took falling backwards into the end zone, falling backwards onto Lynn Hughes, who was trying desperately to bat the ball away. Wayne Barfield's kick was good, and it ended 14-10, Florida.

"It is a game I would like to forget," said Dooley later.

"It meant everything to us," said Graves.

"It was one of my high points," said Spurrier.

It roused the Gators into such spirits they destroyed a pretty good Tulane team 51-13 in Gainesville the next week, and in his upstairs bedroom that night Graves accepted for his team a bid to play in the Sugar Bowl against Missouri, even though games with Miami and Florida remained.

"This is one of the goals I wanted so to achieve," said Graves at the time. "I wanted an SEC championship, and I wanted some major bowls."

It was the first big bowl for Florida outside of the Gator. It would be announced the next week, after victory at Miami, was the plan.

Then a terrible thing happened.

"Did you ever see an alligator with a red face?"

266

That was the lead one newsman put on his story the next Sunday, after the night before when Miami had upset Florida in the Orange Bowl 16-13.

Spurrier had his poorest night to that point, only eight completions in twenty-two attempts, and an off-target pass of his that was intercepted and led to the final prestige-shattering Miami field goal. Miami, which always plays Florida as if the national championship were at stake, played gutty, carefully, with purpose. Florida did not, erring frequently. Indeed it was a Miami punt while Florida led 13-6 that hit unsuspecting Florida defender Dick Kirk and was recovered that led to the tying touchdown for the Hurricanes.

The Sugar Bowl people announced the choice anyway, and put on their thick hides for their return to New Orleans, where LSU that night had smashed Tulane 62-7.

There simply was no trusting these Gators. The previous year Florida, remember, had beaten LSU 20-6 in the delayed game after LSU had accepted a Sugar Bowl bid. Now this.

"Ah," said Sam Corenswet, Jr., present at Miami for the despairing development along with other Sugar Bowl delegates, Monk Simon and Theo Maumus, "ah, maybe Liz Taylor has an answer. A bowl bid is like marriage. It does not always work out."

Now, Florida was suddenly 6-3 and had another game to play—against an FSU team with a 4-4-1 record and inspired by victory the year before. The game was at Gainesville, and 49,000 were there, including the nervous Sugar Bowl delegation.

Two great Harper receptions and a Wayne Barfield field goal put the Gators safely ahead, it seemed, 16-3.

Then suddenly FSU rallied, and it became 17-16, Florida State leading, with FSU quarterback Ed Pritchet looking more like Spurrier than Spurrier himself.

The clock showed 2:02 left in the game, FSU leading by that one big point. A Florida loss would mean a 6-4 record for the Sugar Bowl host Gators.

Spurrier told Graves on the sidelines not to worry. He should have said it on the public address system.

"I never saw anything in my life like Spurrier," Graves said later.

Harper returned the kickoff to the Florida 29. Spurrier threw an incomplete pass, aimed at Casey, then one Casey caught at the Florida 39. Harper went deep next and caught the Spurrier pass falling backwards, at the FSU 43. A minute and 32 seconds were left.

Spurrier ran for five yards and called time. Then he passed complete to Casey for thirteen at the FSU twenty-five. Time left: 1:19.

Now hear Spurrier describe the pass he rates his favorite among all he completed at Florida:

"I rolled to my right and Casey was to juke, then go straight down the sideline in front of me. As I moved right, two important things happened. Don Knapp made a great block on the Florida State end to give me more time to fool around, and I saw that the FSU middle guard had jumped offsides. That would give us five yards and get us closer for Wayne to try the field goal if other things failed. Casey was in front of the defender, Billy Campbell, but with the time I had I motioned for him to go deeper, and I kept threatening to run. Coach Pancoast had told me from the booth that the object was to get close for the field goal, but to play it by ear.

"Campbell stood his ground as Casey went by him, and I threw at Charley. He caught it in the end zone. I won't forget that one."

A quick followup score by the Gators came when Trammell intercepted a deflected pass for a score to make it 30-17, and a deceiving total. The Sugar Bowl people put away their arsenic pills, and Graves returned to favor. His Coronary Kids, as they were known to some, had saved the farm again.

It was off to the Sugar Bowl and another remarkable series of developments. It is among the best remembered and most perplexing yarns in Florida football records.

The favored Tigers of the Big Eight jumped to a 20-0 lead, 17-0 at half time. It was 20-0 with 10:32 left in the game. Yet, in those next minutes Spurrier won the MVP award and the Gators themselves the admiration of the full house and television audience. But a coaching judgment first won a place in that lineup of Florida's Top Ten Dubious Decisions.

Spurrier's passes began working, a beauty to Harper of 22 yards producing six points. Spurrier and Barfield prepared for the extra point kick. They were waved off the field. Offensive chief Ed Kensler had decided to go for two points. In the press box Gator aides Pancoast and Brown held their palms outstretched when asked why the two-point conversion. The Spurrier pass for two points failed. The score stayed 20-6.

Florida had another score in no time and again the try for two points failed.

Now it was 20-12, with 4:58 left, and Spurrier flung it long and into the end zone, Casey catching the ball flying parallel to the ground, arms outstretched. It is a famous photo, the shot of the catch that made it 20-18. Another pass for the two points failed.

It ended that way, 20-18, Missouri. There was no more reliable extra point man in college ball than the one who did not try any in the Sugar Bowl, 1966.

Later Kensler accepted the blame, saying: "Honestly, I thought 20-8 would look better than 20-7. I made a mistake."

Alumni were outraged, the Go-For-Two cry etched in their memories. A call for a math course for coaches was petitioned.

It was a few days later that Graves made the statement that, "After the game in the Sugar Bowl, I told the boys to walk out into the sunshine with their heads high, that they had played well, deserved the victory, and that anyway, four hundred million Chinese didn't even know the Gators had played Missouri," and he paused, and added, "then damned if two days later I didn't get a letter from an alumnus in Hong Kong wanting to know why in the devil we went for two."

That 1964-65 group was a proud and talented bunch. Its members:

Offense: Charles Casey and Paul Ewaldsen, split ends; John Whatley, John Preston, Randy Jackson, and Mike Waxman, tackles; Larry Beckman (captain), Phil Maggio, Jim Benson, and Neal Sneed, guards; Bill Carr and Gary Cliett, centers; Barry Brown and Gary Thomas, tight ends; Spurrier and Harmon Wages, quarterbacks; Jack Harper, Marquis Bacszler, Alan Poe, and John Feiber, backs; Richard Trapp, wideout; Hallie Seymour, punter; Wayne Barfield, field goals.

Defense: Lynn Matthews, Brian Jetter, Don Barrett, and Chip Hoye, ends; Larry Garner, Doug Splane, Wally Colson, and

Don Giordano, tackles; Jerry Anderson and Ed Warner, middle guards; Jack Card, Ron Pursell, Wayne McCall, and Steve Heidt, linebackers; Dick Kirk, Bud Williams, Allen Trammell, Bobby Downs, George Grandy, Tom Hungerbuhler, and Bruce Bennett (captain), backs.

And if 1965 was good, surely, went the word, 1966 would be better, even though some of the heroes—Harper, Matthews, Poe, Bennett, and Casey would be gone.

Spurrier was back, and Trapp, and Ewaldsen. Fullback Graham McKeel had recovered, and Graves and Pancoast, after a massive fight with every college in America, had signed a big, bruising, quiet high school all-American from Tampa who could

Here comes huffin' and puffin' Silent Larry Smith.

not miss. His name was Larry Smith, and he would be a sophomore in 1966.

He did not miss. He became another on the list of great running backs, a fascination to watch, for he ran straight up, bumping people with his chest. He became all-SEC, a first round pro draft choice.

These 1966 Gators were picked to be good, and they were. Graves calls them "my best team, all around."

They polished off Northwestern in the Gainesville heat, 43-7, avenged the defeat of the year before by handling Mississippi State easily, 28-7, and Vanderbilt, 13-0, and setting the stage for a controversial "win."

It was at FSU, and the buildup was staggering. Florida was undefeated (3-0), FSU 1-1, losing barely to Houston but beating tough Miami 23-20 the week before.

It was a whale of a see-saw game with Spurrier and Smith and Trapp brilliant, FSU resolute, and with quarterbacks Kim Hammond and Gary Pajcic to throw to Ron Sellers and Lane Fenner.

Each led the game twice. Florida shot ahead in the final quarter on a Spurrier pass to a wide-open Smith, and a two-point conversion pass to Trapp. It was 22-19, Florida. The two-point conversion had immobilized FSU place-kicker Pete Roberts. It had made an FSU touchdown necessary.

It all got down to one play after Pajcic's passes to Billy Cox, the magnificent Sellers and tackle Jack Fenwick put the ball at the Gator 45. Thirty-two seconds remained. It seemed safe enough. Sellers left the field limping, Florida's two deep men were both ex-quarterbacks: Bobby Downs of Winter Haven and Larry Rentz of Coral Gables.

The play started. Pajcic ran to his right. He had good protection. Cox flew down the field taking some defense. Fenner delayed, then struck out towards the goal, then cut towards the northeast sideline. Downs went back with him, and Rentz cut over from the middle. Official Doug Moseley went with the play too.

Pajcic flung the ball 55 yards in the air at Fenner. Fenner went up in the air close to the northeast playing field pocket, up over the flag. So did the defenders. The ball went through the defenders, who went down. Fenner twisted and took the ball on his shoulder and slammed down to the ground, rolling out of bounds. Cameras recorded the action from several angles.

The FSU fans went crazy at the "completion." Seventeen seconds remained. Florida fans waited, breathless. The official, Moseley, unhesitatingly signalled no catch in bounds—an incomplete pass. It was Florida's game, 22-19.

Coach Bill Peterson first seemed to accept the judgment, but as the hours went on he did not. He spoke of it harshly for all the years he was at Florida State. FSU fans everywhere still do and always will.

Fenner said plainly, "I was in."

Moseley said he was not. There is no question about who wins in a matchup like that.

Photos of the "catch-no-catch" are all over Florida in offices of FSU alumni. But on the books it was, and is, Florida 22-19, and the Gators were 4-0.

They became 5-0 a week later when, in another emergency situation, Spurrier directed a winning drive at North Carolina State with time running out, and with Richard Trapp dazzling on the winning touchdown run with a clutch Spurrier pass. The score was 17-10.

Next the Gators manhandled LSU 28-7 to approach that breath-taker with Auburn, the 30-27 Florida Field squirmer on Spurrier's impossible last-minute 40-yard field goal.

With the 7-0 standard the Gators could win the SEC with following wins over Georgia and Tulane. Tulane was designated as the sixth conference game. There was Cotton Bowl talk, and Orange Bowl, and coaches were laying away gifts for their wives, payment to come out of bowl bonuses. But most of all the elusive SEC title was in sight. Only thing was, within the league Alabama was unbeaten too at that time and so was one other team besides Florida—the Georgia Bulldogs. Dooley's Dawgs, as those Georgia fans called them, were 6-1, a 7-6 loss to Miami, a surprise, the only blemish. Florida was favored with Spurrier and the splendidly balanced team.

Georgia defensive coach Erskine Russell knew he had to do something special. He put in a new defense, and Spurrier read it right off the bat and took Florida to a 7-0 lead. Then it was 10-3, Florida, after a 72-yard kickoff return by Harmon Wages led to a field goal. Then an interception led to a Dog score to knot it 10-10. Another, with a 39-yard touchdown return by the same Lynn Hughes over whom Harper had scored Florida's winning TD a year earlier, built a 17-10 lead. The final score was a cruel, decisive 27-10. The photo of the game was one of Spurrier after it was over, at midfield, on one knee, head down—beaten.

The fine Florida offensive machine had gained only five net yards rushing the second half against a line Bill Stanfill led for Georgia. Spurrier had completed only 29 yards worth of passes in the final two periods. Before the Georgia game

Steve Spurrier kneels in anguish on the Gator Bowl turf on that November Saturday in 1966 moments after Georgia stopped Florida's win streak at seven in a row and the Gator bid for an SEC title. The score: 27-10.

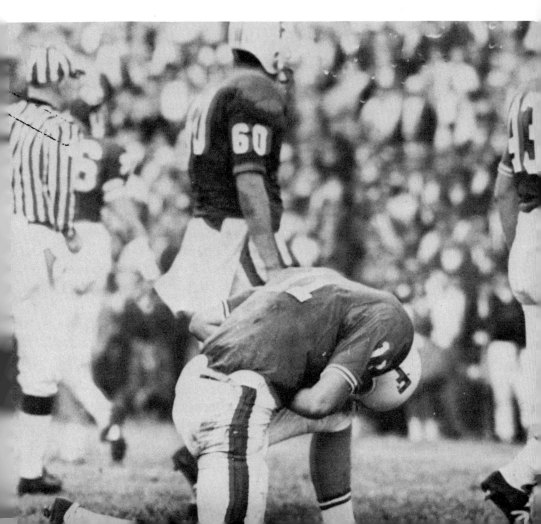

Spurrier had thrown 192 passes. Only two had been intercepted. Georgia intercepted three of six over one span. The defeat was crushing. "My worse," said Spurrier, "my absolute worst." He was blitzed off balance all day.

Graham McKeel said of it, "they played better. We deserved this loss."

Graves said, "I never said we were invincible. I said we were a good team. We're a good team like Georgia, who is 7-1, like us, and UCLA, who is 7-1, and Tennesssee, who is 5-2." But Georgia was not beaten in the SEC and would not be and would end up 6-0-0 in the SEC, 9-1-0 overall, and beat SMU in the Cotton Bowl. Duke at Jacksonville in 1962 had been Graves' bitterest defeat because of the nature of it, but Georgia in 1966 became the bitterest because of the consequences. In 1969 another would occur to round out Graves' Big Three Defeats.

But then, after Georgia, the Gators rallied to master Tulane in Gainesville 31-10 and accept a bid to the Orange Bowl with old rival Georgia Tech as the opponent. But Orange Bowl committeemen like Jack Baldwin, Ben Benjamin, and Jimmy Lewelleyn would cringe the next weekend when they too would have to leave Gainesville and head home.

Miami upset Florida at Gainesville in that final game in 1966, dealing the Gators a stinging 21-16 defeat as defensive end Ted Hendricks of Miami played superbly along with a linebacker named Ken Corbin. It was a bruiser. It came even though Spurrier ended his career with 26 completions in 49 passes for a staggering 227 yards, including a touchdown throw to Paul Ewaldsen. Larry Smith even threw one, a touchdown pass of 37 yards to Trapp, and Barfield set an SEC consecutive extra point record with his 29th. Trapp caught 11 passes in all for 130 yards to beat Casey's season total of 63, for 872 yards. But Miami, a fine team that ended up 7-2-1, including wins over Georgia and Southern Cal but losses to Florida State and LSU, teams Florida beat, then rapped Virginia Tech in the Liberty Bowl.

The Gators went to the Orange Bowl nonetheless with their 9-2 record and handled Georgia Tech effectively, 27-12, Spurrier playing as the Heisman Trophy winner, and playing well enough with 14 completions in 30 passes for 160 yards. He even ran 13 yards once. But, in his final game as a Gator he was

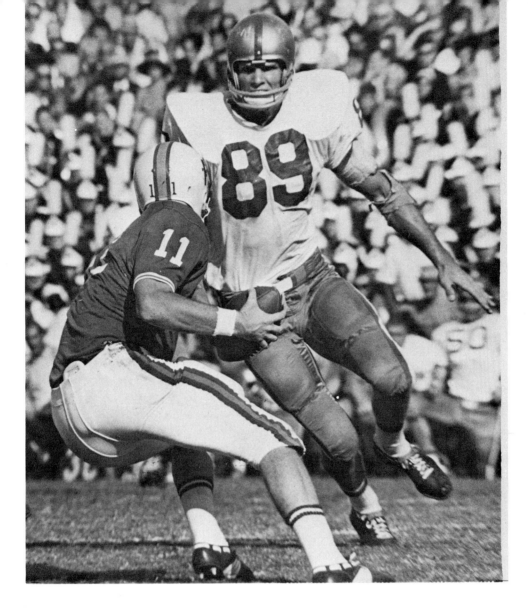

Miami's giant end Ted Hendricks, later to become all-Pro for the Baltimore Colts, bears down on Steve Spurrier in Miami's 1966 upset of Florida.

overshadowed by sophomore Larry Smith who stole the show and almost lost his britches. In the second quarter, down 6-0, Smith suddenly burst through his right tackle and ran 94 yards for a touchdown, his pants inching ever downward with every step until, as he turned into the end zone, they very nearly fell free, photos show.

The national television audience and crowd of 72,426 loved it as Larry Smith, perhaps the most unlikely candidate in the world, came close to being the first Gator Streaker. He was voted the game's most valuable player. The season ended 9-2-0 overall, with 5-1 and a third place finish in the SEC, and the Heisman Trophy winner.

At Florida there had never been anything quite like 1966. And those largely responsible were:

Offense—Spurrier, Trapp, Smith, McKeel, Barfield, Wages, tight ends Jack Coons and Jim Yarbrough, split ends Paul Ewaldsen and Mike McCann, offensive linemen Guy Dennis, Bill Carr, Jim Benson, Terry Morris, John Preston, Steve Clark, Bob Houng, Davd Barnhart, Gary Duven, Wally Colson, backs Harmon Wages, Tom Christian, and Tommy Glenn.

Defense—Linemen Rex Rittgers, Don Giordano, Bill Dorsey, Red Anderson, Brian Jetter, Don Barrett, Mike Santille, Eddie Foster, George Dean, Doug Splane, Bobby Adams, Steve Ely, linebackers Steve Heidt, Jack Card, Wayne McCall, Chip Hinton, and Dan Manry, and defensive backs Tom Hunger-buhler, Bill Gaisford, Bobby Downs, George Grandy, and Larry Rentz.

The Spurrier years—the 23-9 standard and two major bowl years—were history.

The Almost Years

Late in the 1965 season, with the Gators riding high and bowl-bound, a friend of Graves' from Houston, Lou Hassell, phoned the Florida coach. Jess Neely was finally retiring at Rice Institute, and Graves' name had come up as a successor. Was he interested?

Well, he was, and he was not. He was enough that he met with the committee at the Hilton Inn at the New Orleans airport after the Florida State win and arranged for his family to fly to Houston before the Sugar Bowl for talks. They did and liked what they saw and considered it, enough so that the Rice people prepared a contract for Graves and wife Opal to take back to Gainesville while they studied the proposition. Rice was a high echelon school with low heat on coaches. It was tempting, but Graves declined when he came to the conclusion which he passed on to Opal. "If we go there, our goal will be to save money and retire to Florida."

There would be days and nights when Ray Graves, perhaps even wife Opal, in the seasons of 1967 and 1968, may have rued their decision not to go to Rice.

They were not hurrah years, and one, 1968, was supposed to be the so-called Year of the Gator. It was a phrase originated by Sports Editor Bill McGrotha of the *Tallahassee Democrat* after a Graves pre-1968 season speech and interview, and it became a phrase that now is bandied about annually, sometimes seriously, mostly in jest. One wag even offered that the Year of the Gator is from January to September.

Although Larry Smith and other standouts were back for 1967, missing was Spurrier, the first Gator quarterback to be No. 1 for three straight years. Hopes were on Jack Eckdahl, a quarterback from right there in Gainesville, but he tore up his ankle while LSU was beating up on Florida in the third game of the 1967 season, and that was that. When that happened the other quarterback, Harmon Wages, was sitting out a disciplinary action for late hours which Coach Lindy Infante had detected, giving some special drama to a not particularly dramatic year.

The Gators had beaten Illinois 14-0 and Mississippi State 24-7 but been blown out of Florida Field by LSU's three-year revenge machine 37-6, and Eckdahl went down. Since decisions are decisions, and Wages had been sentenced, Graves had to pull Larry Rentz from safety to the quarterbacking job he had not worked since high school. He did a superb job the first time, at New Orleans, guiding Florida over Tulane 35-0, then led the Gators over Vanderbilt 27-22. Auburn won up there again, 26-21, and then the Gators won their BIG game of 1967. They upset Georgia 17-16 at Jacksonville in a great game for spectators, Rentz passing to Trapp who hot-footed most of the 52 yards for a score, and reliable senior Wayne Barfield of Albany, Georgia, kicking a 31-yard field goal for the difference with 34 seconds left. Trapp's run with the Rentz pass was the best of his celebrated career.

The Gators then beat cumbersome Kentucky 28-12 and were 6-2-0, better than the expectations. Graves had labeled it a rebuilding year. It would turn out that way because vengeance would be Florida State's, and Miami would make it three in a row over the Gators, dropping the overall finish to 6-4, despite a 5-2 SEC record, worth third place.

It was after the losses to rivals FSU and Miami and some howls were heard that Graves said: "Only at Florida can a fellow finish third in the SEC and still get fired."

The Florida State victory came before a record Florida Field crowd of nearly 65,000, who saw a gripping game and tense drama. Once more Florida tried a psychological gimmick that backfired. The Gators marched onto the field in rank and solomnly, instead of running out for pre-game workouts. Some thought it was because Graves was on crutches with a banged up leg, but the idea was to show concern.

Coach Ray Graves consoles a warrior sad.

FSU was leading 14-9 and iced the game in the fourth period when Kim Hammond, who had been knocked unconscious by Florida linebacker Tom Abdelnour in the first half, came off the bench. Although still somewhat dazed, he threw first a 41-yard pass to Ron Sellers, then one of 41 for the clinching touchdown. Rentz, Trapp, and Christian tried to save the day, but wound up losing 21-16 despite over 500 total Gator yards, including runbacks.

Miami added the final insult the next weekend 21-14, and 1967 was mercifully over, 6-4.

Nineteen hundred and sixty-eight, though, some said would be The Year of the Gator. It began like it might be, in a way, and ended like it should have been. In between—not so much. It was the year during which Ray Graves decided to coach just one more. He had some crackerjack freshmen on his 1968 frosh squad. And until the Sunday before the opener of 1968, Graves was not rushing to deny that it just could be The Year of the Gator.

He changed his mind because on that Sunday before the Gators were to open against the Air Force Academy in sparkling new Tampa Stadium, his super, senior running back Larry Smith pulled a hamstring muscle. He was never again in college up to his own great standards. In fact things got worse. He injured an arch later in a pitiful Florida effort at Vanderbilt.

But, pulled hamstring or no, the bands were playing and the sun was shining and 52,000 were at Tampa for the start of The Year of the Gator—1968. The publicity could not be stopped.

Florida promptly blew the script and lost the coin flip, kicked off, and Air Force speedster Curtis Martin gave good endorsement to the new Tampa Stadium turf. He went nearly 100 yards for the touchdown.

But Florida won it 23-20 in the game's dying minutes, and the Air Force lost not just the game but its Falcon mascot, if only temporarily. In Tampa search parties scoured the city for days seeking the mascot. It is a fact that Tampa police answered call after call from residents saying they had spotted the bird, who had reneged at the half-time show instead of flying from the press box roof to midfield to his trainer, who was flinging a rope in circles about his head. The pet went south. Tampa police learned the rope trick and spun it day after day after all manner of birds only to learn the falcon, called Mach 1, had not been lost at all. He had spotted the Air Force bus and caught it before the Airmen had left Tampa the afternoon of the game.

Meanwhile, back on the gridiron, the Gators went to Florida State underdogs but won on a day called hotter than a pot of collards, 9-3, on some determined Smith running, some great Florida defense, and some disinclination of FSU to use the weapon it advertised the most, the pass to Ron Sellers.

Next Florida polished off Mississippi State 31-7 and Tulane 24-7 and took its 4-0 and national ranking to North Carolina where another victory seemed assured.

It was a disaster. Continuous rains had soaked the field, and Florida's forte was the running of Smith and Christian. The Gators, on that rainy day in Carolina, set a school record. They lost eight fumbles and each led either to Carolina scores or stopped Florida drives. North Carolina won it 22-7. It was the second biggest upset of that weekend. Biggest was the sudden announcement that Jackie Kennedy, widow of the late President, was marrying Greek richman Aristotle Onassis. Someone wrote that Onassis might be the only living man who could handle the Florida coaching job.

The Gator decline had begun. A tie by underdog Vanderbilt in Nashville, 14-14, followed. Smith injured himself again there. A 24-13 Auburn victory followed at Florida Field, and the once 4-0 Gators were 4-2-1 and talking to themselves. Alumni were buzzing. Graves was frustrated. Undefeated Georgia was next. Graves felt he had to do something.

He did. He made history. At midweek he made an unprecedented swap. He made his defensive chief, Gene Ellenson, his offensive chief, and his offensive chief, Ed Kensler, who had taken a lot of heat, his defensive chief.

Georgia beat Florida that following Saturday 51-0, and one writer wrote:

"Georgia beat Florida 51-0 in the Gator Bowl yesterday in a game in which the offense of Florida played as if it were coached by the defensive coach, and the defense played as if it were coached by the offensive coach, which happened to be the way it was.

"But, the game was not as close as the score indicates."

A dark, dismal hour, after the 51-0 Georgia win over these wet, dispirited 1968 Gators, in the Jax Gator Bowl. That is Coach Gene Ellenson sheperding home the pained Floridians.

It was the most humbling day for Florida players, coaches, and partisans since another Georgia game, 75-0 in 1942. It was a disaster. And it rained throughout, making the passing success of Georgia sophomore Mike Cavan all the more phenomenal. Safety Jake Scott heroed too for Georgia in a game that even Coach Dooley of Georgia wished could have been called by the 10-run rule. It was 42-0 with the second half just begun, and Dooley admits, "it was the longest football game I have ever experienced in a winning cause."

It was awful. And as if it were not enough that the head of offense and head of defense were in jobs unfamiliar to them, the one man who may have kept the offense functioning, Coach Pancoast, backfield coach, was stricken with appendicitis the night before the calamity, underwent an operation, and was helpless 75 miles away in Alachua General Hospital while the slaughter took place. He may, some said, have been the most fortunate of all in the official family. He was warm, and dry, and his pain was only physical.

That remarkable move of department heads moved into the Top Three of the Silver Sixties in Dubious Decisions, moving alongside Go For Two at the Sugar Bowl and the Onsides Kick at FSU in 1964.

Florida was then 4-3-1 and saved some pride by beating Kentucky 16-14, in the rain again, in Lexington, then got by Miami 14-10 in Gainesville. The 6-3-1 finish was a blow to Graves and the state, and he talked of some changes on his staff, then of staying one more year and not changing his staff. He told close friends that was his plan, and then told University President Steve O'Connell that as well.

O'Connell had become president of Florida in 1967 when Dr. Reitz resigned. O'Connell, a determined and articulate man who served during those unsettled campus times of the Vietnam War, came from the Florida Supreme Court to the position as university president. He was a scholar-athlete of the finest tradition. At Florida as a student he had excelled at boxing, a top-notch intercollegiate sport when he was an undergraduate. He maintained his interest in sports always and on his return to Florida favored a strong, balanced athletic program. In the one year of extraordinary football that he was the president, he was as swept up as the next man in the 9-1-1 of 1969 and was a familiar figure in the pre-game huddle with the team.

So it was too that he shared the discomfort and dismay of his first two years, 1967 and 1968, and looked forward with Graves to 1969, which Coach Ray told him was to be his last.

Some fine recruiting in high schools about the state the year before, in 1968, made Coach Graves want one more year. "I don't want to bow out on two seasons like the last two," he told close friends and President O'Connell.

Modern Day Pioneers

Leonard George made University of Florida football history on December 17, 1968, without carrying the ball, making a tackle, or catching a pass. He made it the moment he signed the football scholarship assistant Coach Don Brown put before him in his Tampa home with George's Jesuit High School coach, Bill Minahan, witness. With his signature, Leonard George became the first black Florida Gator.

George was a halfback. The night after he became a Gator, he led Jesuit to the Class A state high school championship. A 5-11, 170-pounder, George had a high (87) grade average at Jesuit. He was a soft-spoken, intense young man who gained 224 yards in one high school game.

The day after Leonard George signed with Florida, Willie Jackson, a fast wide-receiver who high schooled at Sarasota and prepped at Valley Forge, Pennsylvania, signed his grant. He was the second black Florida Gator. Both George and Jackson were effective freshmen team members in 1969, then moved up to the varsity in 1970. Both lettered all three years, and by the time they were seniors no one remembered they were the first, of the then many, blacks on the squad.

George was an offensive halfback his sophomore year, a starting defensive back the next two. Defensively he was a sure tackler and on two occasions broke up passes that would have meant go-ahead scores for the enemy.

But what Leonard George will remember most about his career, perhaps, happened in the third game he played. As a

284

Leonard George of Tampa and Willie Jackson of Sarasota were the first black players signed by the Gators.

sophomore he scored against Alabama at Denny Stadium, in Tuscaloosa, the first of his race to score a touchdown against Alabama at home.

George stayed on after graduation as a student-coach and became deeply involved in religious work.

Willie Jackson was a flashy, all-stops out wideout who had a flare for the spectacular. In 1970 as a sophomore he caught 25 passes for 439 yards and 2 touchdowns. As a junior in 1971, he caught 27 for 334 yards and 2 TDs, and as a senior in 1972 he caught 23 for 397 and 4 TDs.

Jackson's forte was his speed and deception, once he caught the football. He was hampered somewhat by a depth perception problem. He was a dangerous kickoff return man, but his most outstanding single play came with 20 seconds left in the half against Kentucky at Tampa Stadium in the 10th game of that troubled 11-game first season of Coach Doug Dickey. Kentucky had moved ahead 10-3 of the Gators and had the upper hand. Florida badly needed that win, being 6-3 at the time.

Jackson from the left wideout spot cut across the middle. Quarterback John Reaves hit him on the dead run, smack between two Kentucky defenders. Jackson took the ball without juggling it or slowing down and streaked for a touchdown on a rousing 71-yard play, and Florida tied it up 10-10, then rode the momentum Reaves and Jackson cranked up to a critical 24-13 victory.

In no time a black running back would set a school rushing record, and a little later there would be a black quarterback.

285

But Leonard George and Willie Jackson were the pioneers onto this modern-day frontier.

Signing Of The Super-Sophs

In the fall of 1967, when not trying to patch up his many fallen Gators of that year, Coach Graves had his recruiters hard at work. And generally his staff in those days recruited well, particularly the Super Athlete.

In that fall of 1967 Graves had told his staff he must have a rangy, passing specialist from Tampa Robinson named John Reaves. Assistant Coach Lindy Infante told Graves he must let him sign a Cuban refugee in Miami full-named Carlos Alvarez Vasquez Rodriquez Ubieta.

Alvarez was a 5-10, 180-pound all-Miami running back who was sought by most Southern teams, but not exactly coveted, as was Reaves, up in Tampa. Reaves stood 6-3 and was a classic passer who had taken his team into the high school playoffs.

Florida State, Alvarez said, laid off him "because they thought I hurt my knee bad. I'd hurt it playing basketball and it had swelled. But there was no operation and it was fine."

Alvarez scored 491 out of 495 on the state placement test. He was a brilliant student, as fast-thinking as he was fast-moving. His dad, Licinio, had graduated from the University of Havana, but when Fidel Castro moved to "save" Cuba from the American imperialists, lawyer Licinio Alvarez packed up his wife and kids (Carlos was 10) and they made it on one of the last legal ferries across the Florida Straits. Most of their worldly goods they left behind. In Miami they went into the dress-shop business.

He signed with Florida, he said, "because of their wide open style of play."

So did Reaves, on December 23, 1967, at his Tampa home, "because Coach Fred Pancoast promised me we'd play the pro-set and play wide-open, and because in the back of my mind I always wanted to go to Florida," said the Anniston, Alabama-born Reaves.

The last two schools he eliminated in his decision—and everyone in the country wanted him—were Tennessee and Florida State. His good friend and neighbor, former FSU halfback Nelson Italiano, "had convinced me in Florida State, but I changed my mind at the last minute. I was, for a time set. I was going to FSU." Reaves, Florida running back Larry Smith, and Italiano all lived in the same immediate neighborhood. It was Smith that Reaves first told he had settled on Florida, and Smith called Coach Ray Graves to advise him. Then he told Italiano, and then he told two recruiter coaches who visited him in his home the night he made up his mind, but had not signed. The recruiter-coaches were on their way to Miami where their team, Tennessee, was playing Oklahoma in the Orange Bowl.

The recruiter-coaches were Doug Dickey, head Tennessee coach, and Jimmy Dunn, head of Tennessee's offense.

"I told Coach Dickey I'd made up my mind to go to Florida and primarily because of their offense, and because I was a Florida boy. He said he understood and left. I didn't see Coach Dickey again until January, 1970, when he called the first team meeting after being named the new head coach at Florida. I'll never forget it."

Elsewhere around Florida that fall of 1967 other Gator coach-recruiters were reaping a fine harvest. They were signing players named Fred Abbott, Tommy Durrance, Jim Yancey, Bill Dowdy, Bob Harrell, Andy Cheney, Jimmy Barr, Harvin Clark, and, in Georgia, a strong-legged runner named Mike Rich.

Later this crowd would have a name. They would be called the Super-Sophs.

288

Take That!

When the 1969 Southeastern Conference Skywriters tour spent its day in Gainesville with the Gators, the sportswriters found a group of seniors not much interested in talking to the press, and they found a field full of stylish-looking sophomores. But they did not see anything to suggest that anything lay ahead for that crowd but a fair-to-middling season.

Senior cornerback Steve Tannen, in an interview, said, "We'll let our playing do our talking. There's been too much talking in the past."

Just that day someone had brought up in a well-read newspaper the 51-0 Georgia embarrassment heaped on Florida the year before. That happened because the writers had come from Georgia directly to Florida and a Georgia trainer had joked with Florida writers about Gatorade, the newly developed energy replenisher, not having helped the Gators much that rainy day in Jacksonville last season.

The Gators and the Gator staff were sensitive—except the sophomores. They were still wide-eyed and concerned only with the business at hand. There had been talk before the season Coach Graves would make wholesale staff changes. He had told one confidante that he planned to. But in the end he chose to tough it out. There had been considerable criticism over the summer of the two seasons past. Florida alumni could not get Georgia off their minds—51-0 Georgia.

It was about the time of the Skywriters' visit that Graves decided to gamble with his young players where possible.

Gatorade inventor, Dr. Robert Cade, uses Gator linebacker Chip Hinton to test the original mix of his energizing drink.

Offensive chief Pancoast had convinced him he should go with the sophomore quarterback, John Reaves, plus flanker Carlos Alvarez, and others. But going with Reaves, that was the tough decision. Jack Eckdahl was back and sound. He was a senior quarterback and with Southeastern Conference experience, a qualification most head football coaches hold dear.

The 1969 schedule was not to be so tough there was no chance, but the opener surely would be a dilly. It was to be Houston, gratefully at Florida Field and not in the Astrodome. It was to be played September 20, and no matter what happened on the field the Gator treasury would be helped. Graves, the athletic director, had signed Houston years before for a $25,000 guarantee and no share of the gate, and here

Houston was coming to Gainesville picked by pre-season polls high in the Top Ten.

Houston, with its Veer-T, was a solid, more than two-touchdown pick. Florida fans were skeptical of the Gators still, and they did not fill Florida Field for the opener. But, Graves would remember later, "It is the only game I know we kept the ticket booths open well into the fourth quarter. People were riding around listening to the game on radio and liking what they heard and came to the game late." By the time it was over 53,897 showed up.

And what they saw they would never forget. Graves and Pancoast and defensive chief Gene Ellenson put a finely mixed team on the field. There was virtually a senior line in front of Reaves and Alvarez and Tommy Durrance and Mike Rich, the veteran tackle Mac Steen and center Kim Helton, two keys. Split-ends were mixed, senior Paul Maliska and sophomore Andy Cheney. Tight ends were Jim Yancey and Bill Dowdy, both sophomores.

The defense had plenty of experience in frontmen Jack Youngblood, Robbie Rebol, and Bob Coleman, in linebackers David Ghesquierre, Tom Abdelnour, and Mike Kelley, in defensive backs Tannen, Mark Ely, Jack Burns, and Skip Albury. Young defenders in there at the start or soon included tackle Bob Harrell and defensive swifties Jimmy Barr and Harvin Clark.

It was not really THAT MUCH of a SOPHOMORE team. Indeed two of the key ball-carriers, Garry Walker and Jerry Vinsett, had been around. But as it developed, sophs played such a big part in the scoring, that there was general acceptance that this was an all-around young team.

John Reaves quarterbacked the Gators from that day forward for three years, not missing a game in 33. He set a national record. He was involved in controversy. He was extraordinarily cheered. He was booed. He achieved great heights but in the 32 games that followed his very first, he did not, in his own mind, match his deeds and thrills of that first game. He completed 603 total passes in the 33 games. The first of the 603 he remembers the most and cherishes the most. The next to last he completed beat Jim Plunkett's NCAA total yards, the last, the 603rd, also set a national record. But, well, hear John Reaves:

"I can't say what it was, but going into that Houston game I wasn't nervous, or jittery, or anything. It was like going to another practice. Coach Pancoast had us so prepared. I'd been drilled and schooled. I'd even read articles in magazines written by Houston's defensive coaches. I wasn't scared or nervous, as we began that game that day. I wasn't in awe of them. I knew we had some horses too. The week before we had beaten our "B" team 93-0. Coach Graves had tried to make much of that; anybody who scores 93 points against anybody is no slouch, I thought.

"I remember the morning of the game, Carlos and I talked to Coach Pancoast about throwing the bomb early, and he said okay and we got excited. He said he'd been thinking the same thing. He said he would call the plays, and we would do it. So we won the toss, and we got the ball in about the middle of the field. I had the whole first series of downs. We ran two plays off tackle, and that got us on the right hashmark, where Coach Pancoast wanted us. He had studied their defenses and realized they played man for man up close and left two free safeties to cover both sides of the downfield.

"Carlos flanked out and was 40 yards, almost, from our tackle. I knew with that setup there was no way that corner could handle Carlos alone. They had no idea who he was, or that I could throw the ball. Well, he outran the guy. It was a 70-9 play. He ran straight past the guy. I went straight back. I set up, saw him break past him, and I threw it and said to myself, 'Well, it's wobbling a little,' and I got knocked down. I didn't know what happened until I heard the crowd break loose. I jumped up and ran to the side in time to see Carlos running into the end zone. I jumped up in the air about 20 times, ran 80 yards to catch Carlos, and picked him up and carried him off the field."

The first pass play of John Reaves, the first catch of Carlos Alvarez, had covered 70 yards, the pass perhaps 50 yards in the air before Alvarez caught it on a dead run. And their first play produced a touchdown.

On their next offensive opportunity, "it was then I was a little nervous," said Reaves. Only a three-point 26-yard field goal by Richard Franco developed.

Then Reaves passed two yards to Walker for a score, 21 yards to Alvarez for a score. It was 38-6 at the half. Jimmy Barr, another soph, intercepted a pass and legged it 37 yards for the other first half touchdown.

In the second half Reaves passed 46 yards to Durrance for a touchdown, Durrance ran six yards for one, and Reaves passed to him again for three and another TD. Eckdahl came in to run

Gator defensive back Steve Tannen (22) at work against Florida State. Shirt-sleeved gent over No. 23's shoulder is Bill Peterson, FSU coach of that time.

in one touchdown. Richard Franco kicked all the points.

The final score: 59-34, over a good Houston team. What could not happen, had.

Reaves had made his debut with a remarkable five touchdown passes, completing 18 in 30 throws for 342 yards!

"I'll never forget that day," said Reaves. "At the half the students poured out of the stands and lined up to greet us when we came back."

It is fascinating that 32 games later, in his windup as a Gator at Miami, he very nearly duplicated his first game performance with 348 passing yards, and a record-setting show.

"It's the truth," said Reaves. "It was the first and last I remember most. The alpha and omega, sorta."

Yet the start by the Gators-69 apparently really did not surprise Reaves, and it is so documented. The week of the opener Reaves wrote to his good Tampa friend and advisor, Leonard Levy, this remarkable prophecy:

"Today we start final preparation for the University of Houston. At present I count on at least five TD's out of our offense. As you know we demolished the frosh and B's, 93-0 Saturday. Our offensive line has given me fantastic protection, and if I don't choke we shouldn't have any trouble throwing and scoring."

The great victory and great start in 1969 was not the private property, however, of the Super-Sophs. Appreciating it even more were the seniors on that team, the Tannens, and Steens, Heltons, and Maliskas. For two years they had heard some beefs, and they too remembered the 51-0 at Georgia and the upset at North Carolina. For them it was a Take-That sort of a win, as it would be a Take-That sort of a season.

Nine - One - One

Florida fans may be fickle, but they are faithful. They may curse their team and their coaches, but they deny that right to those of other school ties. They may stray, but they never go far and almost never do they go forever.

All was forgotten after that rouser in the 1969 opener, the crunch of a strong Houston team 59-34, and in the best possible way with plenty of offense and lots of long passes.

That the Super Sophs were no fluke was established the next week at Jackson, Mississippi, when they outscored Mississippi State 47-35 as Reaves completed passes for 326 yards, demonstrated some checkoff-at-the-line maturity, and Alvarez caught 12 passes himself.

Bill Bondurant wrote in the *Fort Lauderdale News* of the team, and Bondurant was no hubba-hubba writer, "Florida has an exciting team, one to take to your bosom, one young, aggressive, unaffected, and unabashed of offense, which pleases crowds so." He pointed out the value of the pass-blockers so busy in the two games: Kim Helton, Skip Amelung, Mac Steen (captain), Donnie Williams, and Wayne Griffith. The Pepperman, split end Paul Maliska, was the downfield blocking specialist.

Next came a comfortable 21-6 win over Bill Cappleman-quarterbacked FSU, when Front Four Harrell, Rebol, Youngblood, and Coleman forced two fumbles and three interceptions, when Rich and Durrance ran so well. Harrell said later his technique for getting to Cappleman so often was: "I just folded back my ears and hauled my tail in there."

Now 3-0 and riding high, and a "breather" was coming up at Tampa Stadium—Tulane.

With 2:10 left in the "breather," Tulane led 17-16. Florida had come alive and Durrance had just scored, a leaping Alvarez pass reception keeping that drive going. But he had gone down and out and seemed hurt.

The premier passing combination of John Reaves to Carlos Alvarez sparked the 9-1-1 finale year of Ray Graves in 1969. Above, Reaves prepares to throw. At right, Alvarez catches.

He was badly needed on the two-point conversion attempt, and into the game he went. He had not been hurt, as the big crowd thought and Tulane hoped, but had leg cramps.

"When we got to the line," said Reaves, "I looked at the defense. I was surprised. Usually down on the goal, teams play receivers man-to-man, but they were in a zone. When one of the two men on Carlos checked off, I knew I was going to throw to him."

Alvarez took four steps straight ahead (north) and cut to the sidelines. Paul Ellis had intercepted two Reaves passes earlier. He tried to leap for this one. The ball went through his arms, "missing Ellis' hand a foot," said Alvarez. "Hands don't

bother me. I watch the ball. It was an easy catch."

The final: Florida 18-17, in the breather, before the revenge game with North Carolina, the team that did-in the Gators the year before when they were undefeated.

Florida got even, smashing Bill Dooley's team unmercifully, 52-2, and making him say later, "why blame me for what my brother did?" His brother is Vince Dooley of Georgia, coach of the 51-0 beating of Florida the year before.

An easy 40-20 victory over Vanderbilt followed, and the Gators-69 were the Cinderella team of the nation, 6-0, nationally ranked, going to Auburn where *Sports Illustrated* was poised to do a cover-story on them.

Pat Putnam was the man sent to do the job for SI. He did not have to write a line.

The jinx—and some great linebacking by Auburn and some fine teaming by Auburn's answer to Reaves—Alvarez, Pat Sullivan, and Terry Beasley—stopped the Sophs cold. The final was 38-12. Reaves was intercepted a collegiate record nine times. Five of the pickoffs led to Auburn points. Auburn was hardly a slouch. They were 4-2 and wound up 8-2, beat Alabama 49-26 in the finale, and played in the Bluebonnet Bowl against a team the Gators knew something about— Houston. Houston beat Auburn 36-7, and Gator partisans scratched their heads.

The last time *Sports Illustrated* had sent a writer to do a cover story on a Florida team and a Florida quarterback had been back in 1966, at the Florida-Georgia game, the one Georgia won 27-10 to stop the Gator streak of that year. Like Putnam in 1969, the SI scribe in 1966 wrote nothing, save the bare score.

Now these intriguing Gators-69 were about to experience one more severe blow, one more bloody nose.

While Florida has a half dozen so-called natural rivals, none reaches into history like Georgia-Florida, nor into the gut so deep. In no other series is the result so totally unpredictable, is the house always full for the show. In no other matchup is the house so evenly divided.

The game in 1969 was rated even. How right those making the line were, though the finish emerged only after all matter of drama.

Florida moved ahead 10-0, then fell behind 10-13 with time fleeting and Spike Jones' long Georgia punts not helping. Forgotten in the fury was the fact that Reaves broke Frank Sinkwich's SEC one-season yards-gained record at mid-game with Sinkwich in the stands watching.

It came to be 13-13 when Franco kicked a 21-yard field goal late in the game on a second try. First time he missed it, but an alert official had blown the whistle before the snap when he noticed photographers in the end zone had moved onto the playing field. Georgia newsmen's investigations revealed the photographers represented Florida newspapers, and they made post-game sport of that.

Then with it 13-13, Reaves took Florida to the Georgia 15 where it was fourth and 5, and in came Franco for the winning field goal attempt. He had kicked five of seven in the year, two in the game, one 36 and one 21. He could handle this one of 31 yards easily. The Eau Gallie soph was a walk-on player. He was working for his scholarship. His dad taught him how to kick.

"From that distance, it would be automatic," Franco said later. "I wasn't worried. I was ready for it."

But Nick Sinardi's snap to holder John Schnebly was a tad low and right. Schnebly juggled it. Franco had started forward. He stopped, then started again—too soon. He did not get full impact. The kick was a hair low and off target. "I should have taken more time," he said. "I should have had more poise."

It stayed 13-13, and Graves said: "It is what great rivalries are all about. That's an explanation, but it doesn't make any of us feel any better."

Yet the young Gators showed their mettle. They bounced back to smash Kentucky 31-6 and then Miami with remarkable ease, 35-16, to earn a bid to play Tennessee in the Gator Bowl. And all manner of things were about to happen.

One, and among the least remembered, was that the Gators were going to beat Tennessee, the SEC champs, 14-13. And with the win the Gators-69 would complete a spectacular 9-1-1 record. A crowd of them—Reaves, Alvarez, Durrance, Steen, Ghesquierre, Tannen, Williams—made first or second team all-SEC. Alvarez was a consensus all-American as a sophomore. Tannen would be the only SEC player to go in the first round of the pro draft. The New York Jets grabbed the Miami Beach

Defensive back Steve Tannen beats Tennessee receiver Lester McClain for 1969 Gator Bowl interception.

hurdler.

The exhilaration of the season, the long day at Auburn notwithstanding, and the prospects of so many point-makers, if not the blockers and tacklers, returning were enough to make a coach planning to resign have a second thought.

Graves On Graves

When he is especially sentimental, and he is a sentimental man, Ray Graves thinks back on his 10 years of the Silver Sixties at Florida and says:

"If you'll look on page 73 of the Gator press guide, for 1973, you'll see there on that single page the scores of all my results. Can you imagine all the recruiting, the planning, the coaching, the counseling, the injuries, the heartaches, the joys and thrills, taking up no more than one page in history? One hundred and five games. Can you imagine?"

But jumping out of those bare scores are the recollections of all the happenings, those planned, those unplanned, those smooth, those bizarre, just as looking at them Ray Graves was able to give his superlatives, the best and the worst, and the other "ests" of his Decade.

These are his judgments:

BEST TEAM—1966, which went 5-1 in the SEC, 9-2 overall, and beat Georgia Tech in the Orange Bowl.

POOREST TEAM—1961, his only loser, 4-5-1.

BEST DEFENSE—1960, a 9-2 season, when 11 opponents scored a total of 86 points, no one more than Georgia Tech's losing 17, and when three teams were shut out.

BEST OFFENSE—1969, the 9-1-1 last season, when a total of 343 points were scored in 11 games, an average of 31 points per.

TOP TEN WINS—Georgia Tech 18-17, and LSU 13-10, both in 1960; Texas A&M 42-0, in 1962, after the 28-21 loss to

The Gator Getters, an innovation of the sixties, a corps of coed pretties who assist in recruiting and hostessing around the athletic department.

Duke; Penn State 17-7, Gator Bowl, 1962; Alabama 10-6, 1963; Mississippi 30-14, 1964, because it destroyed a myth; Georgia 14-10, in 1965; Florida State 30-17, in 1965, after loss to Miami and with Sugar Bowl bid in hand; Auburn 30-27, 1966; Houston 59-34, in 1969.

BEST RECRUITING JOB—Signing Steve Spurrier, since he, unlike some of the other standouts like Larry Smith and John Reaves, was not a Floridian.

BEST COACHING JOB—After 0-51 loss to Georgia in 1968, coming back to beat Kentucky 16-14, at Lexington.

WORST COACHING MOVE—Changing offensive and defensive coordinators before the Georgia game in 1968, the 51-0 defeat.

GREATEST LOSSES—Duke, 28-21, in 1962; Georgia Tech, 9-0, in 1963 opener; Alabama 17-14, in 1964; Miami, 16-13, in 1965; Georgia, 27-10, in 1966; North Carolina, 22-7, in 1968; Georgia, 51-0, in 1968; Auburn, 38-12, in 1969; and Georgia, 13-13, in 1969, which was as bad as a loss.

GREATEST RECRUITING LOSS—Back Tucker Frederickson of Fort Lauderdale who went to Auburn because Florida had no School of Veterinary Medicine, which it does now.

THE YEAR WITH THE BEST SHOT AT BEING "YEAR OF THE GATOR"—1968, except for injuries before the season.

MOST PLEASANT COACHING DAY—Houston, 1969, when it was 59-34, and 31-0 before the half, 7-0 after three plays.

GREATEST REGRET—Not winning the SEC title.

But in his 10 years Coach Graves won 70, lost 31, and 4 were tied. The percentage is .667, but it pretty much averages out to a 7-3 decade.

RAY GRAVES PICKS HIS ALL-DECADE TEAM
(Position, Player, Size, Hometown, Years)
SE, Richard Trapp, 6-1, 180, Bradenton, '65-'66-'67
LT, Randy Jackson, 6-5, 230, Lake City, '62-'63-'64
LG, Guy Dennis, 6-2, 250, Walnut Hill, '66-'67-'68
C, Bill Carr, 6-4, 225, Pensacola, '63-'64-'65
RG, Larry Gagner, 6-3, 250, Daytona Beach, '63-'64-'65
RT, Mac Steen, 6-4, 225, Melbourne, '67-'68-'69
TE, Jim Yarbrough, 6-7, 255, Arcadia, '65-'66-'67
QB, Steve Spurrier, 6-1, 194, Johnson City, TN, '64-'65-'66

*Richard Trapp (44), boyish-looking premier pass receiver from
Bradenton, at work.*

RB, Larry Dupree, 5-11, 190, Macclenny, '62-'63-'64
RB, Larry Smith, 6-4, 220, Tampa, '66-'67-'68
F, Carlos Alvarez, 6-0, 188, Miami, '69
P, Steve Spurrier
P, Billy Cash

Defense

LE, Lynn Mathews, 6-3, 215, Tampa, '63-'64-'65

LT, Ronnie Slack, 6-4, 235, West Palm Beach, '60
MG, Bill Dorsey, 5-9, 205, Jacksonville, '66-'67-'68
RT, Jack Youngblood, 6-5, 250, Monticello, '68-'69
RE, Pat Patchen, 6-1, 205, Steubenville, OH, '60
LLB, Tom Abdelnour, 5-9, 206, Miami, '67-'68-'69
RLB, Ron Purcell, 6-0, 200, Tavares, '63-'64-'65
LC, Steve Tannen, 6-2, 200, Miami Beach, '67-'68-'69
SS, Hagood Clarke, 6-2, 196, Miami, '61-'62-'63
FS, Bruce Bennett, 5-11, 180, Valdosta, GA, '63-'64-'65
RC, Allen Trammell, 6-1, 193, Eufaula, AL, '63-'64-'65

Return Of The Native

In the summer of 1969 Douglas Adair Dickey was among the most envied of major college football coaches. He was 36, yet he was the head coach of a giant of the sport, the University of Tennessee. Athletic facilities were unmatched in the South, comparable to any nationally, and he personally had returned Volunteer football to the high place good Tennesseeans thought it deserved. The late General Bob Neyland, most distinguished of Dickey's predecessors, had retired in the early fifties. But there had been, after Neyland, an embarrassing decline toward mediocrity. The Vols even had a couple of losing seasons to go with only a couple of real winners.

Taking charge of the overall program in 1963 was Bob Woodruff, the very man whose star had fallen at Florida after the 1959 season, but who had moved back to coaching and administration at Tennessee after one year of selling gas in Gainesville in 1960. Woodruff became the Tennessee athletic director. He quickly sought out Dickey as the man to lead his Volunteers out of the wilderness. Dickey had been his Gator quarterback on the 1952 Gator Bowl team, and he had been a quarterback who achieved by his wits and wisdom rather than God-given physical ability. Dickey was working for Arkansas' Frank Broyles, who had coached for Woodruff at Florida for a year.

Dickey moved to Tennessee in 1964. He needed just one year to get the house in order. After a 4-5-1 start, Dickey guided Tennessee teams to 7-1-2, then 7-3, then 9-1 (the nine wins in a row after an opening loss), 8-1-1, and 9-1. Dickey became

Doug Dickey, as the 1970s begin.

the SEC Coach of the Year twice, won two SEC championships, and took the Vols to six straight bowls. Dickey was a no-nonsense winner.

In that summer of 1969 Dickey was a contented coach. He had a lock on Tennessee recruiting, had made some extra money on Minnie Pearl Chicken franchises, had pretty wife Jo Ann, and five kids. The press was friendly, TV sponsors were standing in line, and the prospects for the 1969 season were fine—just fine. The spring work had gone well. It was time for some time off. The plan called for a couple of weeks at a North Carolina lodge with some friends. They would play some golf and relax. That would happen in early August, 1969.

It was a time when Doug Dickey was giving no thought to leaving Tennessee for any place. In the last several years he had declined to be interviewed for the jobs as they opened at Michigan State, Georgia Tech, and Oklahoma. Oh, in his daydreaming he had thought of one place in which he might be interested—his old school, the University of Florida. It still had not won the SEC, still had not reached its potential, he thought, though Coach Ray Graves had brought the Gators along. He had in those daydreams thought of the pleasure it would give him to take his Gators to yet-unreached great achievement. After all both he and wife Jo Ann were graduates. His mother lived in Gainesville and her family in Daytona, where she had grown up on a dairy farm.

In late July, 1969, just before the North Carolina trip, Dickey got a telephone call from a man he had never met. His name was Steve O'Connell. He was the president of the University of Florida and had been since 1967. O'Connell told Dickey that Graves, who was both AD and head football coach, had decided to give up his head-coaching job at Florida after the 1969 season, but to remain as athletic director. O'Connell wondered over that telephone line from Gainesville to Knoxville if there was a chance Doug Dickey would be interested in talking about becoming the head football coach at his old school in 1970.

The truth is, Coach Graves, after the two seasons that were disappointing and dispiriting to him (1967 was 6-4-0 and 1968 was 6-3-1 and included that 51-0 embarrassment by Georgia), gave passing thought to resigning before the 1969 season. Then he considered a wholesale change of his staff, because there were grumbles among the influential. That 51-0 lacing by Georgia had been a terrible irritant to the longest-sufferers among veteran Gator watchers. But Graves did not want to resign on a sour note. There had been too many good times to end things during bad times. The sophomore crop was out-standing. He would tough it out another year and seek to return the record to a proper setting for his exit. He had given Florida its best record yet. He wanted to depart under favorable circumstances. The summer of 1969 was not a comfortable one for Ray Graves. With the fine sophomore group coming up he chose to keep his staff and his position, but informed President O'Connell that 1969 would be the last for him.

"I felt," said Coach Graves, "two jobs were for two men, and it would be in the best interest of the athletic program to make this change if everything worked out reasonably satis-factory during the season. President O'Connell indicated at this time that if I felt so strongly this way, he would be making some plans for my replacement. At this time I recommended two or three head coaches, including Coach Doug Dickey and Coach Bill Pace (of Vanderbilt). I also suggested that if we did not go with the head coach, or if a head coach was not available, I would recommend assistant head coach Gene Ellenson on my present staff.

"President O'Connell was very receptive to Coach Dickey with his Florida background and asked if I would talk informally to him about any interest he might have in the position," said Graves.

About this time, with Coach Graves' notice in hand, O'Connell appointed a committee to work with him. On it were himself, Graves, Board of Regents Chairman Burke Kibler of Lakeland, alumni leader Jimmy Kynes of Tampa, and Law Professor Mandell Glicksberg. They had several meetings. They wondered if Dickey were indeed interested. President O'Connell made the call to Knoxville in July, 1969.

"I said to him," Coach Dickey remembered, "I would be glad to talk on an informal basis, but I felt it important to tell my athletic director. I said I didn't want to talk without their knowledge. As it happened President O'Connell was going to vacation in Asheville, North Carolina, the same time I was to be nearby.

"I told Woodruff of the call, and he said fine, go ahead. My wife Jo Ann and I flew to Asheville and met with President O'Connell and his wife Rita in their room in a hotel there. We visited for an hour and a half. He told me Ray was quitting and wondered if I could be persuaded to move. I told him I thought it was the one situation I would have to investigate and give a strong look. But I told him, and he agreed, everything would have to wait until the end of the 1969 season. We parted with that understanding."

Dickey's thoughts were simply that he would be interested because it was home to him, and because Florida had not yet won the Southeastern and/or national championship. "And if I could do that for a school, why not do it for my very own," he said later in explaining the switch that would surprise so many and cause him so much anguish and misunderstanding.

After meeting with O'Connell, "I had a chance meeting

309

with Ray (Graves) a couple of weeks later in Atlanta, and he confirmed to me directly that he was resigning, and that he thought I was the natural person to take the job, with, he said, the least amount of problems."

How wrong that would prove as the unusual drama unfolded in the year ahead.

The 1969 season began with both Florida and Tennessee having great success: Tennessee's expected, Florida's a genuine surprise. But the coaching-change game plan was firm. Graves would resign, and an offer, not yet made, would be put to Dickey, who had said he would be receptive. All this would happen after the season's end.

In truth the selection committee was overjoyed. "Frankly," said Kibler, "I did not at first think Dickey would be available, because his arrangement at Tennessee was so attractive. But we were pleased and would, when the time came, make a strong bid for him. I suppose if we could have picked one man in the country and known he'd have accepted, we would have gone for Doug."

Dickey's Vols streaked to a 7-0 standard, Graves' young sophs to 6-0 before Auburn muzzled them. The Vols were talking Penn State and the Orange Bowl until a mad, mad Mississippi team—angered by Tennessee linebacker Steve Kiner's tag of "mules" on them—and some key Tennessee injuries, resulted in a 38-0 crush of the Vols and the hopes for the trip to Miami. But, as it developed, the Vols could win the SEC title by defeating Kentucky and Vanderbilt and finishing 9-1 overall and 5-1 in the SEC. Florida was going to finish no worse than 8-2-1, perhaps 9-1-1. More bowl talk began. The strangest thing was in prospect—the Gator Bowl wanted Tennessee vs. Florida. How fateful this was.

"If I made one mistake in all this," said Dickey two years later, with time to reflect on the troubled times that followed the Gator Bowl, "it was agreeing to play Florida in the Gator Bowl. We could have played Houston in the Bluebonnet. Houston had beaten Mississippi, who had beaten us. That probably would have been better. Florida offered nothing for Tennessee to play, but a chance to lose to a member of the SEC, and we'd won the championship. But Woodruff urged we go to the Gator Bowl. He said the last time we went there

17,000 of our fans made the trip. Fewer would go to Houston. We agreed to go and so did Florida."

Between the regular season and the December 27, 1969, Gator Bowl there was time to recruit. Some of Dickey's assistants returned from recruiting in Florida and announced to him that the state was full of rumors that he was leaving for the Florida job.

"I leveled with them" said Dickey. "I told them I had been approached, but nothing would happen until after the game. Then I called Ray (Graves) and told him what I had heard. I said I needed to know something. He called me back and said he definitely was going to resign. Then Jim Kynes called and asked if I could meet with the committee in Gainesville Sunday, December 21. I went over. They were all there: President O'Connell, Kynes, Kibler, Glicksberg, and Ray. I said I didn't think they could make an offer, which they had not, without me telling them what I thought it would take to get things going at Florida. I told them we could not compete if players could leave Florida high schools for other SEC schools and play against us because we could not admit them to our school. I told them my salary and fringe benefits. We talked about TV and that was that. The 5 per cent rule was coming in, so that would take care of the academics. The 5 per cent simply means that 145 freshmen per year can score below the 300 minimum on the Florida placement test for seniors and still get in provided they have a C average. We share in that 145." That rule proved essential to the turn-around the Gator program took in two years.

The Gator Bowl game bore down, and the press reports of an impending change increased. Some wrote flatly that Graves would resign after the game and that Dickey would be the coach. Some took up a sword for Ellenson, the longtime chief assistant and good-guy type.

A friend from Tampa called quarterback Reaves at Daytona, where the Gators were camped, and told him it was certain that Graves would retire and Dickey would be the coach. Reaves told an assistant that. The other assistants questioned him. Then the team got uneasy and "some of the defensive players began a move for Ellenson," said Reaves. "But in truth I know so far as I was concerned and some of the others, that was all right. The change. It wasn't unexpected. And Dickey certainly had been a winner."

But, "with the upcoming game," Graves said, looking back, "I made positive statements that I was still head coach and director of athletics and would continue in this position. There were a lot of traumatic experiences with the players, and staff, and news media, which helped to add pressure and confusion to the problem and which changed my thinking about my resignation." The night before the game President O'Connell told the squad that Coach Graves "still is the head coach and will be indefinitely," one player reported.

Then Dickey was asked point-blank by Marvin West, a respected Knoxville newsman, if he had had a firm offer from Florida. "I told him I had had no offer," said Dickey, "and then he asked me if I had been contacted. I said at first I didn't think it was the time to discuss it, then called him back. I had always been treated fairly. I had to be honest. I always have been. I told Marvin I had been contacted, but that no formal offer had been made, and nothing would happen until after the game."

Meanwhile Coach Graves was having some thoughts on reconsideration of his decision to resign. Then Florida beat Tennessee 14-13; beat the SEC champion; beat the man who was supposed to come and coach the Gators. It was sticky. And it got worse.

"The next morning, Sunday, the Tennessee faculty board met in Jacksonville and called me," said Dickey. "I told them I had been contacted by Florida, as I had told Woodruff always. He knew the progress. I don't think Woodruff ever thought I would leave. I told them I had no firm offer but probably would discuss one. I felt I had earned that right. I had declined offers of interviews by Tech, Oklahoma, and Michigan without telling anyone. I went home, and President O'Connell made a firm offer by telephone call that night, Sunday, after the Gator Bowl. But I was not to make a final decision until Ray resigned."

Meanwhile Graves said in Gainesville, "I told the president and the board it seemed under the circumstances, and with all the problems that had arisen, it might be best if I continued a couple of more years as head coach and athletic director. I also told the players after the game I was still the head coach, that

312

I'd tell them first of any other decision. I asked President O'Connell for until Friday, January 2, to make a final decision. He agreed," Graves recalled.

"But then I began to see the plight of my assistant coaches. They were confused and needed a quicker answer. I told Coach Ellenson to call a staff meeting for Monday morning, December 29, and told them I was resigning. I then told President O'Connell and asked that he announce it the next day so I could contact my players. I did. I wired them. I think all things I did were in the best interest of the school and team. It did wind up complicated, however, with Florida and Tennessee meeting in the Gator Bowl."

It wound up more than complicated. Some of the players felt they had been deceived. They made that feeling public later, and helped create for Dickey's return to his alma mater an atmosphere other than the happy-times circumstance that

Head Coach Doug Dickey (front and center) and his first Florida staff, 1970.

might have been.

"When we were informed of Ray's resignation," said Dickey, "Jo Ann and I had another session. Then we decided to take the Florida job. I thought I could bring all things together at Florida, stabilize the program, and produce a champion. I always have. I took the job because it was an opportunity to go home, and home was a place where great things could be achieved that had not been achieved. It also would allow me to plant my own family's roots back in Florida.

"Think," said Dickey, "how less complicated and trying this all might have been had Tennessee played Houston in the Bluebonnet and not Florida in the Gator Bowl."

But, complicated or not, Dickey became head coach of the Florida Gators. He brought with him most of his staff from Tennessee, including former quarterback Dunn, and his chief of offense, Doug Knotts. There were nervous, uncomfortable times ahead, nights when Dickey turned sleeplessly and thought about the waltz he had had at Tennessee, and the wonder then was, did he make the right decision. Did Florida?

Troubled Start

There was no dancing in the streets of Gainesville for Coach Doug Dickey's arrival. Had the circumstances of his agreement with Florida been handled differently, he might have found a much more receptive air, but as it was he arrived instead to find a group angry because Assistant Coach Gene Ellenson had not been elevated to head coach. The student newspaper, the *Alligator*, was outraged, and all-American flanker Carlos Alvarez, a sensitive young man, was quoted in the headlines of the state's newspapers as saying he and the team had been betrayed. Alvarez kept it up and eventually became involved with an objecting organization called the League of Athletes, which flurried at first, then fell aside.

"The whole atmosphere," said Dickey, "had turned 180 degrees from what I thought it would be. But we were there to make friends and do our best. The complaining didn't stop right away."

Though it was not his doing, the decision to increase student ticket prices for home games placed him in further disfavor. Yet he gained ground as he met people.

"I remember Coach Dickey's first meeting with the squad," said John Reaves. "I was impressed. I think we all were. It was the first time I had seen him up close since he was in my home my senior year in high school, when I told him I was going to Florida, not Tennessee (where Dickey was then coaching) because of the offense. I was a passer and didn't suit his offense, I told him. Now here he was my coach. I remember

That first, nervous, historic moment, when new head coach Doug Dickey met the 1970 Gators he inherited.

he came straight over and shook my hand, and I appreciated that. Then the ice was broken when Rocky Robinson, a lineman, went up and slipped Coach Dickey the SAE grip. It caught him off guard, but it was the kind of thing Rock would do, and it loosened things up."

Alvarez first told Sports Editor John Crittendon of the *Miami News* that he had been betrayed. He said it was wrong and that he would never again pray in the same pre-game huddle with University President O'Connell.

After Dickey's first few squad sessions, Alvarez told the *Tampa Tribune*:

"Coach Dickey and his staff are fantastic. Already he's made the players feel like we're really going to win. He has us all inspired and ready to play. They know their stuff. Coach Dickey looks you in the eye and tells you how it is, and that's what my dad taught me to do.

"He made believers with his positive attitude. I think he inspired everybody, even those on the B team and with injuries. He made them feel they had a shot again. I don't think we

316

could ask for more. Already we're impressed with the plans and the assistants that came."

But the young, intense, probing Alvarez again and again questioned the coach, and spoke for the League of Athletes. He always disagreed with being told the old coach was staying when he was not.

Yet it was not really so much Carlos Alvarez' state of mind as his physical state that figured so vitally in his own future and that of Dickey and the Gators. Early in 1970, he injured a knee practicing starting from blocks on a running track. He was never again the Carlos Alvarez of the 59-34 win over Houston. He was never again the Carlos Alvarez of the Super Sophs of 1969. He

The nagging knees of receiver Carlos Alvarez.

Tackle-end Robert Harrell will not let go of North Carolina quarterback Dennis Britt.

never again approached the deeds he recorded against Miami in the Orange Bowl that year when he caught 15 passes for a staggering 283 yards. In time, degenerative arthritis set into his knee and gradually slowed him down, despite treatment and patience.

But nobody knew then what was happening to Alvarez, just as nobody knew what was happening to Andy Cheney. Cheney was the split end opposite Alvarez in 1969. He was a disciplined receiver, so often the safety valve. Cheney helped make Alvarez and Reaves all-SEC. But he went down on a crumpled knee in that 35-16 rout of Miami in the last game of the 1969 season.

Dickey's problems began to look far more serious than any editorial in the *Alligator*. Alvarez had hurt his knee, and Cheney looked finished too. The roster contained many familiar names—Alvarez, Reaves, Durrance, Rich, Yancey, Youngblood, and Abbott—but the offensive line was gone and so was the defensive secondary.

"I know now," said Reaves much later, "that it was the loss of Alvarez and Cheney, and our offensive line that had given me so much time in 1969, that was responsible for what happened to us in 1970 and 1971. It wasn't any quote by anybody. No lack of speeches and emotion. We lost players we couldn't afford to lose. But nobody wants to say that. It's too simple an answer. No drama there."

It truly was some kind of winter, spring, and summer for Dickey before he put his first team on the field. It was a wonder he hung around to do it. Between the time he made the move from cozy Tennessee, and before his first game in September, 1970, Dickey:

Was investigated by the NCAA ethics people for the manner in which he departed Tennessee for Florida.

Heard and read the furor about Gene Ellenson not getting the job he did, heard and read what Alvarez and some other members of the team said, heard and read what some sports writers said.

Saw student leaders threaten to boycott games because of an admission charge, the beefers demonstrating at his first spring game.

Winced when adult ticket prices were jumped from $6 to $7.

Saw his playing field chewed up by a rock festival that lasted through a downpour. That came before artificial turf.

Read where his quarterback, Reaves, publicly stated that Tennessee running back Curt Watson could not carry Tommy Durrance's jock strap. Florida was playing Tennessee in Knoxville a bit later on.

Learned that they had banned alcohol of any kind, including beer, from Florida Field, meaning that when his fans got mad, they would be entirely sober and know precisely what was going on.

Had a terrible time lining up the television show that was supposed to make him extra money to make up for what he had lost in leaving the lucrative Tennessee post.

With a new offensive line, a slower defense, and a slower Alvarez, the Gators faced the 1970 season. They beat Duke in the opener 21-19, in Jacksonville, then handled Mississippi State 34-13. But the weaknesses showed up in a 46-15 loss to Alabama. Dickey regrouped the Gators to beat North Carolina State 14-6 in the fourth quarter, then Florida State and Richmond fell 38-27 and 20-0.

In that Florida State game a Reaves-to-Yancey combo clicked to help in the third straight win over the Seminoles, but Reaves-to-Alvarez was there again, too. Alvarez caught four for 69 yards and Yancey caught two for 99 yards. Reaves had thrown 13 completions in 22 tries for 244 yards and a 31-7 lead

Tight end Jim Yancey heads for FSU goal with John Reaves reception in 1970.

when a sophomore named Gary Huff began tossing bombs for Florida State to make the final a respectable 38-27. Big Jack Youngblood, who grew up in Monticello, not far from Tallahassee, helped rub it in on the Seminoles. Near the end of the game the giant lineman stood on the retaining wall in front of the FSU students and did a hula, waggling his backside, naturally, in their direction.

But when the Gators beat Richmond, they were 5-1 and headed for Knoxville to face the Tennesseans who thought Dickey had run out on them. Tennessee fans were mad enough to throw oranges on the field before the game. Then the team Dickey left behind (most of whom came over to wish him well) proceeded to have themselves a day. Bill Battle, chosen by Woodruff to succeed Dickey, had his bunch ready. Youngblood was heroic on defense, but the Volunteers won 38-7. The Gators gained a net 8 yards rushing, although they did pick up 263 passing.

The hard times were not over. The next week, Auburn, 5-1, loser the week before to LSU, invaded Gainesville with the Pat (Sullivan) and Terry (Beasley) Show. They gave Florida the worst beating in hometowners' recollection, playing absolutely as well as a team can for the first half. It was 21-0 at the end of the first quarter, 35-0 at the half, 56-7 after three periods, and an astonishing 63-14 when it was finally over.

Florida partisans were accustomed to defeats, but not like that, not like the losses to Alabama, Tennessee, and Auburn, not with a combined score of 174 to 36 in three games.

Florida was 5-3 with Georgia, Kentucky, and Miami remaining and spirits dragging. But, "In the first two tough years," said Dickey, "I had two high points. One was about to happen."

He did not know that, though, as he got his team ready to face a good Georgia team. That was where Fred Pancoast had gone to coach.

Victory came because Reaves and Alvarez played as they had during most of 1969 for offensive coach Pancoast. This time they played that way against him.

"That was definitely one of the low points in my career," said Georgia Head Coach Vince Dooley. "We had played well, and I thought we were about to put the game on ice early in the

321

Defensive lineman Jack Youngblood, a great one, leaves game in Tampa, temporarily.

fourth quarter. At that moment we fumbled the ball on the one-yard line, when a touchdown would have given us a fourteen-point lead. In any event we lost the football, and then, thanks to two great plays by two super athletes, Reaves and Alvarez, we lost the ball game." The final score was 24-17.

Both Reaves and Alvarez rushed to Pancoast to embrace him, and he said, "If we had to lose I'm glad it was to you two guys."

The win juiced Florida up for an easy 24-13 rap of Kentucky in Tampa, and Liberty Bowl talk blossomed. A win over Miami, suffering through a bad year, would mean 8-3 despite the severe beatings by Tennessee, Alabama, and Auburn. But, as always, Miami played better than it could against the

Gators, and in the game's dying moments, with one chance at victory, a Florida player who seldom erred, especially in the thick of it, let a floater from Reaves bounce off his chest in the end zone. With that dropped touchdown pass by Tommy Durrance, Miami won 14-13 on a dreary, rainy afternoon. This meant no bowl for Florida, a 7-4 finish rather than 8-3, and another seige of gloom.

The gloom, though based on the past, could have been a forecast of the future, for 1971 got worse. Alvarez was almost ineffective and there was no sophomore help. With Reaves a senior and a Heisman Trophy candidate, the Gators began by losing to Duke in Tampa 12-6 as the Blue Devils kicked four field goals. Then Mississippi State won 13-10, Alabama prevailed 38-0, and Tennessee took a 20-13 victory in what was the Gators' best effort to that point in the season. LSU won 48-7 to make the record 0-5.

With its worst record since 1946 Florida prepared to take on the Seminoles of Florida State, coming to town with a 5-0 worksheet and solidly favored for the first time in the series. Huff was the FSU quarterback, matching two Tampans, Reaves and Huff, as opposing signal-callers.

Florida won the game 17-15, largely on four fumbles by FSU and a 26-yard touchdown run by Jimmy Barr with one of those fumbles which he picked off in mid-air. A change in Florida offensive planning worked, too. The Gators stayed on the ground, gaining 152 yards rushing and only 44 passing.

"That was the other high point of the first two seasons," said Dickey. "The Georgia win in 1970 and this one, when we were 0-5 and in danger of going without a win."

Florida then managed a win over Maryland, but lost big at Auburn 40-7 as the Tigers made it three straight over Reaves and protected Cliff Hare's chastity from Gators.

Dooley, Pancoast, and Georgia got revenge on the Gators to the tune of 49-7, making the record 2-7, and the situation deteriorated even more. It did not help that Dickey was not the natural socializer that Graves had been. And it had not helped that Dickey had chosen not to use alumni as much as Graves had, utilizing instead members of his own staff for recruiting.

Things looked grim. The terrible beatings of the last two seasons had shocked longtime Florida fans. It was not so much

Doug Dickey after the 49-7 loss to Georgia in the troubled year of 1971.

the losses, they said, as the degree of them. But Florida managed to beat Kentucky 35-24 and entered the season finale at 3-7. The last game of the Super Sophs approached, and Gator fans felt that a loss would be catastrophic.

Dickey, on a recruiting trip to West Palm Beach during the extra week off before the Miami game, was in a Florida refreshment parlor with a friend. The lighting was not too good. A man came up to Dickey and said, "By God, man, you are the spitting image of the Florida coach, Doug Dickey."

Yeah? Dickey offered. He did not need any conversation.

"Yeah. Really. If you get to Gainesville, go by and see for yourself. You could pass for his double. And I'll tell you what, that poor so-and-so needs all the help he can get!"

The Great Laydown

On a Monday night, early in the 1970 season, Fran Curci was being flown by his friend Tom Stewart from a Daytona Beach Quarterback Club speaking engagement back to Tampa where the ambitious young former Miami quarterback was having a successful third season as head coach of the Tampa Spartans. Aloft, about Walt Disney World, Curci said to a writer-friend who had been picked up after he had spoken to the DeLand Quarterback Club:

"I may have made a mistake tonight. I don't know whether there were any reporters in the audience, but when somebody asked me if I had any opinion on the problems at Florida I said something about the Gators being cry-babies."

The writer-friend assured Curci he had made a mistake. He was right. There had been a reporter at the Daytona meeting. He had written a story carrying the "cry-baby" statement. It had made the wire services, and it was in newspapers in Gainesville the next day for all of the Florida Gators to read. Those who did not read it heard about it.

They remembered it a year and two months later. On the eve of the 1971 Florida-Miami game at the Orange Bowl, the last of the season, Sports Editor Edwin Pope of the *Miami Herald* interviewed Florida quarterback John Reaves. By then Curci was head coach at Miami. His year had been up and down, but so had Florida's at 3-7. On the team were many members of that 1970 team Curci had called cry-babies. Reaves was one of them, of course, and while the game's outcome could be of little interest or significance to anyone save the team members and partisans of the two schools, Reaves had two things going for him.

The first, about which Sports Editor Pope began the interview, was the slight chance Reaves had at breaking the national career passing record in that final game against Miami. Jim Plunkett of Stanford had set the career record two years before. His total was 7,544 yards. That meant Reaves would need to pass for 344 yards in the final game in order to top Plunkett's total. Reaves told Pope it would be nice to beat the record, but that was not the most important thing about the game to him and the players.

"We are coming down here to teach Fran Curci a lesson," Reaves said. "I still remember him calling us a bunch of cry-babies. As far as Fran Curci is concerned," Reaves told Pope, "he always has been nice and courteous around me, but I've read and heard some of the bad things he has said about the University of Florida. Then there was that time he called us cry-babies."

Later Reaves said of that statement, "Well, when I read it in print it looked tougher than when I said it. But, well, we'd had a week off, and it was the last game of our careers, some of us. So the night before the game I remember we saw a movie and then all gathered around the pool. Tommy Durrance said a few things, then I did. I remember I said we didn't just need to beat Miami for the school and the coaches, but because of what Curci had said and because we needed to win it for ourselves. We'd been through so much, we needed to go out with class. Our omega needed to be like our alpha," that opening win over Houston when Reaves, Alvarez, Durrance, and so many of them were sophomores.

Coach Dickey said he was aware of the chance John had at the record, but it seemed pretty remote—344 yards. "The problem we faced was winning," said Dickey, looking back.

But "I saw the enthusiasm like I'd not seen in a long time," said Reaves, of the pre-game dressing room scene. He also saw a game plan that called for pass-first, run-second that was not going to be changed, that was going to work right away. The Gators came out passing, and the Gators came out catching. "It was like the old days," said Reaves. "We shot ahead. Hollis

Boardman was catching everything, and so were Willie Jackson, Durrance, and Vince Kendrick coming out of the backfield, and Carlos was catching them again, and running better."

Just before the half Florida assistant Jack Hall ran up to Reaves on the sideline and said, "You've got about 170 yards. You can get Plunkett's record in the second half." Dickey said he checked with assistant Jimmy Dunn, and confirmed that John "had a shot now. I wanted to get one more score to put the game on ice, then we'd go for a record," Dickey said.

The half-time score was Florida 17, Miami 0. The Gators did as Dickey wanted. They scored in the second half and then began a run at the Plunkett passing record that concluded in one of football's most bizarre and most theatrical performances.

When Reaves was within 13 yards of breaking the record, Miami had possession of the ball, and Curci's newly installed wishbone offense was grinding out enough yards for first downs and eating up the clock. Finally a punt was forced, leading to a classic bit of irony. Harvin Clark, a co-captain and close friend of Reaves' returned the punt all the way for a touchdown.

"It was a great run," said Reaves. "Harvin hurdled two guys for the score," and then ran off the field and straight to Reaves to apologize for going all the way. The score meant Miami would receive the kickoff and keep the ball away from Florida and Reaves with time fleeting.

The Hurricanes returned to their time-consuming wishbone. When they were inside the Florida 20, in fourth-down territory, only two minutes remained in the game. Florida began calling time out after each play, and during each time out Clark ran to Dickey on the sidelines asking permission to let Miami score so Florida and Reaves could get the ball back.

The Florida partisans in the stands sensed the situation and began chanting to let Miami score. The Miami radio network announcers even predicted that it might happen. Finally, on third down at the seven with 1:20 left on the clock, Dickey gave in to Clark's request. Reaves was standing right beside him, but said nothing. Other players had. With the word, Clark raced back in.

"I never thought they'd do it the way they did," said Dickey later. "We have many practice plays where we brush but don't tackle. I thought they'd do that."

Miami quarterback John Hornibrook took the snap and rolled out on a keeper. He even slowed at the corner as he looked at the scene before him. The Gators made not the slightest effort to hide their purpose. They simply flopped flat on the ground at their positions. It was as if they had been machine-gunned. Hornibrook scored, Miami kicked off, and in went Reaves with the offense and the need for 13 passing yards.

"The first play was a quick screen nine," he recalls. "I faked to the fullback, spun around, and threw to Durrance coming out of the backfield. The ball hit Durrance in the chest and bounced into the arms of the Miami linebacker coming over quick. For an instant my heart sank. Then the linebacker didn't hold onto the ball.

"Next I simply rolled out. Carlos broke over the middle. With that bad knee he wasn't the Carlos of old but, by the standards of just good receivers he was flying. Carlos was trying. I threw it to him and he had it and 15 yards, and we had the national record and our pride back.

"Carlos and I had finished for a touchdown, my last for a national record. I felt then like I hadn't felt since that first touchdown pass."

Reaves left the game to a great ovation from most, but stares from the Miami bench. But he was quickly sent back into the game to throw a 3-yarder to Boardman just in case the statisticians had made an error. They had not. He had thrown 50 passes that important night. Thirty-three of them were caught for a total of 348 yards, and a final score of 45-16. The win also meant a 4-7 finishing record that was so much better than 3-8, and with his completions John Reaves' career yardage production on passing wound up 7,549, 5 yards more than Plunkett.

It was a moment of redemption for those Gator seniors in the Orange Bowl that night, those seniors who experienced such agonies, were so maligned at times, so beaten on occasions by the Auburns, the LSUs, and the Alabamas the two previous years, after hitting the acme of 9-1-1 their sophomore year.

At the fever pitch they were, and needing to wind down, the entire Gator squad swept down the Orange Bowl after the final whistle, running towards the pond and fountain at the south end, the pond where Miami Dolphin mascot "Flipper"

John Reaves, record-setting Gator quarterback from 1969-71, shows his style.

frolicked each time the Dolphins scored.

"I remember it was Robert Harrell," a big defensive end from Jacksonville, "who picked me up by himself and flung me into the pool," said Reaves. "I didn't care. Nobody cared. Everybody got into the pool and danced, or whatever they wanted to do. I know Carlos Alvarez climbed the flagpole."

There came from some in the days ahead cries of poor sportsmanship with the lowdown trick or the Gator Flop as it came to be known. Cheap record, some would call it, and Curci said it was "bush," that he had lost all his respect for Coach Dickey.

Dickey said: "I found it no different from an intentional pass in baseball or a late game basketball decision to let a man shoot to regain possession, or intentionally fouling. We did not do it because it was Miami or Curci. We did it for John and for our team. Our needs were great then. This helped in some small way to serve them."

Reaves said, "I loved it. I loved it because my friends were doing something for me. And the funny thing is, if Fran Curci hadn't called us cry-babies that year ago, I doubt if we'd have played good enough for us to get into the position to break that record against his team. What it did for us was give that 1969 team a chance to go out like we came in, with a flourish."

The Turnaround?

They were gone, the last of the Super-Sophs of 1969 Dickey had inherited, the last of personal memory of the 1969 Gator Bowl and his challenged succession to the position Graves had.

The 1972 Gators and those thereafter would be his—Dickey's Gators. He could perform or not with his own. If he said run-first and pass-second, well that was the basis on which he recruited. Despite the exigencies of the job change, Dickey and his aides had recruited well. They also had moved in to take advantage of that 5 per cent break that allowed the university some promising athletes who may not have been able to make it a few years back, but would have been able to enroll in rival SEC schools. Dickey also had gone after the stellar black athletes so important to his program.

With few victory parties to attend the first two seasons Dickey had kept his staff on the road recruiting—Jimmy Dunn, Doug Knotts, Ken Hatfield, Jack Thompson, Don Brown, Dave Fuller, Jack Hall, Allen Trammell, Charley Fulton, Bill Carr—and Don Deal and Jimmy Haynes, before they left the school for other positions. The rule allowing freshmen to play varsity football was in effect too, and that helped. The recruiting brought such prizes as linebacker Ralph Ortega of Coral Gables, tackle Dave Starkey of Troy, Ohio, quarterback David Bowden of Lakeland, Clearwater's Sever brothers, Tyson and Glenn, Clearwater's Parker brothers, Joel and Paul, defensive linemen John Lacer of Brandon and David Hitchcock of Winter Haven,

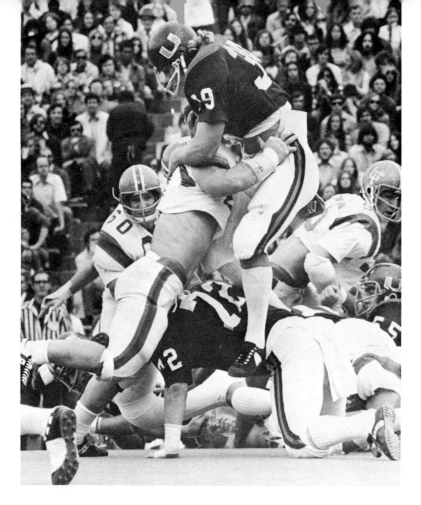

Florida tackle David Hitchcock puts the stops on Miami back Tom Smith.

David Poff of Titusville, and Ricky Browne of Longwood. Dickey found a punter in Buster Morrison, secondary speed in Jim Revels, Tyson Sever, Alvin Butler, and Leonard George. He found Vince Kendrick of Miami as a big fullback, and Vince brought along brother Preston, a mean fellow at end.

Then there happened to Dickey one of the greatest strokes of good fortune in his career. An old playing pal at Florida was coaching basketball at South Dade Junior College in Miami. In January, 1972, when Dickey's spirits were so low, the friend, Bob McAlphin, called and said he had a young man on his basketball team who would graduate in June and wanted to play football again. He played at Miami Jackson a few years

334

back, then went to the University of Tennessee at Martin and played a year of football there. He did well but grew homesick. He returned to Miami, sat out of school a year, and drove a truck delivering Kosher food on Miami Beach. He enrolled in South Dade JC, was a fine basketball player, and was worth Dickey's look for a possible specialist: a split-end, punt return, and kick return man. Dickey dispatched Lindy Infante, now at Memphis State, to look over Nat Moore, only 5-10 and 175.

"I watched him play basketball, then I got out some films of him in high school. He had the moves. I thought he was worth it," said Infante, the fellow who had signed Alvarez when only one other school expressed interest.

Nat Moore was not able to enroll in Florida until September, 1972, and thus did not participate in spring drills.

Florida defenders turn tiger on Auburn Tigers.

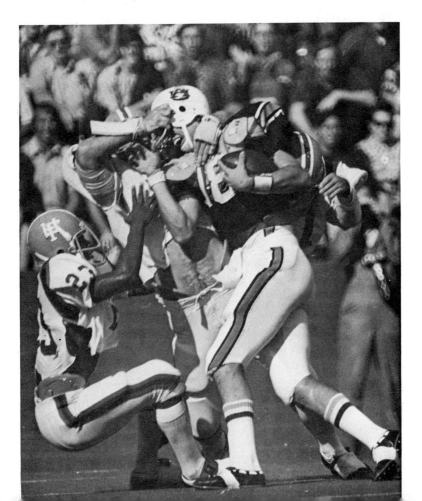

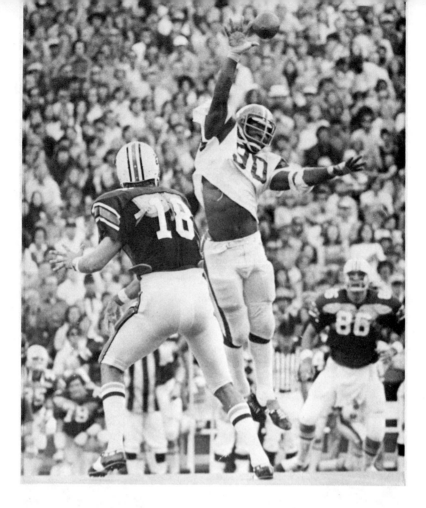

Defensive end Preston Kendrick just misses batting down Auburn quarterback Randy Walls' pass.

He reported cold in September when the team was pretty much set for the opener in Tampa September 23 against Southern Methodist.

Nat Moore was not in the 1972 press guide, not in the Tampa-Southern Methodist program. But he was on the field in his No. 38. Dunn said they recruited him figuring he could "be a spot receiver, run back punts and kickoffs, and relieve Lenny Lucas at running back some. We had not seen much of him and had no idea he'd be the great player he became." There were whispers before the season that Florida had a phenomenon named Nat.

He was just that. With SMU well out in front in the

opener, 21-0, Dickey changed quarterbacks from Chan Gailey to young Bowden, and worked Moore in as a back-receiver. Bowden was a hummingbird quarterback, a darter, a last-second man. He seemed to lack polish, but he got things done. He and Moore pulled the game to 21-14; close but not out of the fire.

Moore caught a five yard touchdown pass from Bowden to score the first points in 1972 for the Gators. It was as it should have been. When the season was done at 5-5-1, Moore became all-Southeastern Conference and received all-America consider-

Great Gator find of the 1970s, Nat Moore, long-strides it toward North Carolina goal in 1972.

ation. He became the most exciting runner in Florida's history, some say in the modern SEC.

By the year's end Nat Moore had carried the ball 145 times for 845 yards, breaking the Florida single season rushing record of Chuck Hunsinger in 1948. It was nearly 100 yards more than recent Gator ball-carriers of note—Larry Smith and Larry Dupree. He was a specialist in long plays, one of which he made in each game. He also led the team in pass receptions with 25, for 351 yards. He scored 13 touchdowns and 78 points, 4 TDs receiving passes, 9 rushing. He returned kickoffs an average of 20.8 yards.

Dooley of Georgia flatly called him "the most complete back I have seen in the SEC." Moore was "a picture back. If we drew on a blackboard what we wanted in a back, it would come out Nat Moore," said Dooley. Yet his Bulldogs contained Moore better than any of the 11 opponents in 1972. Moore could run with the ball with speed, strength, and deception. He could block, he could catch passes. He also had that undetectable talent all recruiters seek. He was a game-breaker. He earned berths on virtually all pre-season all-America line-ups for 1973.

With Moore and Bowden, Kendrick, a new aggressiveness in the offensive line, speed in the secondary, and a defense of angry men who figured in 50 turnovers, with Fred Abbott there at middle linebacker as captain, it was conceded by mid-season that Dickey had started to turn it around. His era was beginning in 1972. It was not the record. That was but 5-5-1, while in fact his cumulative record for the troubled years of 1970 and 1971 was a dead-even 11-11. It was the performance of the team against an agonizing schedule, the muscle and speed and interest in aggression that impressed, gave new hope for the future, the kind Alligator Athletic Editor Shackleford foresaw after the 1912 season.

The SMU loss was a shakedown game. Then came a 28-13 victory over Mississippi State, and another upset of snakebit Florida State. That was not just an upset. It was a 42-13 rout in a game that was supposed to be close. Played in Tallahassee before the FSU homefolks, with Huff and his fine receiver Barry Smith as seniors and the Seminoles undefeated going in, there was no way to predict the outcome. Florida State fumbled and saw its passes intercepted a total of nine times.

Florida won it by a staggering score that so affected FSU Coach Larry Jones that he pledged before the next season to install a get-tougher policy at FSU. Whatever he instituted caused sufficient adverse newspaper reports to attract an investigation from the National Collegiate Athletic Association, and caused Jones to resign after the 1973 season. It is clear the beginnings of that feud came after the embarrassment of the defeat by Florida.

Florida, with Moore such a hero and the defense intense, beat Mississippi handily, 16-0, in Oxford, and Kentucky, 40-0, and Miami, 17-6, but lost to Alabama, 24-7, Georgia, 10-7, Auburn, 26-20, and North Carolina, 28-24, for the 5-5-1

Linebacker David Poff intercepts Gary Huff pass headed for Barry Smith in shocking 42-13 upset of 1972 Florida State at Tallahassee.

standard. A highpoint was the 3-3 tie in a downpour with LSU, quarterbacked by all-American Bert Jones. That happened at Gainesville where linebackers Abbott, Poff, and Oretega played matchlessly, Abbott blocking a within-range field goal attempt by LSU in the closing seconds.

"I believe of my losses those first three years, that one the first year to Miami, when we could have won with the late pass completion and gone to the Liberty Bowl, and the loss in 1972 to Georgia when we fumbled it away, were the worst two defeats for me," said Dickey. "The ones you regret the most are the ones you should have won. We should have won those. A win at Georgia in 1972 may have meant a 7-3-1 record for us," he said.

Dickey had completed his third year at Florida with a record of 16-16-1. But even he believed "our program has gotten on a stable footing. I think now we can look anybody in the eye, and I must say we have people on our schedule who are willing to get down and eyeball us right back."

In those three years he had been beaten 63-14 and 46-15, been 0-5 at one point, had oranges thrown at him at his old homeplace of Knoxville, been cussed, discussed, helped, hurt, bad-mouthed by some of his own players, praised by others. He had been through injuries to his very best people, seen student ticket prices raised, seen athletes try to organize into a union on his campus, been called "bush" by another coach, Fran Curci, a machine without emotion by some, had had players quit and come back, or just quit. He had even fallen down the stairs while on crutches recovering from an operation on his own knee to correct an old injury sustained while he was trying to win football games for Florida.

But Dickey had not just survived; he was quietly building a stable program he promised, changing entrance requirements a bit, getting a new artificial playing field, new locker and training facilities for his players, and putting together the staff he felt he needed, helped lately by the addition of offensive talent Don Breaux. He had installed a weight program and whatever else it took to make his own 1972 team play with uncommon ferocity, indeed with ferocity unknown at Florida heretofore, old hands agreed. Florida's defense in 1972 was an angry one.

As 1973 approached, the Gators were being touted as SEC

contenders and as national Top Ten contenders, and Dickey was not backing away. Most of the important ones—save Abbott, Poff, and George were returning for 1973 and great expectations.

In fact, "yes, I believe we have stablized it," said Dickey as 1973 approached. "We look forward to this year. I'd have to say I too think we have turned it around, so to speak. It remains to be seen how fast now we can move out in that right direction towards that 'next year' achievement anyone ever associated with Florida has always sought so, myself included."

Perhaps more than any other single thing, Dickey and Florida had Nat Moore coming back for another year.

Dr. J. Wayne Reitz, President.

The Split Season
Before Auburn
End Of A Curse
A November To Remember

Doug Dickey began his fourth season at Florida with a dead-even cumulative record 16-16-1. He also began it looking ahead to some special circumstances. His first two opponents were head-coached by old Tennessee assistants of his, Vince Gibson at Kansas State, and P. K. Underwood at the University of Southern Mississippi. Mississippi State was next on the schedule. Then followed a staggering lineup—one of the nation's most awesome—in a row there would be LSU, Alabama, Mississippi, Auburn, Georgia, and Kentucky in the SEC, then windups with traditional rivals Miami and FSU.

But Dickey's material looked fine, he said, putting it this way: "Things are better than they have been."

He was coaching his first Gator team that was comprised almost entirely of young athletes he had recruited. Included were some standouts from the year before, like the uncontainable Nat Moore, unanimous all-SEC, and little premier pass receiver Lee McGriff. Vince Kendrick was back at fullback. The offensive line looked big, and Doug Knotts' marvelous defense was returning almost intact. Biggest losses were all-SEC Fred Abbott, the 1972 team captain, and according to Dickey "one of the finest leaders I have ever had on my team. Abbott led by example. If his teammates didn't perform, he told them about it, then showed them how it should be done." Yet this was the same young Brooksvillian who left the team briefly as a sophomore, then dispirited. He returned quickly, "realizing my mistake," he said later, was voted back on the team, and made the incredible climb to squad captaincy in 1972.

Abbott and linebacker David Poff were gone, but Knotts was proud and pleased of the defenders returning. In 1972 Gator patrons seemed to enjoy the slashing Florida defense every bit as much as Moore's darts and McGriff's leaps with receptions.

And for 1973 Dickey had returning young David Bowden of Lakeland, the No. 1 quarterback when 1972 ended. Bowden handled the ball well and, though he threw side-armish, had a way of making things happen. He seldom ran the ball, but then who needed to with Moore, Kendrick, and Jimmy DuBose around?

Nobody picked Florida to win the SEC except *Playboy Magazine* which picked Dickey the pre-season Coach of the Year, nationally. Mostly the Gators were regarded as outside shots for honors. But Florida followers, always a hopeful and optimistic lot, had that old feeling, and it was not squelched by the Florida coaching staff. If Moore could have another year like 1972...

The Gators beat Kansas State on a hot, damp, clammy Florida Field night, 21-10, not by the run, but by the pass: three Bowden touchdown passes to Moore, McGriff, and Tyson Sever.

Next the Gators beat Southern Mississippi at Tampa with two more Bowden passes, both in the second period, to win it nervously, 14-13. Southern Miss had lost the week before to East Carolina. It was a second win, but...

Tragedy struck the Gators-73 at Memorial Stadium, Jackson, Mississippi, September 29, about 8:05 p.m. The marvelous Moore went down on the game's first offensive play. He went down and out and by ambulance to the hospital.

The sight of Moore leaving the field, then the scene, was shocking to the Gators. He had been the guts of the running game for 13 straight games. Before the shock wore off Florida was down 0-14 to Mississippi State, a team with an explosive offense.

Next Kendrick went down. Wingback Glenn Sever had been lost the week before. The offense was gutted. Yet Florida hung in until the final period. The final score was a stark Mississippi State 33, Florida 12. Florida had not lost to M-State

Reliable Florida fullback Vince Kendrick often flew over trouble.

since 1965.

Moore had returned to the field before the game's end, but on crutches. He had a strained arch and would not be the same until the season's 11th game.

Dickey tried to revamp his offense for LSU at Baton Rouge. It was no dice. LSU manhandled the Mooreless Gators 24-3.

"I know how Dickey feels," said LSU Coach Charley McClendon after the game. "Three years in a row I lost my quarterback to injuries."

Florida was 2-2 and had a date coming up at Gainesville with Paul Bryant's undefeated, bulldozing, triple-option Alabama Crimson Tide. Word was Moore could play for the Gators, and play he did before that Florida Field record crowd of 64,864. And he played well, as did the Gators, for a while. Moore left the game with a new hurt to his old one in the second quarter. He would not return at all until Florida State in the finale. Bowden's two TD passes kept it close, 14-21, against the vaunted Tide, until the team that would make it to an historic date with Notre Dame in the Sugar Bowl blew it open in the final period.

More Gators were hurt. The squad was truly crippled. The record was 2-3, but hope lay ahead. Mississippi was coming to town, and Mississippi was having its troubles too.

Then there happened a most bizarre series of events in the Mississippi game at Florida Field. Without Moore, and Kendrick lame but gamely trying to be the tailback, Florida's only weapon seemed to be the pass. Mississippi knew that too. And Mississippi had some spirit going. Head Coach Billy Kinard had been fired two weeks before, and the veteran John Vaught was back head coaching.

Yet Florida *was* ahead 10-6 with about four minutes to go and driving, when a Bowden pass was intercepted by Harry Harrison. The Gator defense resisted and forced a third and goal at the Florida 8. Quarterback Bill Malouf threw the ball up for grabs in the end zone. Florida defender Randy Talbot wanted to make sure nobody caught it. He batted it away into the arms of Rick Kimbrough for six points.

It was Ole Miss 13-10, and more was to come.

With 1:26 left, Florida had moved the ball to the Ole Miss

345

33, where it was fourth and 5. Young Bowden, in the frenzy, had lost count of the downs. He quickly took the snap and flung the ball out of bounds, trying to stop the clock. "Well, I thought we had made a first down," he said after the game. "I kept asking the other players if they realized it."

It was a cruel manner of defeat, and the loss was to a team having troubles too. As the game was ending, the largest chorus of boos yet heard at Florida Field rained down "aimed at me," said Dickey later. "I am the coach. I am responsible."

The Gators had lost four in a row, all in the SEC. They were 2-4 overall and troubled. Auburn was next—at Cliff Hare in Auburn, where Florida had never won. Criticism of Dickey flooded in from all quarters.

He had a private meeting with Florida Alumni President Witt Palmer and Athletic Committee Member Red Mitchum. They talked long into the night in a Jacksonville motel room.

Fortunately the Gators had a week off, before facing Auburn.

Dickey called a press conference. Speculation was he might resign. There even was a rumor Ray Graves was unretiring. Or was it Fred Pancoast being summoned from his head job at Memphis State? It was none of those. It was what was characteristic of Dickey.

He stuck out his jaw and said he was putting down all rumors. He was staying. He had four more years on his contract. He was firing no assistants. Nobody had asked for his resignation. Nobody had quit the squad. He was disappointed too, but there *had* been crippling injuries. He was not giving up. There were five games to play. He did not want sympathy from anyone, but he was asking those loyal Florida supporters to step forward. Now was the time to come to the aid of the school, he said.

He said: "None of us has changed thoughts that we can produce a champion at Florida. I came here to do that. I came here thinking I can do that. I still believe I can. When the time comes I don't think I can, then I'll step aside."

The team jumped behind their coach. "Blame the team," said linebacker Glenn Cameron. "He has no eligibility. It's not his fault if he shows us, tells us, and we don't do it. It's no more fun for us to lose than for those in the stands."

McGriff said: "I don't remember Coach Dickey fumbling all year."

Defensive tackle John Lacer said: "There is no strife. It's mistakes, nothing more. Frankly I think we are going to beat Auburn."

With the week off Dickey called for closed practice and made major changes. He elevated a black, sophomore quarterback named Don Gaffney to first team, and moved big, reliable Vince Kendrick, recovered from his injuries, to tailback and Jimmy DuBose to fullback. He also changed the offense to take advantage of Gaffney's elusive running talents and set up the kind of operation Dickey and Dunn preferred. Gaffney, with the running ability that Bowden lacked, added another dimension to the Gator offense.

The flight to Auburn was routine, except that the pilot said over the public address system that he was a Florida alumnus and directed the Gators to go "give-'em-hell." Later the bus driver ferrying the team from the Columbus airport said that he was an Alabama fan, so he wanted Florida to beat Auburn.

Auburn, fresh from a rugged 7-0 upset of Houston, was riding high and that was cause for concern as far as Auburn President Dr. Harry Philpott was concerned. Watching the Gators work out Friday afternoon, he observed: "You are catching us at just the right time. I fear we are ripe for upset."

He said it standing on the field where no Florida team had ever won, Cliff Hare Stadium until it was recently renamed Jordan-Hare Stadium to honor Auburn's longtime coach, Ralph Jordan.

Ray Graves heard Philpott and then predicted to Gator network announcer Otis Boggs and several sportswriters: "I tell you what. If I live until tomorrow, we'll see it."

Somebody laughed. Not Dickey, nor any of the players, for they were hard at it.

Later that night Dickey offered this look-ahead to the crucial game: "We are going with Gaffney because he can put the pressure outside. He's a running threat. We can't let them jam the middle. All I really pray for is time for Gaffney and the rest to settle down. I'm hoping for a little breathing room. We can't give up the big play early. We can afford no early fumbles, no blocked punts. We've got a good chance to win this ball game," said Dickey.

David Hitchcock, defensive tackle from Winter Haven, said, "We're ready. We will win. Our defense can handle them."

The defense for the day, Coach Knotts said, "is simple. We call it the A and E Defense." He meant Posteriors and Elbows Defense, or words to that effect.

It was a sellout, and the "Waa-a-a-r-r-r Eagles" were being shouted.

The Plainsmen won the toss, but on Auburn's first possession Florida's John Lacer slammed into the ball exchange and forced a fumble. Ricky Browne recovered. In came Gaffney and his team. It was his first start ever for the Gators, and there he was with all the pressure of four straight defeats, never a

Sophomore Don Gaffney brought Florida back from straight losses to Mississippi State, LSU, Alabama, and Mississippi in 1973, to a first win ever at Auburn's Cliff Hare Stadium, then wins over Georgia, Kentucky, FSU, and Miami.

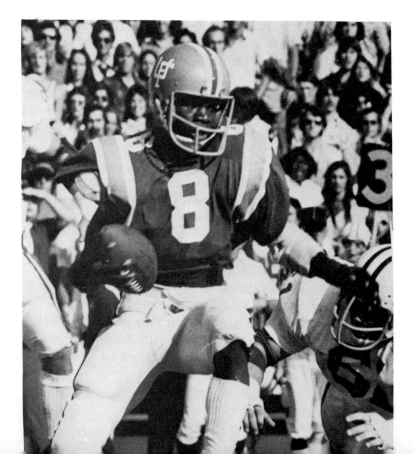

victory on that field, the underdog, and in a must situation.

Don Gaffney played as if he were in his own backyard in a pickup game with the neighborhood kids. Even though the Gators missed a 29-yard field goal after a Gaffney-led first drive, the game was never in doubt. Don Gaffney took Florida to a total victory over Auburn. Florida's offense was superior. Florida's defense was far superior. Buster Morrison kicked out of sight. Kendrick had his best day ever, 119 yards in 23 carries, including a five-yard burst for a third-period touchdown to make it 12-0.

Gaffney ran and passed like a pro. He shot a pass to Joel Parker in the second quarter for the first score. The 22-yard pass capped a 69-yard drive, and when the point-try failed, the score stood 6-0 until Kendrick's touchdown.

Gaffney completed six of ten for 70 yards, with no interceptions. Parker caught four for 55 yards. James Richards gained 33 yards with but two carries, and DuBose got 31 yards.

The final score was 12-8, Florida, with the Tigers' score coming late when young Gaffney made a mistake that he cried about later. He fumbled while holding the ball unnecessarily high in the air on a sprint-out. That happened with forty-three seconds left, and Auburn scored on the game's last play, then added two points for the 12-8 tally.

Florida's total yards: 308; Auburn's: 119.

The Gators had taken far brighter teams to Cliff Hare Stadium down through the years, but this time they took a club that was winless in four straight, dead-last in the Southeastern Conference, bad-mouthed by many. It was led by a slender black quarterback who had never before started a college football game. And it broke the Curse of Cliff Hare.

"They beat the tar out of us," said Coach Jordan.

Parker, who caught the touchdown pass, said: "It means we now have a jinx over Auburn at Jordan-Hare Stadium."

Dickey was so happy and anxious to get home that he ordered the bus away from the stadium early, and it left without the university registrar, Dick Whitehead, whose friendship Dickey needs. But the coach held the plane, and over the P-A system he told his triumphant warriors: "You men have just had a great victory. Nobody appreciates it more than I do. It was a great job. It was a great win."

He paused. "But a great win means for one thing that there's a chance for a greater one ahead. I guess you all know Georgia (the next opponent) beat Tennessee 35-31 (a major upset) this afternoon. That means you'll have 72,000 in the Gator Bowl to watch you play Saturday."

The Gators' landing at the Gainesville Airport was greeted by a big crowd, including a woman whose sign read:

"Dickey-Hare Stadium."

Dickey was right. A full house, 72,000, jammed into the Gator Bowl to see 4-3-1 Georgia play 3-4 Florida. ABC, which had put the contest on its original regional television schedule, was going to cancel until Florida beat Auburn and Georgia upset Tennessee the week before.

It was a great battle. The Bulldogs led 10-3, with 9:36 left, with the Gators starting a new possession at their own 20. Florida's offense had been sluggish, but it was time for an awakening.

An interference call got a first down at the 26. Thom Clifford banged for six more yards. Then Gaffney threw the ball far down the east sidelines, and Lee McGriff, the smallest starting player in the SEC at 5-8 and 150, reached farther than he was able to and caught it as he fell at the Georgia 36.

Gaffney worked the ball to a fourth down at the 17, then tossed toward McGriff over the middle in front of the goal posts. The ball was a good 10 feet off the ground at the point of reception, but the leaping McGriff caught it for a touchdown.

That made it 10-9 in a go-for-two situation.

This time Gaffney connected with Hank Foldberg Jr., son of the former Gator coach who was in the stands watching. It was only the fifth catch for the big tight end all season but it was good for an 11-10 victory.

The "new" Gators-73 had won two games over two favorites by a total of five points. They made it seven the next week at Gainesville by beating Kentucky 20-18 and frustrating Fran Curci again. Curci had moved from Miami to the head job at Kentucky during the off-season.

Curci almost had his first win over Florida that day. Nearly 56,000 saw trouble begin when the opening kickoff was returned 95 yards for an apparent touchdown, then was nullified because of an offsides charge. Even so Florida moved

Wide receiver de luxe, Lee McGriff, was a walk-on who won his scholarship and then as a junior in 1973, all-SEC honors.

ahead 20-3—six of the points coming from a new field goal man, walk-on David Posey of Boca Raton.

But Curci's team suddenly came to life with running back Sonny Collins leading the way and the score closed to 20-18. Kentucky was moving toward a winning field goal when three things happened to prevent it. First, Hitchcock, on Kentucky's first down at the Florida 22, with 32 seconds left, flung Ernie Lewis for a seven-yard loss. Then Lewis threw incomplete. That made it third down at the 29 with 18 seconds left. In the second aid to Florida's victory, Curci decided to throw one more pass to get the ball closer for kicker Ron Steel, who had kicked one of 46 yards earlier. Lewis passed, and Florida defender Wayne Field shot straight up at his corner and intercepted to preserve the win.

Florida beat Miami in the Orange Bowl the next week by a nervous seven. Final was 14-7, but it was closer than that. The

Tight end Hank Foldberg clutches two-point conversion pass that beat Georgia 11-10 at the Gator Bowl in 1973.

count was 14-0, then 14-7, with Miami dominating the game after the first period. In the second half the Gators netted 10 offensive yards, Miami 143. But with a first down inside the Gator 10 and time running out, the Hurricanes had four plays to move through a tough Florida defense. They gave up the ball on the eight.

Florida had rebounded to a 6-4 record by winning four straight in November and making it the Month of the Gator,

Kentucky Coach Fran Curci (left) congratulates Coach Doug Dickey after narrow 1973 Florida win.

anyway. Next came a Florida State team that was winless in ten games under Larry Jones, a former Dickey assistant at Tennessee.

Florida was an overwhelming favorite. FSU was gambling with a new quarterback, Billy Prescott of Fort Walton Beach, but Seminole fans expected the worst. Two thousand tickets to the game at Gainesville were returned by FSU—a first. Two thousand FSU students did not pick up their tickets—also a first.

Florida won 49-0 when it could have been 100-0.

Nat Moore returned to duty and gained 105 yards in 15 carries as the Gators whipped the Seminoles for the sixth straight time, administering the worst defeat ever for a Florida State team. Coach Jones resigned after the season.

The Gators had it completely turned around. Victory in the season's last five games meant a 7-4 record and hiked Dickey's four-year mark at Florida to 23-20-1.

In Orlando the Tangerine Bowl people, with the help of Athletic Director Graves, had prevailed upon the NCAA extra events committee to move that contest to Florida Field for the one year. Under those circumstances Florida would be invited to play the University of Miami of Ohio there in the bigger plant. The T-Bowl seated only about 25,000, and enlargement plans had bogged down. Miami of Ohio had just finished a 10-0 season for the first perfect record there in 85 years of trying. Coach Bill Mallory's team was nail-tough on defense.

Florida patrons were divided on the decision to go to the Tangerine Bowl—or rather, bring the Tangerine Bowl to the Gators. Some labeled it the Orphan Bowl, the Displaced Bowl, or Backyard Bowl. Some asked: "Is This Trip Necessary?" after the five big wins. But Dickey said it was something for the boys, a reward. They spent the week being entertained in Orlando, then returned to Gainesville on the night of December 22 to lose to Miami 16-7 before about 35,000 spectators in 26-degree weather.

The 7-4 season had slipped to 7-5, but Dickey was still 23-21-1 after four years and as confident as ever. He told Florida Sports Information Director Norman Carlson in March, 1974: "We came here to produce a champion. We still are here to produce a champion. There have been a couple of unexpected problems since the day I told Steve O'Connell by telephone I would come from Tennessee to Florida. But we're on the right track, I'm sure. Put it this way: We coaches and the Gators look forward to *next* year, and as usual, I am sure so do the Gator fans."

As it was in the beginning, is now, and ever shall be. World without end.

Pres. Stephen C. O'Connell.

THE FOLLOWING SIX DRAWINGS SHOW HOW
LONGTIME GATOR ARTIST, LAMAR SPARK-
MAN, VIEWS THE SIX PERIODS OF FLORIDA
FOOTBALL.

GO GATORS

University of Florida Facts

Location	Gainesville, Fla. 32601
Enrollment	24,100
School Colors	Orange & Blue
First Year of Football	1906
Nickname	Gators
Conference	Southeastern
Stadium	Florida Field (61,200)

LOCATION

Gainesville is located in north-central Florida, about equidistant from the Atlantic Ocean and the Gulf of Mexico. It is 72 miles southwest of Jacksonville, 120 miles northwest of Orlando and 150 miles southeast of Tallahassee, capital of Florida.

HISTORICAL STATEMENT

In 1853 the foundation work of the present University of Florida was laid in Ocala when a small private school, East Florida Seminary, was opened. Florida Agricultural College was established at Lake City in 1883 and by 1905 six colleges were at least partially state-supported. With the passage of the Buckman Act in 1905, the University of Florida was established at Gainesville. There have been six presidents: Dr. Andrew Sledd (1905-09), Dr. Albert A. Murphree (1909-28), Dr. John J. Tigert (1928-47), Dr. J. Hillis Miller (1947-53), Dr. J. Wayne Reitz (1955-67) and Stephen C. O'Connell (1967-).

COLLEGES

The University's colleges are: Agriculture, Architecture and Fine Arts, Arts and Sciences, Business Administration, Dentistry, Education, Engineering, Health Related Professions, Journalism and Communications, Law, Medicine, Nursing, Pharmacy, Physical Education, Health and Recreation and University College. A College of Veterinary Medicine is being planned for the future. Schools are: Forestry and Graduate.

GENERAL INFORMATION

The University of Florida is one of the largest landgrant institutions in the South with a faculty of 2,500 and student body of

362

more than 24,000. The physical plant is valued at $200 million and includes more than 700 buildings on 2,000 acres.

In addition to numerous research projects in the various colleges, schools and divisions, the University has established a number of specialized laboratories. These agencies carry on continuous basic research in the fields of engineering, science, agriculture, forestry, business, economics, public administration, communications and statistics, making significant contributions to private industry and government research.

A broad program in medical education, research and patient care is being carried out in the University's J. Hillis Miller Health Center. Expansion totaling $42 million will provide space by 1974 to house the College of Dentistry and to accommodate more medical and health related students.

FLORIDA'S PAST SCORES

1901
Coach: James M. Farr

Fla.
0—Stetson 6

G	W	L	T	PT	OP
1	0	1	0	0	6

1902
Coach: James M. Farr

Fla.
0—Stetson 0
5—Stetson 22
6—Fla. Col. Tallahassee ... 0

G	W	L	T	PT	OP
3	1	1	1	11	22

1903
Coaches: Fleming & Humphreys

Fla.
5—Stetson 6
0—Fla. Col. Tallahassee .. 12

6—East Fla. Seminary 5

G	W	L	T	PT	OP
3	1	2	0	11	23

1904
Coach: M. O. Bridges

Fla.
0—Alabama 29
0—Auburn 44
0—Georgia 51
0—Georgia Tech 77
0—Fla. Col. Tallahassee .. 23

G	W	L	T	PT	OP
5	0	5	0	0	224

1905
Coach: C. A. Holton

Fla.
6—Julian Landon 0

G	W	L	T	PT	OP
1	1	0	0	6	0

1906
Coach: Jack Forsythe

Fla.
16—Gainesville AC 6
3—Mercer 27
6—Rollins 0
19—Jax AC 0
2—Savannah AC 27
10—Athens AC 0
0—Rollins 6
39—Jax AC 0

G	W	L	T	PT	OP
8	5	3	0	95	66

1907
Coach: Jack Forsythe

Fla.
6—Columbia AC 0
0—Mercer 6
21—Jax AC 0
9—Rollins 4
17—Jax AC 0
0—Rollins 0

G	W	L	T	PT	OP
6	4	1	1	53	10

1908
Coach: Jack Forsythe

Fla.
0—Mercer 24
4—Jax AC 0
37—Gainesville AC 5
0—Rollins 6
6—Columbia College 0
6—Stetson 0
37—Jax 0
0—Stetson 0

G	W	L	T	PT	OP
8	5	2	1	90	40

1909
Coach: G. E. Pyle

Fla.
5—Gainesville AC 0
14—Rollins 0
0—Stetson 26
28—Rollins 3
11—Olympics 0
5—Stetson 5
28—Olympics 0
26—Tallahassee AC 0

G	W	L	T	PT	OP
8	6	1	1	117	34

1910
Coach: G. E. Pyle

Fla.
23—Gainesville Gds. 0
0—Mercer 13
52—Georgia A & M 0
6—Citadel 2
38—Rollins 0
34—Col. Charleston 0
33—Columbia College 0

G	W	L	T	PT	OP
7	6	1	0	186	15

1911
Coach: G. E. Pyle

Fla.
15—Citadel 3
6—South Carolina 6
6—Clemson 5
9—Columbia College 0
27—Stetson 0
21—Col. Charleston 0

G	W	L	T	PT	OP
6	5	0	1	84	14

1912
Coach: G. E. Pyle

Fla.
13—Auburn 27
10—South Carolina 6
7—Georgia Tech 14
78—Col. Charleston 0
23—Stetson 7
0—Mercer 0
44—Tampa AC 0
28—Vedado Clb. 0

G	W	L	T	PT	OP
8	5	2	1	203	54

1913
Coach: G. E. Pyle

Fla.
144—Southern 0
0—Auburn 55
39—Maryville 0
3—Georgia Tech 13
0—South Carolina 13
18—Citadel 13
24—Mercer 0

G	W	L	T	PT	OP
7	4	3	0	228	94

1914
Coach: Charles McCoy

Fla.
0—Auburn 20
36—Kings College 0
0—Sewanee 26
59—Southern 0
36—Wofford 0
7—Citadel 0
14—Mercer 0

G	W	L	T	PT	OP
7	5	2	0	152	46

1915
Coach: Charles McCoy

Fla.
0—Auburn 7
0—Sewanee 7
45—Southern 0
0—Georgia 39
6—Citadel 0
14—Tulane 7
34—Mercer 7

G	W	L	T	PT	OP
7	4	3	0	99	67

1916
Coach: Charles McCoy
Fla.
```
 0—Georgia .............. 21
 0—Alabama .............. 16
 0—Tennessee ............ 24
 0—Auburn ............... 20
 3—Indiana .............. 14
G   W   L   T   PT   OP
5   0   5   0    3   95
```

1917
Coach: A. L. Busser
Fla.
```
21—South Carolina ....... 13
 0—Tulane ............... 52
19—Southern .............. 7
 0—Auburn ............... 68
 7—Clemson ............... 55
 0—Kentucky ............. 52
G   W   L   T   PT   OP
6   2   4   0   47  247
```

1918
Coach: A. L. Busser
Fla.
```
 2—Camp Johnson ......... 14
G   W   L   T   PT   OP
1   0   1   0    2   14
```

1919
Coach: A. L. Busser
Fla.
```
33—Georgia A & M ......... 2
48—Mercer ................ 0
 0—Georgia .............. 16
 0—Southern .............. 7
 2—Tulane ............... 14
64—Stetson ............... 0
13—South Carolina ........ 0
14—Oglethorpe ............ 7
G   W   L   T   PT   OP
8   5   3   0  174   46
```

1920
Coach: William Kline
Fla.
```
21—Newberry .............. 0
13—Southern .............. 0
30—Mercer ................ 0
 0—Tulane ............... 14
26—Stetson ............... 0
 0—Georgia .............. 56
21—Stetson ............... 0
0—Oglethorpe ........... 21
 1—Rollins ............... 0
       (Forfeit)
G   W   L   T   PT   OP
9   6   3   0  112   91
```

1921
Coach: William Kline
Fla.
```
 6—U. S. Infantry ........ 0
33—Rollins ............... 0
 0—Carlstrom Fly. ....... 19
 7—Mercer ................ 0
 0—Tennessee ............. 9
34—Howard ................ 0
 7—South Carolina ........ 7
 9—Alabama ............... 2
 7—Mississippi College ... 7
21—Oglethorpe ............ 3
10—North Carolina ....... 14
G    W   L   T   PT   OP
11   6   3   2  134   61
```

1922
Coach: William Kline
Fla.
```
 6—Furman ................ 7
19—Rollins ............... 0
14—American Legion ....... 0
57—Howard College ........ 0
12—Oglethorpe ............ 0
47—Clemson .............. 14
 0—Harvard .............. 24
27—Tulane ................ 6
58—Mississippi College ... 0
G   W   L   T   PT   OP
9   7   2   0  240   51
```

1923
Coach: J. A. VanFleet
Fla.
```
 0—Army ................. 20
 7—Georgia Tech .......... 7
28—Rollins ............... 0
16—Wake Forest ........... 7
19—Mercer ................ 7
27—Stetson ............... 0
53—Southern .............. 0
13—Mississippi State .... 13
16—Alabama ............... 6
G   W   L   T   PT   OP
9   6   1   2  179   60
```

1924
Coach: J. A. VanFleet
Fla.
```
77—Rollins ............... 0
 7—Georgia Tech .......... 7
34—Wake Forest ........... 0
 7—Texas ................. 7
27—Southern .............. 0
 7—Army ................. 14
 0—Mercer ............... 10
27—Mississippi State ..... 0
10—Drake ................. 0
16—Washington and Lee ... 6
G    W   L   T   PT   OP
10   6   2   2  212   44
```

1925
Coach: H. L. Sebring
Fla.
```
24—Mercer ................ 0
 9—Southern .............. 0
22—Hampden-Sydney ........ 6
 7—Georgia Tech ......... 23
24—Wake Forest ........... 3
65—Rollins ............... 0
42—Clemson ............... 0
 0—Alabama .............. 34
12—Mississippi State ..... 0
17—Washington and Lee ... 14
G    W   L   T   PT   OP
10   8   2   0  222   80
```

1926
Coach: H. L. Sebring
Fla.
```
16—Southern .............. 0
 6—Chicago .............. 12
 7—Mississippi .......... 12
 3—Mercer ................ 7
13—Kentucky ............. 18
 9—Georgia .............. 32
33—Clemson ............... 0
 0—Alabama .............. 49
 0—Hampden-Sydney ........ 0
 7—Washington and Lee ... 7
G    W   L   T   PT   OP
10   2   6   2   94  137
```

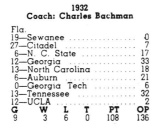

1932
Coach: Charles Bachman
Fla.

19—Sewanee					0
27—Citadel					7
6—N. C. State					17
12—Georgia					33
13—North Carolina					18
6—Auburn					21
0—Georgia Tech					6
13—Tennessee					32
12—UCLA					2
G	W	L	T	PT	OP
9	3	6	0	108	136

1936
Coach: Josh Cody
Fla.

20—Citadel					14
0—South Carolina					7
32—Stetson					0
0—Kentucky					7
7—Maryland					6
8—Georgia					26
18—Sewanee					7
14—Georgia Tech					38
0—Auburn					13
0—Mississippi State					7
G	W	L	T	PT	OP
10	4	6	0	99	125

1933
Coach: D. K. Stanley
Fla.

28—Stetson					0
31—Sewanee					0
0—N. C. State					0
9—North Carolina					0
6—Tennessee					13
0—Georgia					14
7—Georgia Tech					19
14—Auburn					7
19—Maryland					0
G	W	L	T	PT	OP
9	5	3	1	114	53

1937
Coach: Josh Cody
Fla.

0—LSU					19
18—Stetson					0
6—Temple					7
21—Sewanee					0
13—Mississippi State					14
7—Maryland					13
6—Georgia					0
9—Clemson					10
0—Georgia Tech					12
0—Auburn					14
6—Kentucky					0
G	W	L	T	PT	OP
11	4	7	0	86	89

1934
Coach: D. K. Stanley
Fla.

13—Rollins					2
20—VPI					13
12—Tulane					28
14—N. C. State					0
0—Maryland					21
0—Georgia					14
13—Mississippi					13
14—Auburn					7
13—Georgia Tech					12
14—Stetson					0
G	W	L	T	PT	OP
10	6	3	1	113	110

1938
Coach: Josh Cody
Fla.

14—Stetson					16
0—Mississippi State					22
10—Sewanee					6
7—Miami					19
33—Tampa					0
0—Boston College					33
6—Georgia					19
21—Maryland					7
0—Georgia Tech					0
9—Auburn					7
12—Temple					20
G	W	L	T	PT	OP
11	4	6	1	112	149

1935
Coach: D. K. Stanley
Fla.

34—Stetson					0
7—Tulane					19
6—Mississippi					27
6—Maryland					20
0—Georgia					7
6—Kentucky					15
20—Sewanee					0
6—Georgia Tech					39
6—Auburn					27
22—South Carolina					0
G	W	L	T	PT	OP
10	3	7	0	113	154

1939
Coach: Josh Cody
Fla.

21—Stetson					0
0—Texas					12
0—Mississippi State					14
7—Boston College					0
7—Tampa					0
14—Maryland					0
0—South Carolina					6
2—Georgia					6
13—Miami					0
7—Georgia Tech					21
7—Auburn					7
G	W	L	T	PT	OP
11	5	5	1	78	66

1940
Coach: Thomas J. Lieb

Fla.
7—Mississippi State 27
23—Tampa 0
0—Villanova 28
19—Maryland 0
0—Tennessee 14
18—Georgia 13
46—Miami 6
16—Georgia Tech 7
7—Auburn 20
0—Texas 26

G	W	L	T	PT	OP
10	5	5	0	136	141

1941
Coach: Thomas J. Lieb

Fla.
26—Randolph Macon 0
0—Mississippi State 6
46—Tampa 6
0—Villanova 6
12—Maryland 13
7—LSU 10
3—Georgia 19
14—Miami 0
14—Georgia Tech 7
27—UCLA 30

G	W	L	T	PT	OP
10	4	6	0	149	97

1942
Coach: Thomas J. Lieb

Fla.
7—Jax NAS 20
45—Randolph Macon 0
26—Tampa 6
6—Auburn 0
3—Villanova 13
12—Mississippi State 26
0—Maryland 13
0—Georgia 75
0—Miami 12
7—Georgia Tech 20

G	W	L	T	PT	OP
10	3	7	0	106	·185

1944
Coach: Thomas J. Lieb

Fla.
36—Mayport NAS 6
6—Mississippi 26
26—Jax NAS 20
0—Tennessee 40
13—Maryland 6
13—Miami 0
12—Georgia 38

G	W	L	T	PT	OP
7	4	3	0	106	136

1945
Coach: Thomas J. Lieb

Fla.
31—Infantry, 63rd 2
26—Mississippi 13
6—Tulane 6
0—Vanderbilt 7
6—Miami 7
45—So. Western La. 0
0—Auburn 19
0—Georgia 34
41—Presbyterian 0
0—US Amphibs 12

G	W	L	T	PT	OP
10	4	5	1	155	100

1946
Coach: Raymond B. Wolf

Fla.
7—Mississippi 13
13—Tulane 27
0—Vanderbilt 20
13—Miami 20
19—North Carolina 40
14—Georgia 33
20—Villanova 27
6—N. C. State 37
12—Auburn 47

G	W	L	T	PT	OP
9	0	9	0	104	264

1947
Coach: Raymond B. Wolf

Fla.
6—Mississippi 14
12—N. Texas State 20
14—Auburn 20
7—N. C. State 6
7—North Carolina 35
34—Furman 7
6—Georgia 34
7—Tulane 7
7—Miami 6
25—Kansas State 7

G	W	L	T	PT	OP
10	4	5	1	125	156

1948
Coach: Raymond B. Wolf

Fla.
0—Mississippi 14
28—Tulsa 14
16—Auburn 9
41—Rollins 12
7—Georgia Tech 42
39—Furman 14
12—Georgia 20
15—Kentucky 34
27—Miami 13
28—Alabama 34

G	W	L	T	PT	OP
10	5	5	0	213	206

367

1949
Coach: Raymond B. Wolf

Fla.
13—Citadel					0
40—Tulsa					7
14—Auburn					14
17—Vanderbilt					22
14—Georgia Tech					43
28—Furman					27
28—Georgia					7
0—Kentucky					35
13—Miami					28
13—Alabama					35

G	W	L	T	PT	OP
10	4	5	1	180	218

1950
Coach: Bob Woodruff

Fla.
7—Citadel					3
27—Duquesne					14
13—Georgia Tech					16
27—Auburn					7
31—Vanderbilt					27
19—Furman					7
6—Kentucky					40
0—Georgia					6
14—Miami					20
13—Alabama					41

G	W	L	T	PT	OP
10	5	5	0	157	181

1951
Coach: Bob Woodruff

Fla.
13—Wyoming					0
27—Citadel					7
0—Georgia Tech					27
40—Loyola					7
13—Auburn					14
33—Vanderbilt					13
6—Kentucky					14
6—Georgia					7
6—Miami					21
30—Alabama					21

G	W	L	T	PT	OP
10	5	5	0	174	131

1952
Coach: Bob Woodruff

Fla.
33—Stetson					6
14—Georgia Tech					17
33—Citadel					0
54—Clemson					13
13—Vanderbilt					20
30—Georgia					0
31—Auburn					21
12—Tennessee					26
43—Miami					6
27—Kentucky					0
14—Tulsa					13

(Gator Bowl)

G	W	L	T	PT	OP
11	8	3	0	304	122

1953
Coach: Bob Woodruff

Fla.
16—Rice					20
0—Georgia Tech					0
13—Kentucky					26
45—Stetson					0
60—Citadel					0
21—Louisiana State					21
7—Auburn					16
21—Georgia					7
7—Tennessee					9
10—Miami					14

G	W	L	T	PT	OP
10	3	5	2	200	113

1954
Coach: Bob Woodruff

Fla.
14—Rice					34
13—Georgia Tech					12
19—Auburn					13
7—Clemson					14
21—Kentucky					7
7—Louisiana State					20
7—Mississippi State					0
13—Georgia					14
14—Tennessee					0
0—Miami					14

G	W	L	T	PT	OP
10	5	5	0	115	128

1955
Coach: Bob Woodruff

Fla.
20—Mississippi State					14
7—Georgia Tech					14
0—Auburn					13
28—George Washington					0
18—L. S. U.					14
7—Kentucky					10
19—Georgia					13
0—Tennessee					20
6—Vanderbilt					21
6—Miami					7

G	W	L	T	PT	OP
10	4	6	0	111	126

1956
Coach: Bob Woodruff

Fla.
26—Mississippi State					0
20—Clemson					20
8—Kentucky					17
7—Rice					0
21—Vanderbilt					7
21—L. S. U.					6
20—Auburn					0
28—Georgia					0
0—Georgia Tech					28
7—Miami					20

G	W	L	T	PT	OP
10	6	3	1	158	98

1957
Coach: Bob Woodruff

Fla.
- 27—Wake Forest 0
- 14—Kentucky 7
- 20—Mississippi State 29
- 22—L. S. U. 14
- 0—Auburn 13
- 22—Georgia 0
- 14—Vanderbilt 7
- 0—Georgia Tech 0
- 14—Miami 0

G	W	L	T	PT	OP
9	6	2	1	133	70

1958
Coach: Bob Woodruff

Fla.
- 34—Tulane 14
- 7—Mississippi State 14
- 21—U. C. L. A. 14
- 6—Vanderbilt 6
- 7—L. S. U. 10
- 5—Auburn 6
- 7—Georgia 6
- 51—Arkansas State 7
- 21—Florida State 7
- 12—Miami 9
- 3—Mississippi 7

(Gator Bowl)

G	W	L	T	PT	OP
11	6	4	1	174	98

1959
Coach: Bob Woodruff

Fla.
- 30—Tulane 0
- 14—Mississippi State 13
- 55—Virginia 10
- 13—Rice 13
- 6—Vanderbilt 13
- 0—L. S. U. 9
- 0—Auburn 6
- 10—Georgia 21
- 18—Florida State 8
- 23—Miami 14

G	W	L	T	PT	OP
10	5	4	1	169	105

1960
Coach: Ray Graves

Fla.
- 30—George Washington 7
- 3—Florida State 0
- 18—Georgia Tech 17
- 0—Rice 10
- 12—Vanderbilt 0
- 13—L. S. U. 10
- 7—Auburn 10
- 22—Georgia 14
- 21—Tulane 6
- 18—Miami 0
- 13—Baylor 12

(Gator Bowl)

G	W	L	T	PT	OP
11	9	2	0	156	66

1961
Coach: Ray Graves

Fla.
- 21—Clemson 7
- 3—Florida State 3
- 14—Tulane 3
- 10—Rice 19
- 7—Vanderbilt 0
- 0—L. S. U. 23
- 0—Georgia Tech 20
- 21—Georgia 14
- 15—Auburn 32
- 6—Miami 15

G	W	L	T	PT	OP
10	4	5	1	97	136

1962
Coach: Ray Graves

Fla.
- 19—Miss. State 9
- 0—Georgia Tech 17
- 21—Duke 28
- 42—Texas A&M 6
- 42—Vanderbilt 7
- 0—LSU 23
- 22—Auburn 3
- 23—Georgia 15
- 20—FSU 7
- 15—Miami 17
- 17—Penn State 7

(Gator Bowl)

G	W	L	T	PT	OP
11	7	4	0	205	132

1963
Coach: Ray Graves

Fla.
- 0—Georgia Tech 9
- 9—Miss. State 9
- 35—Richmond 28
- 10—Alabama 6
- 21—Vanderbilt 0
- 0—LSU 14
- 0—Auburn 19
- 21—Georgia 14
- 27—Miami 21
- 7—FSU 0

G	W	L	T	PT	OP
10	6	3	1	130	119

1964
Coach: Ray Graves

Fla.
- 24—SMU 8
- 16—Miss. State 13
- 30—Ole Miss 14
- 37—South Carolina 0
- 14—Alabama 17
- 14—Auburn 0
- 7—Georgia 14
- 7—FSU 16
- 12—Miami 10
- 20—LSU 6

G	W	L	T	PT	OP
10	7	3	0	181	98

369

1965
Coach: Ray Graves

Fla.
24—Northwestern 14
13—Miss. State 18
14—LSU 7
17—Ole Miss 0
28—N. C. State 6
17—Auburn 28
14—Georgia 10
51—Tulane 13
13—Miami 16
30—FSU 17
18—Missouri 20
(Sugar Bowl)

G	W	L	T	PT	OP
11	7	4	0	239	149

1966
Coach: Ray Graves

Fla.
43—Northwestern 7
28—Miss. State 7
13—Vanderbilt 0
22—F.S.U. 19
17—N. C. State 10
28—L.S.U. 7
30—Auburn 27
10—Georgia 27
31—Tulane 10
16—Miami 21
27—Georgia Tech 12
(Orange Bowl)

G	W	L	T	PT	OP
11	9	2	0	265	147

1967
Coach: Ray Graves

Fla.
14—Illinois 0
24—Miss. State 7
6—L.S.U. 37
35—Tulane 0
27—Vanderbilt 22
21—Auburn 26
17—Georgia 16
28—Kentucky 12
16—F.S.U. 21
13—Miami 20

G	W	L	T	PT	OP
10	6	4	0	201	161

1968
Coach: Ray Graves

Fla.
23—Air Force 20
9—FSU 3
31—Miss. State 14
24—Tulane 7
7—North Carolina 22
14—Vanderbilt 14
13—Auburn 24
0—Georgia 51
16—Kentucky 14
14—Miami 10

G	W	L	T	PT	OP
10	6	3	1	151	175

1969
Coach: Ray Graves

Fla.
59—Houston 34
47—Mississippi St. 35
21—Florida State 6
18—Tulane 17
52—North Carolina 2
41—Vanderbilt 20
12—Auburn 38
13—Georgia 13
31—Kentucky 6
35—Miami 16
14—Tennessee 13
(Gator Bowl)

G	W	L	T	PT	OP
11	9	1	1	343	200

1970
Coach: Doug Dickey

21 Duke (53,841)* 19
34 Miss. St. (55,674)* 13
15 Alabama (58,138) 46
14 N.C. State (53,068)* 6
38 FSU (42,704) 27
20 Richmond (51,471)* 0
7 Tennessee (64,069) 38
14 Auburn (63,560)* 63
24 Georgia (70,294) 17
24 Kentucky (45,102) 13
13 Miami (50,149)* 14

G	W	L	T	PT	OP
11	7	4	0	224	256

1971
Coach: Doug Dickey

6 Duke 12
10 Miss. State 13
0 Alabama 38
13 Tennessee 20
7 LSU 48
17 FSU 15
27 Maryland 23
7 Auburn 40
7 Georgia 49
35 Kentucky 24
45 Miami 16

G	W	L	T	PT	OP
11	4	7	0	174	298

1972
Coach: Doug Dickey

14 SMU 21
28 Miss. State 13
42 FSU 13
7 Alabama 24
16 Ole Miss 0
20 Auburn 26
7 Georgia 10
40 Kentucky 0
3 LSU 3
17 Miami 6
24 North Carolina 28

G	W	L	T	PT	OP
11	5	5	1	218	144

370

1973
Coach: Doug Dickey

21 Kansas State 10
14 So. Mississippi 13
12 Miss. State 33
3 LSU 24
14 Alabama 35
10 Miss 13
12 Auburn 8
11 Georgia 10
20 Kentucky 18
14 Miami 7
49 FSU 0

G	W	L	T	PT	OP
11	7	4	0	180	171

A Gator Touchdown Leap.

371

Records

LONG DISTANCES

Longest run from scrimmage: 91 (Herb McAnly vs. Sewanee, 1932)

Longest TD pass: 81 (John Reaves to Jim Yancey vs. FSU, 1970)

Longest TD punt return: 96 (Hal Griffin vs. Miami, 1946)

Longest TD kickoff return: 100 (Pat Reen vs. Miami, 1940)

Longest TD intercepted pass: 100 (Jackie Simpson vs. Mississippi State, 1955 and Joe Brodsky, 1956)

Longest punt: 92 (Ark Newton vs. Mississippi State, 1924)

SINGLE GAME

Most plays: 68 (Reaves vs. Auburn)†

Average gain per play: (Min. 60) 5.3 (Reaves vs. Auburn)†

Most runs from scrimmage: 31 (Larry Dupree vs. FSU, 1963).

Most yards rushing: 218 (Leroy "Red" Bethea vs. Chicago, 1930)

Most yards rushing and passing: 361 (John Reaves vs. Auburn, 1969)

Best rushing average (12 or more rushes): 11.5 (Leroy "Red" Bethea vs. Chicago, 1930)

Most passes attempted: 66 (Reaves vs. Auburn, 1969)†

Most passes completed: 33 (Reaves vs. Miami, 1971)†

Most TD passes: 5 (Reaves vs. Houston, Vanderbilt)†

Most yards passing: 369 (Reaves vs. Auburn, 1969)

Most yards returned for intercepted passes: 3 for 162 yards (Joe Brodsky vs. Mississippi State, 1956) good for two TD's*

Most passes caught: 15 (Carlos Alvarez vs. Miami, 1969)†

Most yards caught passes: 283 (Alvarez vs. Miami, 1969)†

Average gain per catch: 15.8 (Alvarez vs. Miami)

Most times punted: 23 (Bud Walton vs. Georgia Tech, 1938)

Best punting average: (7 or more) 53.0 (Fred
Montsdeoca vs. Alabama, 1949)
Most field goals: 3 (Earle "Dummy" Taylor vs.
Columbia College, 1911)
*Led Nation   **National Record   †SEC Record.

Records

CAREER RECORDS

Most runs from scrimmage: 520 (Larry Smith, 1966-7-8)
Most net yards rushing: 2,186 (Larry Smith, 1966-7-8)
Best rushing average (350 or more runs): 5.8 (Charlie
Hunsinger, 1946-7-8-9)
Most yards rushing and passing: 7213 (John Reaves,
1969-71)
Most passes attempted: 1128 + (John Reaves)
Most passes completed: 603 + * (Reaves)
Best pass completion average (150 or more): .566
(Spurrier)
Most touchdown passes: 54 + (Reaves)
Fewest passes had intercepted (300 or more passes): 15
(Haywood Sullivan, 1950-51)
Most yards passing: 7549 (Reaves)*
Most passes caught: 172 (Carlos Alvarez, 1969-71)
Most yards caught passes: 2,563 (Alvarez)
Most TD receptions: 19 (Alvarez)
Most times punted: 173 (Fred Montsdeoca, 1948-49-50)
Best punting average (100 or more): 42.9 (Bobby Joe
Green 100, 1958-59)
Best punt return average (25 or more): 18.6 (26/484) (Hal
Griffin, 1946-47-48-49)
Most field goals: 16 (Earle "Dummy" Taylor,
1908-9-10-11-12)
Most extra points: 77 (Wayne Barfield, 1965-66-67)
Most consecutive extra points: 52 (Wayne Barfield,
1965-66-67)

+ SEC Record
*National Record

Season Records

Most Points: 110 (Tommy Durrance, 1969)

Most runs from scrimmage: 217 (Walter Mayberry, 1937)

Most yards rushing: 845 (Nat Moore, 1972)

Most yards passing: 2,896 (John Reaves, 1969)†

Most yards running and passing: 2,852 (John Reaves, 1969)†

Best rushing average (75 or more runs): 7.3 (Charlie Hunsinger, 1948)

Most passes attempted: 396 (Reaves, 1969)†

Most passes completed: 222 (Reaves, 1969)†

Best pass completion average (25 or more): 616 (Spurrier, 1966)

Most TD passes thrown: 24 (Reaves, 1969)†

Best Average Gain Per Game: 285.2 (Reaves)†

Average Gain Per Play: 6.7 (Reaves)† (Min. 300)

Most passes caught: 88 (Carlos Alvarez, 1969)†

Most yards caught passes: 1,329 (Carlos Alvarez, 1969)†

Most TD passes caught: 12 (Alvarez, 1969)†

Average Gain Per Game Receiving: 132.9 (Alvarez, 1969)†

Average Gain Per Catch: 15.8 (Alvarez)†

Most passes intercepted by: 7 (John Clifford, 1970)

Most yards returned pass interceptions: 5 for 244 (Joe Brodsky, 1956)*

Most times punted: 83 (Bud Walton, 1938, Buster Morrison, 1972)

Best punting average (50 or more): 44.8 (Bobby Joe Green, 54 in 1959)**

Most punt returns: 41 (Wallace Brown, 1934. Average: 11.2)

Best punt return average: 26.7 (Hal Griffin, 10 in 1947)** (National record for 10 or more)

Most field goals: 8 (Earle "Dummy" Taylor, 1911)

Most extra points: 33 (Richard Franco, 1969)

Most fumbles recovered: 5 (Bob Flowers, 1950; Charles LaPradd, 1951)

Most blocked punts: 3 (Steve Tannen, 1968)

*Led Nation **National Record †SEC Record.

Gator Team Records

Most points: 144 (Florida Southern 0, 1913)
Greatest victory margin: 144 (Florida Southern 0, 1913)
Greatest defeat margin: 0-75 (Georgia, 1942)
Most first downs: 32 (vs. Tulane, 1967)
Most runs from scrimmage: 73 (Georgia Tech, 1954)
Most first downs allowed: 28 by Kentucky, 1950
Fewest first downs allowed: 2 by South Carolina, 1936
Most yards rushing: 489 (vs. Citadel, 1953)
Most yards passing: 369 (vs. Auburn, 1969)
Most yards net rushing and passing: 651 (484 rushing, 167 passing, vs. Mercer, 1928)
Most yards allowed rushing: 363 (Alabama, 1971)
Most yards allowed passing: 372 (Loyola, 1951)
Most yards allowed rushing and passing: 593 (Georgia, 1942)
Fewest yards allowed rushing:—8 (vs. F.S.U., 1969)
Fewest yards allowed passing:—1 (vs. Vanderbilt, 1958)
Most passes attempted: 66 (vs. Auburn, 1969)
Most passes completed: 33 (vs. Auburn, 1969)
Most passes intercepted by Florida: 6 (Clemson, 1952)
Most punts by Florida: 23 (vs. Georgia Tech, 1938)
Most Turnovers Forced 10 (US, FSU, 1972)

SINGLE SEASON

Highest scoring: 336 (9 games, 1928)
Most wins: 9 (1960, 1966, 1969)
Most losses: 9 (1946)
Most first downs: 237 (1969)
Most runs from scrimmage: 609 (11 games, 1952)
Most yards net rushing: 2,388 (11 games, 1952)
Most yards rushing and passing: 4,348 (1969)
Average gain per game: 434.8 (1969)
Most passes attempted: 413 (1969)
Most passes completed: 233 (1969)
Most yards passing: 3,016 (1969)
Fewest passes had intercepted: 5 (1957)
Most passes had intercepted: 22 (1940)
Most passes intercepted: 23 (1972)
Most TD passes: 24 (1969)*
Most punts by Florida: 110 (1937)
Most Fumbles Recovered: 25 (1972)
Most Turnovers Forced: 50 (1972)
*SEC Record

THROUGH THE YEARS

Year	W	L	T	Pts.	O. Pts.	Coach	Captain
1906	5	3	0	95	66	Jack Forsythe	T. G. Hancock
1907	4	1	1	53	10	Jack Forsythe	Roy W. Corbett
1908	5	2	1	90	40	Jack Forsythe	Wm. W. (Gric) Gibbs
1909	6	1	1	117	34	G. E. Pyle	Ralph Rader
1910	6	1	0	186	15	G. E. Pyle	Demmy Taylor
1911	5	0	1	84	14	G. E. Pyle	N. S. Storter
1912	5	2	1	203	54	G. E. Pyle	Sam Buie
1913	4	3	0	228	94	G. E. Pyle	Louis Tenny
1914	5	2	0	152	46	Charles McCoy	John Sutton
							Puss Hancock
1915	4	3	0	99	67	Charles McCoy	A. A. Lotspeich
1916	0	5	0	3	95	Charles McCoy	Rex Farrior
1917	2	4	0	47	247	A. L. Busser	Arthur Fuller
							S. A. B. Wilkinson
1918	0	1	0	2	14	A. L. Busser	Gordon Clemons
1919	5	3	0	174	46	A. L. Busser	J. Sparkman
1920	6	3	0	112	91	William Kline	Paul Baker
1921	6	3	2	134	61	William Kline	"Tootie" Perry
1922	7	2	0	240	51	William Kline	F. H. Duncan
1923	6	1	2	179	60	J. A. VanFleet	Robbie Robinson
1924	6	2	2	212	44	J. A. VanFleet	"Ark" Newton
1925	8	2	0	222	80	H. L. Sebring	Edgar Jones
1926	2	6	2	94	137	H. L. Sebring	Lamar Sarra
1927	7	3	0	164	96	H. L. Sebring	Bill Middlekauf
1928	8	1	0	336	44	Charles Bachman	Ernest J. Bowyer
1929	8	2	0	193	73	Charles Bachman	Rainey Cawthon
1930	6	3	1	199	61	Charles Bachman	L. R. Bethea
1931	2	6	2	74	168	Charles Bachman	E. N. Parnell
1932	3	6	0	108	136	Charles Bachman	Joe Jenkins
1933	5	3	1	114	53	D. K. Stanley	Sam Davis
1934	6	3	1	113	110	D. K. Stanley	Chuck Rogers
1935	3	7	0	113	154	D. K. Stanley	W. W. Chase, Jr.
1936	4	6	0	99	125	Josh Cody	Julian Lane
1937	4	7	0	86	89	Josh Cody	Walter Mayberry
1938	4	6	1	112	149	Josh Cody	Frank Koscis
1939	5	5	1	78	66	Josh Cody	Clark Goff
1940	5	5	0	136	141	Thomas J. Lieb	W. L. (Bud) Walton
1941	4	6	0	149	97	Thomas J. Lieb	Bill Robinson
1942	3	7	0	106	185	Thomas J. Lieb	O'Neal Hill
1943		No Team			No Team		
1944	4	3	0	106	136	Thomas J. Lieb	Joe Graham
1945	4	5	1	155	100	Thomas J. Lieb	Hugo Miller
1946	0	9	0	104	264	Raymond B. Wolf	William Raborn
1947	4	5	1	125	156	Raymond B. Wolf	Charlie Fields
1948	5	5	0	213	206	Raymond B. Wolf	Fletcher Groves
1949	4	5	1	180	218	Raymond B. Wolf	Jimmy Kynes
1950	5	5	0	157	181	Bob Woodruff	Angus Williams
1951	5	5	0	174	131	Bob Woodruff	Jim French
							Carroll McDonald
1952	8	3	0	304	122	Bob Woodruff	Bubba Ware
							Charlie LaPradd
1953	3	5	2	200	113	Bob Woodruff	Jack O'Brien
							Rick Casares Sonny May
1954	5	5	0	115	128	Bob Woodruff	Jerry Bilyk
							Larry Scott
1955	4	6	0	111	126	Bob Woodruff	Steve DeLaTorre
							Ray Brown
1956	6	3	1	158	98	Bob Woodruff	John Barrow
1957	6	2	1	133	70	Bob Woodruff	Charlie Mitchell
1958	6	4	1	174	100	Bob Woodruff	Don Fleming
1959	5	4	1	169	107	Bob Woodruff	Dave Hudson
1960	9	2	0	157	86	Ray Graves	Bill Hood
1961	4	5	1	97	146	Ray Graves	Jim Beaver
1962	7	4	0	221	139	Ray Graves	Lindy Infante
							Bruce Culpepper
1963	6	3	1	130	120	Ray Graves	Jimmy Morgan
1964	7	3	0	181	98	Ray Graves	Larry Dupree
1965	7	4	0	239	149	Ray Graves	Bruce Bennett
							Larry Beckman
1966	9	2	0	265	147	Ray Graves	Bill Carr
							Jerry Anderson
1967	6	4	0	201	161	Ray Graves	Graham McKeel
							Wayne McCall
1968	6	3	1	151	175	Ray Graves	Bill Dorsey
							Guy Dennis
1969	9	1	1	329	187	Ray Graves	Mac Steen
							Tom Abdelnour
1970	7	4	0	224	256	Doug Dickey	Donny Williams
							Mike Kelley

376

1971	4	7	0	174	298	Doug Dickey ...... Tommy Durrance
						John Reaves Harvin Clark
1972	5	5	1	218	144	Doug Dickey .... Fred Abbott
1973	**7**	**5**	**0**	**180**	**171**	**Doug Dickey**

A Good Day At Florida Field.

FLORIDA YEAR-BY-YEAR RANK
IN SEC STANDINGS

*—Tie

1933-7*	1945-8*	1957-3*	1969-4
1934-6	1946-11	1958-7*	1970-5
1935-10	1947-9	1959-7	1971-8
1936-10	1948-9*	1960-2	1972-6
1937-8	1949-10*	1961-4	**1973-5**
1938-6*	1950-8	1962-5	
1939-8	1951-6*	1963-7	
1940-8*	1952-6	1964-2*	
1941-10	1953-6	1965-3	
1942-8*	1954-3*	1966-2	
1943-No Team	1955-8	1967-3*	
1944-9	1956-3	1968-6*	

ALL-TIME OPPONENTS

Opponent	Games	Fla. W	Fla. L	Tied	First Game
Air Force	1	1	0	0	1968
Alabama	18	5	13	0	1916
American Legion	1	1	0	0	1922
Arkansas State	1	1	0	0	1958
Army	2	0	2	0	1923
Athens, A. C.	1	1	0	0	1906
Auburn	50	18	30	2	1912
Baylor	1	1	0	0	1960
Boston College	2	1	1	0	1938
Camp Johnson	1	0	1	0	1918
Carlstrom Flyers	1	0	1	0	1921
Chicago	2	1	1	0	1926
The Citadel	12	12	0	0	1910
Clemson	13	9	3	1	1911
College of Charleston	3	3	0	0	1910
Columbia College	3	3	0	0	1908
Davidson	1	0	1	0	1927
Drake	1	1	0	0	1924
Duke	3	1	2	0	1962
Duquesne	1	1	0	0	1950
Florida State	16	13	2	1	1958
Furman	6	4	2	0	1922
Gainesville A.C.	3	3	0	0	1906
Gainesville Guards	1	1	0	0	1910
George Washington	2	2	0	0	1955
Georgia	51	19	30	2	1915
Georgia A&M	2	2	0	0	1910
Georgia Tech	34	7	22	5	1912
Hampden-Sydney	2	1	0	1	1925
Harvard	2	0	2	0	1922
Houston	1	1	0	0	1969
Howard College	2	2	0	0	1921
Illinois	1	1	0	0	1967
Indiana	1	0	1	0	1916
Jacksonville A.C.	6	6	0	0	1906
Jax Naval Air Station	2	1	1	0	1942
Kansas State	2	2	0	0	1947
Kentucky	24	12	12	0	1917
Kings College	1	1	0	0	1914
LSU	20	7	11	2	1937
Loyola (L.A.)	1	1	0	0	1951
Maryland	13	8	5	0	1927
Maryville	1	1	0	0	1913
Maypora N. Air Station	1	1	0	0	1944
Mercer	17	10	6	1	1906
Miami	35	18	17	0	1938
Miami (O)	1	0	1	0	1973
Mississippi	13	4	8	1	1926
Mississippi College	2	1	0	1	1921
Mississippi State	28	14	12	2	1923
Missouri	1	0	1	0	1966
Newberry	1	1	0	0	1920
North Carolina	9	2	6	1	1921
N. C. State	12	8	3	1	1927
Northwestern	2	2	0	0	1966
North Texas State	1	0	1	0	1947
Oglethorpe	4	3	1	0	1919
Olympics	2	2	0	0	1909
Oregon	1	1	0	0	1929
Penn. State	1	1	0	0	1962
Presbyterian	1	1	0	0	1945
Randolph Macon	2	2	0	0	1941
Rice	5	1	4	0	1953
Richmond	2	2	0	0	1963
Rollins	16	13	2	1	1906
Savannah, A.C.	2	1	1	0	1906
Sewanee	9	7	2	0	1914
SMU	2	1	1	0	1964
South Carolina	12	6	3	3	1911
Southern	14	13	1	0	1913
So. Miss	1	1	0	0	1973
Southwestern La	1	1	0	0	1945
Stetson	19	15	2	2	1908
Syracuse	1	0	1	0	1931
Tallahassee A.C.	1	1	0	0	1909
Tampa	5	5	0	0	1938
Tampa A.C.	1	1	0	0	1912

Temple	2	0	2	0	1937
Tennessee	15	2	13	0	1916
Texas A&M	1	1	0	0	1962
Texas	3	0	2	1	1924
Tulane	19	11	6	2	1915
Tulsa	3	3	0	0	1948
U.C.L.A.	4	2	2	0	1931
U.S. Amphib. Navy	1	0	1	0	1945
U.S. Infantry	2	2	0	0	1921
Vanderbilt	19	11	6	2	1945
Vedada Club (Havana)	1	1	0	0	1912
Villanova	4	0	4	0	1940
Virginia	1	1	0	0	1959

Please Go Gators.

TOTAL OFFENSE FOR CAREER

	Passing	Rushing	Total
John Reaves (1969-71)	7549	246	7213
Steve Spurrier (1964-65-66)	4848	442	5290
Larry Smith (1967-67-68)	141	2186	2327
Tommy Harrison (1939-40-41)	1170	963	2133
Walter Mayberry (1936-37-38)	713	1306	2019
Chuck Hunsinger (1946-47-48-49)	0	2017	2017
Haywood Sullivan (1950-51)	2016	-24	1992
Tom Shannon (1962-64)	1766	137	1903

TOTAL OFFENSE FOR SEASON

	Passing	Rushing	Total
John Reaves (1969)	2896	-44	2852
John Reaves (1970)	2549	-118	2431
Steve Spurrier (1965)	1893	230	2123
Steve Spurrier (1966)	2012	66	2078
John Reaves (1971)	2104	-104	2000
Larry Rentz (1967)	1031	194	1125
Tommy Harrison 1941	679	428	1107
Haywood Sullivan (1950)	1134	-28	1106
Steve Spurrier (1964)	943	146	1089
Walter Mayberry (1937)	201	818	1019

RUSHING FOR CAREER

	No.	Yards
Larry Smith (1966-68)	520	2186
Chuck Hunsinger	391	2017
Larry Dupree (1962-64)	405	1725
Tommy Durrance (1969-71)	448	1640
Mike Rich (1969-71)	379	1402
Jackie Simpson (1953-54-55-56)	207	1310
Walter Mayberry	415	1306
Rick Casares (1951-52-53)	361	1163

RUSHING FOR SEASON

	No.	Yards
Nat Moore (1972)	145	845
Chuck Hunsinger (1948)	116	842
Walter Mayberry (1937)	164	818
Chuck Hunsinger (1949)	122	774
Bobby Forbes (1947)	118	766
Larry Smith (1967)	205	754
Larry Dupree (1963)	189	745
Larry Smith (1966)	162	742

COMPOSITE RECORD OF ALL GATOR
FOOTBALL COACHES

Period	Coach	Seasons	W	L	T	Pct.
1906-1908	Jack Forsythe	3	14	6	2	.636
1909-1913	G. E. Pyle	5	26	7	3	.788
1914-1916	Charles McCoy	3	9	10	0	.474
1917-1919	A. L. Busser	3	7	8	0	.467
1920-1922	William Kline	3	19	8	2	.704
1923-1924	Gen. VanFleet	2	12	3	4	.800
1925-1927	H. L. Sebring	3	17	11	2	.607
1928-1932	Charles Bachman	5	27	18	3	.600
1933-1935	D. K. Stanley	3	14	13	2	.519
1936-1939	Josh Cody	4	17	24	2	.415
1940-1945	Tom Lieb	5	20	26	1	.435
1946-1949	Ray Wolf	4	13	24	2	.351
1950-1959	Bob Woodruff	10	53	42	6	.554
1960-1969	Ray Graves	9	70	31	4	.671
1970-	Doug Dickey	3	16	16	1	.500

No team in 1943.

DICKEY'S HEAD COACHING RECORD

1964	Tennessee	4-5-1		1971	Florida	4-7-0
1965	Tennessee	8-1-2 (Bluebonnet Bowl, SEC Coach of Year)		1972	Florida	5-5-1
				1973	Florida	7-5-0 (Tangerine Bowl)
1966	Tennessee	8-3-0 (Gator Bowl)				
1967	Tennessee	9-2-0 (Orange Bowl, SEC Coach of Year, SEC Champion)		Totals		69-36-5
1968	Tennessee	8-2-1 (Cotton Bowl)				
1969	Tennessee	9-2-0 (Gator Bowl, SEC Champion)				
1970	Florida	7-4-0				

GATOR RECORDS

FLORIDA'S BOWL RECORD (5-3)

GATOR BOWL, JACKSONVILLE, FLORIDA

1953—	Florida	7	7	0	0—14
	Tulsa	0	0	7	6—13
1959—	Florida	3	0	0	0— 3
	Mississippi	7	0	0	0— 7
1961—	Florida	0	13	0	0—13
	Baylor	0	0	0	12—12
1963—	Florida	3	7	0	7—17
	Penn State	0	7	0	0— 7
1969—	Florida	7	0	7	0—14
	Tennessee	0	10	0	3—13

SUGAR BOWL, NEW ORLEANS, LA.

1966—	Florida	0	0	0	18—18
	Missouri	0	17	3	0—20

ORANGE BOWL, MIAMI, FLORIDA

1967—	Florida	0	7	7	13—27
	Georgia Tech	6	0	0	6—12

TANGERINE BOWL, GAINESVILLE, FLORIDA

1973—	Florida	0	0	0	7-7
	Miami (O)	3	0	10	3-16

GATOR ALL-SOUTHERN PLAYERS

Robbie Robinson, Tackle 1923
Ark Newton, HB 1923
Goldy Goldstein, Guard 1923, 1924, 1925
Edgar Jones, QB 1924
Clyde Crabtree, QB 1928
Dale Vansickle, End 1928
James Steele, Guard 1930

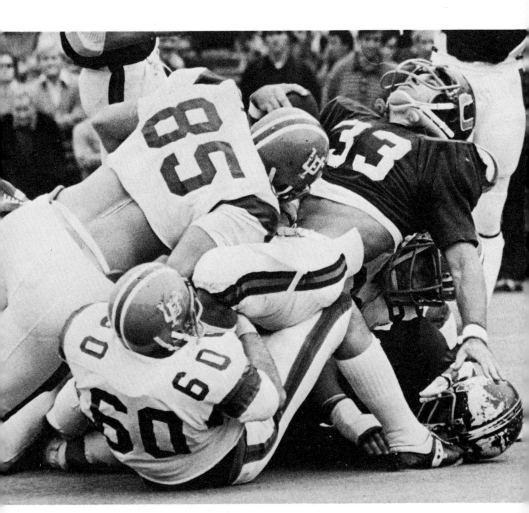

The Gators On Defense.

ALL-SOUTHEASTERN CONFERENCE FIRST TEAM

Walter Mayberry, HB 1937; Jimmy Kynes, Center, 1949; Charlie Hunsinger, FB 1948, 1949; Joe D'Agostino, Guard 1952; Charles LaPradd, Tackle 1952; Steve DeLaTorre, LB 1955; John Barrow, Guard 1956; Jim Rountree, HB 1957; Don Fleming, End 1958; Vel Heckman, Tackle 1958; Dave Hudson, End 1959; Vic Miranda, Guard 1960; Pat Patchen, End 1960; Larry Travis, Guard 1962; Larry Dupree, FB 1962, 1963, 1964; Bill Richbourg, MG 1964; Bruce Bennett, Safety 1964, 1965; Charles Casey, End 1964, 1965; Larry Gagner, Guard 1964, 1965; Larry Beckman, Guard 1965; Steve Spurrier, QB 1965, 1966; Larry Smith, TB 1966, 1967, 1968; Richard Trapp, Flanker 1966, 1967; Jim Benson, Guard 1966; Bill Carr, Center 1966; Wayne Barfield, Kicker 1967; Guy Dennis, Guard 1967, 1968; Steve Tannen, DHB 1968, 1969; David Ghesquiere, End 1969; Carlos Alvarez, Flanker 1969; John Reaves, QB 1969; Tommy Durrance, TB 1969; Mac Steen, Guard 1969; Jim Yancey, TE 1970; Jack Youngblood, DE 1970; TB Nat Moore, 1972; LB Fred Abbott, 1972; Ralph Ortega, LB 1973; Jim Revels, S 1973; Ricky Browne, DE 1973.

GATOR ALL-AMERICANS

NO.	YEAR	NAME	POSITION
1.	1928	Dale Vansickle	End
2.	1952	Charlie LaPradd	Tackle
3.	1956	John Barrow	Guard
4.	1958	Vel Heckman	Tackle
5.	1964	Larry Dupree	Fullback
6.	1965	Bruce Bennet	Safetyman
7.	1965	Charles Casey	End
8.	1965	Larry Gagner	Tackle
9.	1965	Lynn Matthews	End
10.	1965	Steve Spurrier	Quarterback
11.	1966	Bill Carr	Center
12.	1968	Guy Dennis	Guard
13.	1968	Larry Smith	Fullback
14.	1969	Carlos Alvarez	Flanker
15.	1969	Steve Tannen	Defensive Back
16.	1970	Jack Youngblood	Defensive End

Gator Fans Start Early.

A Florida Businessman Has Become A Legend With His Spontaneous Cheerleading At Gator Games. His Nickname: Two-Bits, Naturally.

A

Abbott, Frederic Marshall '70, '71, '72

Abdelhour, Thomas Allen '67, '68, '69

Adams, Lawrence Herbert '71

Adams, Roger '44

Adkins, Mitty '48, '49

Agee, Joseph Ryan, III '69

Albury, Charles D. '68, '69

Alderman, Tom '06

Allen, Joseph Louis, '73

Allen, Major General Chester '28

Allen, Richard Archer '59

Allen, Richard B. '55

Alvarez, Carlos '69, '70, '71

Amelung, Frank Albert, Jr. '67, '68, '69

Anderson, Anthony Leon, '73

Anderson, B. G. '20

Anderson, C. A. '19, '20

Anderson, Jerry David '64, '65, '66

Anderson, Kris Hoffman '71, '72, '73

Anderson, R. T. '31

Anderson, Tom '31

Anderson, W. F. '25

Arfaras, Nicholas John '60, '61

Ash, Terry Dean '70

Aust, Clifton Elwood '71, '72, '73

Ayers, William '57, '58

B

Baeszler, Marquis C. '64, '65, '66

Bagwell, Archie '40

Bail, Clinton Robert, '73

Baker, Henry '08, '09

Baker, P. O. '16, '19, '20

Balas, Leonard Charles '50, '51, '52

Barber, John '42

Barber, Vernon Stanley, '73

Barchan, Joseph '22

Barfield, John Wayne '65, '66, '67

Barker, Allie '31

Barnes, Donald L. '52

Barnhart, David L. '68

Barr, Jimmy Darrell '69, '71

Barrett, Donald James '64, '65, '66

Barrington, Glenn '42

Barris, Albert '06

Barrow, John B. '56

Bartleson, Charles '08

Bass, Billy '52, '53, '54

Batten, Thomas E., Jr. '61

Battista, Julius B. '38, '39, '40

Beach, James Eldridge '48

Beaver, James Edward '59, '60, '61

Beck, Cecil '25, '26, '27

Beck, George '33

Beckman, Lars Eric '64, '65

Beckwith, Jack '33, '34, '35

Beeler, P. R. '12

Belden, Douglas R. '47

Bell, Reed '44

Bennett, Bruce '64, '65

Bennett, Franklin '36

Beno, Andy '39

Benson, James Edward, Jr. '64, '65, '66

Bentfrou, W. '21

Bernhard, Drayton '31, '32, '33

Bernhardt, James Thomas, III '64

Berry, John J. '38

Bethea, L. R. '30

Beusse, Carl '65, '66

Bie, O. A. '22

Bilinski, Leo '33

Bilyk, Gerald L. '52, '53, '54

Bishop, Homer '25

Bishop, Howard '25, '26, '27

Bishop, Thomas W. '46, '47, '48, '49

Blair, Richard Howard '57

Blalock, Jack '37, '38
Blank, Ralph '41
Blavi, Richard H. '57
Bludworth, David Howard '61
Boardman, Hollis Cassell '71, '72, '73
Boedy, Robert Frederick '72, '73
Bolton, William Oakley, Jr. '54, '55, '56
Bond, John S., Jr. '24
Bond, William B. '28
Boney, Clark Howell, Jr. '55, '56, '57
Bono, Louis '27, '28
Booker, William Edward '56, '57, '58
Booth, James Kenneth '71
Bowden, David Raymond '72, '73
Bowen, Hunter Stephen '69, '70
Bowyer, Ernest J. '26, '27, '28
Bracken, Andrew J. '41, '42
Branch, Harold T. '46
Brannon, C. S. '17
Brannon, Hill '50, '51, '52
Brantley, Richard Allen '57, '58, '59
Bray, H. Thompson '47, '48
Bretsch, Kenneth P. '57
Brinson, Larry Sylvesta '73
Broadus, Loren A. '47, '48, '49, '50
Brodsky, Joe '53, '54, '55, '56
Brock, Paul '36, '37
Brooks, Hubert E. '50, '51, '52
Brown, Aaron '48, '49
Brown, Donald E. '49, '50, '51
Brown, J. Alton '33, '34, '35
Brown, Joseph Barry '64, '65
Brown, Merrell Russell '61, '62, '63
Brown, Paul '32
Brown, Ray Thomas '52, '53, '54, '55
Brown, Richard '23, '24, '25
Brown, Wallace '33, '34
Browne, Richard Scott '71, '72, '73
Brumbaugh, Carl '27, '28
Brumby, Robert '24
Bryan, Joe '27, '28

Bryan, William Emory '32, '33
Bryant, G. K. '25
Bryant, Thomas W. (honorary) '62
Bucha, Mike '38, '39, '40
Buchanan, Richard Alvin '69, '70, '71
Buck, Shaw '31
Buie, A. P. '10, '11, '12, '13
Bullock, Carlos E. '33
Bullock, J. R. '11, '12, '13
Burford, Robert Ray '54, '55, '56
Burgess, John E. '52, '53, '54, '55
Burke, William C. '54
Burnett, John '25
Burnett, R. H. '21
Burns, Jack C. '68, '69, '70
Burroughs, John '35
Bushnell, Byron '15
Butler, Alvin Bernard '72, '73
Butler, Gene '32
Butz, Clyde Owen '59
Byers, Bernarr M. '68
Byrge, Earl '65
Byrd, C. Y. '22

C

Cahill, Leo '39, '40, '41
Callahan, Melton Victor '65
Cameron, Glenn Scott '72, '73
Canova, W. F. '17
Cansler, Dale Bruce '58, '59
Card, Jack Dennis '64, '65, '66
Carlton, James M. '52
Carlton, R. A. '22
Carlton, T. Hoyt '20, '21
Carpenter, Darrell Franklin, '73
Carte, B. S. '44, '45, '46
Carr, William Curtis '64, '65, '66
Carver, Corlis R. '47, '48, '49
Cary, Stanley '42
Casares, Richard J. '51, '52, '53
Case, Lawrence '23
Casey, Charles Arthur '64, '65
Cash, William K. '60, '61, '62

Cassidy, Arch W. '53, '54
Cawen, William '41
Cawthon, Rainey '27, '28, '29
Champlon, Ralph '25
Chandler, Don Gene '54, '55
Chaplin, Charlie '30
Chaplin, James '24, '25, '26
Chapman, Howard Garland '52, '53
Charles, William '32
Chase, L. C. '22
Chase, W. W. '33, '34, '35
Cheney, Andrew Bruce '69, '70
Cherry, H. Spurgeon '30, '31
Chesser, Joe E. '45, '46, '47
Chorniewy, Thomas Francis, '73
Christian, Floyd '34, '35, '36
Christian, Floyd T., Jr. '66, '67, '68
Christie, W. M. '12
Cianci, Tony '39, '40, '41
Clark, Caroll Harvin, Jr. '69, '70, '71
Clarke, Hagood, III '61, '62, '63
Clemons, Gordon '17, '18, '19, '20
Clemons, Justin '26, '27, '28
Clemons, W. N. '28, '29, '30
Cliett, Gary '64, '65
Clifford, John Jerome '70, '71, '72
Clifford, Thomas Alan, '73
Clifton, William '62
Coarsey, J. M. '11, '12, '13
Cobbe, Charles T. '32
Cochran, James '49
Cody, Ernest '38
Coe, Harry '06
Cole, Alan Marshall '69, '70
Cole, John '64, '65, '66
Cole, Samuel '48
Coleman, Robert Wesley '68, '69
Collins, Chester T., Jr. '59, '60, '61
Collins, P. F. '15, '16
Colson, Gordon Wallace '64, '65
Coons, John D. '66, '67
Condon, Thomas Franklin '71
Connell, H. R. '17, '18, '19

Conrad, Gene Gray '70, '71
Corbett, Roy '06, '07, '08
Cornwall, Sam '23, '24
Corry, William W. '40, '41, '42
Cowans, Alvin Jeffrey, '73
Cowen, J. William '39, '40, '41
Cowsert, J. T. '14
Cox, Abner '35
Cox, Asa Joseph '57, '58, '59
Cox, John O'Neal, Jr. '48, '49
Cox, John O'Neal '21
Crabtree, Clyde '27, '28, '29
Crabtree, John M. '37, '38
Crawford, Jeff '61
Culler, John '31
Culpepper, J. Blair '57, '58
Culpepper, Philip Bruce '60, '61, '62
Cummings, Robert C. '51
Cummins, John R. '51
Cummins, Richard '51
Curtis, Reid A. '32
Cutfliffe, C. Paige '66

D

D'Agostino, Joe A. '51, '52, '53
D'Aguile, Frank '42
Daniel, Marvin Raymond '57
Darby, Alvis Russell, '73
Daty, Arthur '22
David, Claude Lee '52
Davidson, Peter Bertel '56, '57, '58
Davis, Clyde '24, '25, '26
Davis, F. G. '09, '10, '11
Davis, Joseph P. '51
Davis, Nelson P. '37
Davis, Robert Gene '52, '53, '54
Davis, Robert Stanley, '73
Davis, Sam F. '31, '32, '33
Deal, Don Lee '58, '59, '60
Dean, George R. '66, '67, '68
Dean, Thomas Floyd '60, '61
Dearing, Ashley (honorary) '62
Dearing, William Howard '53
Dedge, Al '29

388

DeHoff, Donald '27
DeHoff, Willie '26, '27, '28
DeLaney, Paul '37
DeLaTorre, Stephen J. '52, '53, '54, '55
Dempsey, James Frank '46, '47, '48, '49
Demro, Conrad (honorary) '62
Dennis, Guy Durrell '66, '67, '68
Dent, John C. '61, '62, '63
DeVane, O. C. '15, '16, '17, '18, '19
Dewell, John '37
Dickey, Douglas Adair '52, '53
Didio, Nick '64, '65, '66
Dilts, Russell Joseph '58, '59
Dingman, Virgil '45
Dixon, Ray C. '22
Dodd, Frank '18
Dodd, Robert Lee, Jr. '60, '61
Doddridge, Rock Edward '70
Dodds, Frank '18
Doel, Duane Paul '70
Doll, Ronald David '72
Donnelly, Jay '65
Dorminy, Albert Clayton '72
Dorsett, Luke M. '29, '30, '31, '32
Dorsey, William J. '66, '67, '68
Doty, Arthur E. '21, '22
Douglas, E. Dewayne '51, '52
Dowdy, William Ernest '69, '70, '71
Dowling, Ham '15
Downs, Bobby C. '66, '67
Drew, Horace '45
Driggers, R. '20
DuBose, Jimmy Dewayne, '73
DuHart, Paul '42
Duncan, Fred H. '21, '22
Dunn, Edgar McAuley, Jr. '61
Dunn, James Howard '56, '57, '58
Dunn, Henry Hampton, Jr. '69
Dupree, L. B., Jr. '45
Dupree, Lawrence Wallace '62, '63, '64

Durrance, Thomas Louis '69, '70, '71
Duven, Gary G. '66, '67, '68
Dyal, Lawrence E. '52
Dye, Dewey '18
Dyer, James A. '44, '45

E

Earman, J. B. '06
Eastman, Ward Taylor, '73
Eaton, James Millard '55, '56
Eckdahl, Jack Lee '67, '68, '69
Edgington, Dan Thomas '57, '58, '59
Edmonds, Maurice '50, '51, '52
Eggart, Dan '64
Eggerton, D. C. '09, '10
Ellenburg, James S. '58, '59
Eller, Paul '38, '39, '40, '41
Ely, Mark M. '67, '68, '69
Ely, Stephen '68
Embry, W. E. '14, '15
Emmelhainz, Allen E. '31
Ennis, Bob (Golden Era)
Entzminger, Percy '41
Entzminger, Wade Denton '61
Eppert, Kenneth '34, '35
Evans, Frank '23
Evans, James H. '41
Evans, John '37
Ewaldsen, Paul H. '65, '66
Ewell, Cecil Davis, Jr. '60, '61

F

Faix, John V. '68, '70, '71
Fannin, David Earle '58, '59
Farmer, Henry B., Jr. '61, '62
Farrior, J. Rex, Jr. '13, '14, '15, '16
Favata, Dr. John J. '45
Feiber, John Kincaid '64, '65
Ferguson, Forest '39, '40, '41
Ferrazzi, W. J. '31, '32, '33
Ferrigno, Carmen '39, '40, '41
Field, Michael Scott '70
Fields, Charles '42, '46, '47
Fields, Wayne '72, '73
Fleming, Charles '33

Fleming, Dan '58
Flowers, Robert J. '50, '51
Foldberg, Henry Christian '71, '72, '73
Forbes, Robert G. '44, '46, '47
Foster, R. Edmund, III '68
Force, Wilbur H. '47
Ford, Herbert G. '20
Fountain, Johnny '31
Franco, Richard Joseph '69, '70, '71
Freeman, H. E. '14
Freeman, Judson '34
Freeman, Wilson '38
French, James '49, '50, '51
Fuller, A. H. '14, '15, '16, '17
Fuller, General Tom '27
Fuller, William Leonard '70, '71

G

Gaffney, Donald George, '73
Gagner, Larry '64, '65
Gailey, Thomas Chandler '71, '72, '73
Gaisford, William J. '67, '68
Gardner, Alex '47, '48, '49
Gardner, Earl '36
Gardner, Gordon '37, '38
Geiger, Carey Harris '71, '72, '73
George, Leonard '70, '71, '72
Gerber, Myron '49
Getzen, James Glenn '70
Ghesquiere, George David, Jr. '67,
    '68, '69
Gholsen, Davis '42
Giannamore, Lawrin Ferd '57, '58,
    '59
Gibbs, W. W. '06, '07, '08
Gilbert, John W. '46, '47, '48
Gilbert, Robert W. '46
Giles, Donald Ralph '58
Gill, Charles Wilson, Jr. '60
Gilmartin, W. H., Jr. '44, '45
Giordano, Donald M. '65, '66, '67
Glenn, Thomas E. '67
Godwin, Russell J. '48, '49
Goff, Clark '37, '38, '39

Golden, Ben '36
Goldstein, Goldy '23, '24, '25
Goldstein, Mark '26, '27
Golsby, Jack K. '14, '15, '16, '17,
    '18, '19
Goodbread, Royce '27, '28, '29
Goodman, Donald Eugene '59, '60,
    '61
Goodyear, E. D. '31, '32, '33
Gowland, Jan Eric '70, '71, '72
Graham, Joe G. '44
Gramling, Donnie Lamar '68
Grandoff, Bert '28
Grandy, Stuart George '64, '65, '66
Graves, Homer Eugene '58, '59
Green, Kaye Carl '54, '55
Green, Samuel Lee '72, '73
Green, Tom '25, '26
Greene, Bobby Joe '58, '59
Greene, Harry '28, '29
Gregory, Leo '33
Gregory, Thomas Ray '60, '61
Griffin, H. H. '46, '47, '48, '49
Griffin, James A. '62
Griffin, Skil '64
Griffith, Clinton Douglas, Jr. '72, '73
Griffith, Todd Wayne, Jr. '67, '68,
    '69
Groves, Fletcher '44, '46, '47, '48
Gruetzmacher, Robert '47, '48, '49
Gunn, Errett F. '21, '22
Gunn, W. W. '19, '20
Gunter, William Bruce '71
Gurkin, Van Michael '70

H

Hackney, Robert Ross '72
Haddock, Thomas Eugene '52, '53
Hadley, James Frederick '67, '68
Hager, Teddy C. '68, '69, '70
Haines, Webber '29
Hall, Brady '45
Hall, H. E. '17
Hall, James Elwood, Jr. '62, '63, '64

390

Hall, Joe '30
Hall, John Lewis, Jr. '50, '51, '52
Hall, Kenneth '44
Hamilton, Elton Cecil '55
Hamilton, Kenneth '44, '45
Hammack, Malcolm '53, '54
Hammock, John Ellis '51, '52
Hancock, A. Roy '10, '11, '12, '13, '14
Hancock, Frank '34
Handcock, Tom '06
Hanna, E. B. '39
Hansberry, William '61
Hanserbauer, Edward P. '41, '42
Harden, M. C. '45
Hardwick, Joe '36
Harlow, Joseph Greg '70, '72
Harper, Jack Ridley '64, '65
Harrell, Robert Steven '69, '70, '71
Harrison, John B. '41
Harrison, Thomas '39, '40, '41
Harry, Cadillac '25
Hassett, Buswell '37
Hatch, Donald James '52, '53, '54
Hatcher, F. '16
Haughton, Mal '06, '07, '08
Hausenbauer, E. P. '42
Hawkins, Joe '48
Hawkins, Robert Alexander '58, '59
Haygood, Attice Curt '52, '53, '54
Hayman, W. P. '17
Hazelwood, Harold '48, '49
Healey, Michael Joseph '67, '68
Heckman, Velles Alvin '56, '57, '58
Heidt, William Steven '64, '65, '66
Heiner, Webber '29
Helton, Charles Kimberlin '67, '68, '69
Henderson, Jack '33
Henderson, W. B. '13, '14, '15, '16
Hendricks, Ray '44
Hendricks, T. M. '36
Henry, Robert '42

Hergert, Joseph Martin '56, '57, '58
Hester, Grant '44
Hester, H. S. '13
Hewlett, Robert F. '51
Hickenlooper, Walter Andrew '60, '61, '62
Hickland, A. J. '33, '34, '35
Hicks, Dashwood '28, '29
Hicks, Donald Henry '55, '56, '57
Hicks, Louis Edwin '61
Hill, Buster Eugene '54
Hill, O'Neal '42
Hipp, Brian '68
Hitchcock, David Philip '71, '72, '73
Hobbs, Harry M. '45, '46
Hobbs, Russell D. '44
Hodges, G. H. '20, '22
Hogan, Fred '45
Hokenstad, Lloyd '22
Holland, Walter Samuel '60, '61, '62
Hontas, Mark James '72
Hood, Charles Henry '70
Hood, William Kenneth '58, '59, '60
Hoover, Robert Raymond '60, '61, '62
Horner, Ray '39, '40
Horsey, James F., Jr. '42
Horton, Robert Elmore '50, '51, '52
Horvath, Robert D. '49
Hosack, Robert Lee '61, '62
Houghtaling, Doc '13
Houser, M. S. '28, '29
Houston, Hubert '39, '40
Howard, '09
Howell, E. G. '38
Howell, W. E. '37, '38
Hoye, Francis O. '65
Hudson, William David '57, '58
Huerta, Marcelino '47, '48, '49
Huggins, Floyd '50, '51
Hughes, Carlisle '34, '35
Hughes, Jimmie E. '31, '32, '33
Hull, Milton '39, '40, '41

Hungerbuhler, Tom J. '66, '67
Hunsinger, Charles Ray '46, '47, '48, '49
Hunter, Daniel M. '50, '51, '52, '53
Hunter, Jim '08
Hurse, William D. '52
Hutcherson, Dale Lee '69, '70, '71

I

Iannarelli, Ronald John '72
Ihrig, Elmer '25
Infante, Gelindo '61, '62
Ives, Thomas Wilbur '53
Ivey, R. H. '35, '36

J

Jackson, James '49, '50
Jackson, R. B. '64, '65
Jackson, Willie B. '70, '71, '72
James, James A. '49
James, J. Wilbur '28, '29
James, John Wilbur, Jr. '70, '71
Jamison, W. K. '42, '46
Jenkins, Joe P. '35
Jetter, Brian L. '65, '66, '67
Johns, Edwin C. '57
Johnson, E. Julian, Jr. '65
Johnson, Fal L. '47, '48, '49
Johnson, John W. '56, '57
Johnson, Kent '06
Johnson, Leslie '10
Johnson, Pat '06
Johnson, R. G. '10
Johnson, Robert E. '38
Jones, A. J. '41, '42
Jones, C. Jerome '61, '62, '63
Jones, Edgar C. '23, '24, '25
Jones, Jackie Dwight '59
Jones, Jesse D. '34
Jones, Richard E., III '61, '62
Jordan, Jimmy Andrew '64
Jumper, Arlen N. '51, '52

K

Kaplan, Phillip '42
Karaphillis, Mike John '53

Katz, Jack '62, '63, '64
Kelley, James Michael '68, '69, '70
Kelley, Tommy Rogers '61, '62
Kelly, Mikey '50, '51, '52, '53
Kelly, T. Paine, Jr. '31, '32
Kelly, William James '70
Kelman, Ralph '38, '39
Kendrick, Preston '72, '73
Kendrick, Vincent '71, '72, '73
Kennell, Thomas Henry '69
Kensler, Richard Byard '70, '71
Kicliter, Harry J. '35, '36
Kiley, James Michael '68, '69
Killer, Clyde '64
King, Mark '71
King, Roswell '11
King, William Curtis '50, '51, '52
Kirchner, Clarence '27
Kirk, Dick '64, '65
Kirk, James '06
Kirkpatrick, Wesley '61
Klickovich, Walter '41
Klutka, Nick '40, '41, '42
Knapp, Donald Otis '64, '65, '66
Knight, Robert V. '50, '51, '54
Knowles, Hanford '49
Kocsis, Frank '36, '37, '38
Konesty, Floyd '40, '41, '42
Konrad, Wayne (Golden Era)
Krejcier, Charles '36, '37
Kruse, Kim Paul, '73
Kuss, Ferdinand '45
Kynes, James Hiatt '72, '73
Kynes, Jimmy '46, '47, '48, '49

L

Lacer, John '71, '72, '73
Lager, Willie '62, '63
Lamb, Doug '66
Lance, Robert F. '54, '55
Lane, Benny '39, '40, '41
Lane, Julian '34, '35, '36
Lane, Thomas '32, '33
LaPradd, Charles W. '50, '51, '52

Lasky, Francis J. '62, '63
Lasmis, H. E. '17
Latsko, William '40, '41, '42
Laurent, Eugene '36
Lavin, Charles G. '33
Lawless, Richard Burton '72, '73
Lawler, S. W., Jr. '11, '12
Lee, Eugene O. '42
Lee, Herbert C. '57
Lee, William L., Jr. '69
Lenfesty, Sidney G. '33
Lewis, Lazarous '47, '48, '49
Libertore, Lawrence Paul, Jr. '60, '61, '62
Lightbown, Lynn E. '37, '38
Lightsey, Spec '23, '24
Litherland, C. J. '31
Livingston, Archibald '25
Lockhart, Welton Perry '53, '54
Long, Buford Eugene '50, '51, '52
Loomis, H. E. '17
Loper, Gerald Calvin, '73
Lotspiech, A. A. '13, '14, '15
Lorenzo, Frank M. '46, '47, '48, '49
Lucas, Leonard LaVann '71
Lucey, Don Truesdale '58, '59
Lyle, Robert Telford, Jr. '62, '63, '64

M

MacBeth, Jon Lowell '58, '59, '60
Mack, Joe '39, '40, '41
Mack, Sam Harry '61
MacLean, Sydney Wade '62, '63, '64
Madigan, James '32
Madison, W. '18
Maggio, Phillip James '65, '66
Mahood, Jack '65, '66
Maliska, Paul Wm. '67, '68, '69
Mallory, LeRoy Thornton '71, '73
Mann, Thomas David '67, '68
Manning, Charles H. '52, '53, '54
Manning, C. W. '10
Manning, Ed, Jr. '36, '37

Manry, Daniel S., Jr. '65
Marshall, A. P. '17
Martin, Bruce '45
Martin, Hubert Bodie, Jr. '52, '53, '54, '55
Martin, Richard Charles '53, '54
Matheny, Charles '35
Matthews, Jack '23
Matthews, Lynn '64, '65
Matthews, Preston '66
May, Aurist '51, '52, '53
May, Jon Mardi '56
Mayberry, Walter '35, '36, '37
Maynard, Jack '37
Maynard, Zollie '34, '35
McAnly, Herbert '33, '35
McBride, William A. '68
McCall, Wayne C. '64, '66, '67
McCampbell, George '32, '33, '34
McCann, George H. '66, '67
McCarron, Pat '65, '66
McCarty, John '36
McClellan, Broward '30, '31
McClure, James '57
McCord, Guyte '06
McCoun, Joseph Chrisman '71, '72, '73
McCravy, Daniel Wesley '71
McDaniel, Ray '39
McDonald, Carroll Wilks '49, '50, '51
McEwen, J. Milton '28, '29, '30
McGhee, Warren '37
McGonigal, Elroy Edward '56
McGowan, William Albert '50, '51
McGriff, Lee Colson '72, '73
McGriff, Perry Colson, Jr. '58, '59
McIver, Larry Leroy '54
McKeel, Frederick Graham '64, '66, '67
McLean, Cecil '32
McLean, Kenneth '44
McMillan, Ralph Wendell '70
McMillan, Red '08
McNeal, Raymond '41

McRae, Walter A., Jr. '41, '42
McRae, W. A. '28, '29, '30
McTheny, Guy Corbett '67, '68, '69
Medved, George P. '52
Meisch, Edmond '20
Merrin, George '25, '26
Merrin, J. F. '19, '20, '21
Merrin, Joe '23, '24
Merritt, G. '12
Midden, Ray E. '55, '56, '57
Middlekauf, Walter '33, '34
Middlekauf, William '23, '24, '27
Milby, Robert Vance '58, '59
Miller, Hugo '42, '45
Miller, H. M. '45
Miller, Waring T. '35
Mims, William O. '42
Miranda, Victor Russell '57, '58, '60
Mitchell, Carl '39, '40, '41
Mitchell, Charles Foster '55, '56, '57
Mitchell, Dr. W. H. '08
Mitchell, Fondren '40, '41, '42
Mitchum, William Jewell '50, '51
Montsdeoca, Fred '48, '49, '50
Moody, John '08
Mooney, Ottis A. '44, '45
Moore, Eddy Lynn '70, '71, '73
Moore, Michael Lindsey '71, '72, '73
Moore, Nathaniel '72, '73
Morgan, Jimmy S. '62, '63
Morgan, L. Z. '18, '19
Morgan, Ralph '46
Morris, Billy Frank '50, '51, '52
Morris, John '64
Morris, Ralph Larry '70, '72
Morris, Terry E. '66, '67, '68
Morrison, Sherwood C. '72, '73
Mortellaro, Paul '44, '45, '46, '47
Moseley, G. R. '13, '14
Mounts, Mervin '21, '22
Moye, George '32, '33, '34
Mueth, Robert Henry '52
Mulcahy, James '37

Mullins, L. D. '36, '37, '38
Muniz, Frank L. '46
Murphy, Alvin Dennis '62, '63, '64
Murphree, John A. H. '23, '24

N

Nalls, Ronnie '61, '62
Natyshak, John '47, '49
Neilson, Alfred '06
Newbern, William Alfred '56, '57, '58
Newcomer, Gerald Carl '62, '63, '64
Newton, R. D. '21, '22, '23, '24
Nichols, Jack Clyde '50, '51, '52
Nolan, Jimmy '28, '29, '30
Norfleet, Joe '30, '31
Norris, Kenneth Leroy '59, '60
North, Merle '30, '31
Norton, Clyde '23, '24, '25
Norton, Oscar H. '18, '19, '20
Nugent, William Scott '72, '73

O

O'Brian, Jack E. '51, '52, '53
Occhiuzzi, Anthony '45
Odham, Glenn '45
Odom, Gerald Spessard '60, '61, '62
    '63
O'Donnell, James Dennis '61, '62, '63
Oliva, John Ernest '61
Oosterhoudt, Frank '24, '26
Oosterhoudt, Sam '50, '51, '52
Ortega, Ralph '72, '73
Osgood, Simon '31
Oswald, Douglas H. '48, '49
Overman, C. H. '09
Owens, George '36
Owens, Tom '26, '27, '28
Oxford, James '36, '37

P

Padgett, Aubrey Gary, Jr. '72, '73
Page, Edward Eugene '59, '60
Palahach, Michael '69
Pappas, Jackie Louis '50, '51
Parham, Harry '40, '41
Parker, Joseph Lee '71, '72, '73

Parker, Paul '08
Parker, Paul Plenge '72
Parker, Wendell C. '46, '47, '48
Parker, W. E. '48
Parnell, Ed '52
Parnell, Edward '29, '30, '31
Parnell, Sidney '38, '40
Parrish, Bernie Paul '56, '57
Partin, Walter Douglas '58, '59, '60
Pasteris, Joseph D. '66, '67
Patchen, Patrick N. '58, '59, '60
Patsy, John '50, '51
Paulson, Gunnar Fortune '69
Payne, W. D. '16
Peacock, Harold E. '68
Pearson, James Fred '61, '62, '63
Pedrick, Jack '51
Pedrick, Jack '27
Peek, David Hudgins '70, '71
Peek, Eugene G. '67, '68
Peek, Scott I. '51
Pelham, Louis Daniel '56, '57
Pennington, Fonia '36, '37
Perry, Carl E. '16, '19, '20, '21
Perry, Henry '21
Peters, Anton Berdette, Jr. '61, '62
Petersen, Gary Lee '70, '71
Pettee, Roger '62, '63, '64
Petty, Richard Allen '50, '51
Pharr, George M. '45
Pheil, Clarence E. '29, '30, '31
Pickels, Richard Clayton '57
Pilcher, Ray C., Jr. '70, '71
Piombo, John '38, '39, '40
Pippin, Charles '66
Pittman, O. W. '24
Platt, Eugene A. '42
Platt, Harry T., Jr. '41, '42
Pless, Glenn '27
Poe, Alan '64, '65
Poff, William David '70, '71, '72
Pomeroy, Stewart '21, '22, '23
Porch, Ben '35

Poucher, Gordon Leroy '50
Pounds, Hoyle '11, '12
Powell, Brad '68, '69, '70
Pracek, Robert Louis '59
Pratt, E. A. '42
Preston, John Harvey '64, '65, '66
Price, Carl A. '24
Price, J. C. '12
Price, T. E. '09, '11, '13
Priest, Ernest '34
Proctor, Carlos '29, '30
Proctor, Ralph '25
Puleston, Charles '06
Purcell, Robert Eugene '55
Pursell, Ron '64, '65

Q

Quinn, Reed G. '51, '52

R

Raasch, Ezra '24
Raborn, W. W. '46
Radar, Ralph '06, '08
Ramsdel, A. W. '13, '14, '15
Ramsey, James '30
Ramsey, Watson '38
Rawls, Dr. James A., Jr. '51
Rawls, Vernon C. '26
Rayborn, William '41, '42, '46
Reaves, Thomas Johnson '69, '70, '71
Rebol, Richard '68, '69
Reddell, Billy '51
Reen, Patrick '38, '40
Reeves, Alex '27, '28, '29
Reeves, A. J. '50, '51
Reid, A. L. '14
Renfroe, W. '21
Rentz, Ralph Larry '66, '67, '68
Revels, James C., III '71, '72, '73
Rhyne, James Robert '58, '59
Rich, Michael Lee '69, '70, '71
Richards, Henry '31
Richards, James Thomas, '73
Richbourg, William Britton '62,
   '63, '64

Rickett, Robert '33, '34, '35
Ringgold, Donald Wayne '60, '61
Ripley, Wayne '26
Rittgers, Rex Von '66
Roberts, Charles Avery '56, '57, '58
Robinson, Harold '33
Robinson, James '46
Robinson, Leffie Fred '52, '54
Robinson, Rocky '70
Robinson, William B. '41
Robinson, W. M. '21, '22, '23
Robles, O. S. '15, '16
Rogero, A. L. '30, '31
Rogers, Charles B. '32, '33, '34
Rood, R. S. '16
Root, Charles '34, '35, '36
Rose, J. R. '24
Rosenhouse, M. '21
Rosenthal, J. D. '16
Ross, Hugh A. '44
Ross, Ira Joseph '54
Roubles, O. S. '16
Rountree, James Woodrow '55, '56, '57
Rowe, Harold '34, '35, '36
Rowe, Richard Lew '50
Royal, Robert Daniel, Jr. '58, '59, '60
Rozelle, Frederick Edward '50
Rushing, Dewell '44, '47
Russell, Kenneth Wayne '62, '63, '64

S

Santille, D. Michael '66
Sapp, E. B., Jr. '44, '45
Sarra, Lamar '24, '25, '26
Sarris, George Tony '52
Sauers, Robert '39, '40
Sauls, Charles E. '28, '29, '30
Saunders, J. L. '30, '31
Sawyer, Ross C. '05
Scarborough, Earl '45
Scarborough, Truman C. '35
Schirmer, Ernest '32
Schmidt, Carl Frederic '70

Schmidt, Robert '44
Schnebly, John Martin '69, '70, '71
Schultz, Fred William '56, '58
Schucht, Hubert '34, '35
Schuman, Carl '32, '33
Schwartzburg, Jim H. '52, '53, '54
Scott, Ivan W. '21, '22
Scott, James '25
Scott, Laurence Clyde '52, '53, '54
Scott, Tom '38, '39
Scott, William R. '40
Seals, Roger Kyle '59, '60
Sears, Edwin R. '55, '56, '57
Seay, Homer '29, '30, '31
Senterfitt, Donald Richmond '59, '60
Sever, Tyson Lee '72, '73
Sever, William Glenn, '73
Sewell, '18
Seymour, Harold Daily '64, '65
Seymour, Kenneth Earle '57
Shackleford, T. W. '10
Shands, A. G. '13
Shands, William A. '07
Shannon, Thomas Joseph, Jr. '62,
   '63, '64
Shearer, Welcome '32, '33, '34
Sheer, Thomas Lee '56, '58
Sheppard, Joseph Earl '71, '72
Shouse, A. G. '33, '34
Sikes, Michael Daniel '56
Silman, John Spencer '70
Silsby, Link W. '29, '30, '31
Simpson, Clay '31, '32
Simpson, Jackie M. '53, '54, '55, '56
Sinardi, Nick Joseph '69
Skelly, Richard James '60
Skoldowski, Ziggy '45
Skrivanek, Britt Edward '67, '68, '69
Slack, Arthur Ronald '58, '59, '60
Smith, Charles Edward '50
Smith, Glenn '44
Smith, Horace '23, '24
Smith, James '49

Smith, John G. '38, '39
Smith, Michael Bernard, '73
Smith, Mills '27
Smith, Robert Dean '54
Smith, Thomas Ruel, Jr. '59, '60, '61
Smith, W. Lawrence '66, '67, '68
Smoak, D. Frank '38, '39, '40
Sneed, Neal '64, '65
Sorenson, Douglas '69, '70, '71
Sparkman, James K. '14, '15, '16, '19
Spears, Harry Gordon '53, '56
Spiers, W. H. '31
Splane, T. Douglas '65, '66, '67
Spurrier, Stephen Orr (Heisman
   Trophy) '64, '65, '66
Stadler, John '29
Stanfield, Michael David '72, '73
Stanley, Dennis K. '26, '27, '28
Stanley, Will A. '25
Stanly, George '21
Stanly, Richard Lee '21
Staples, Russell F. '61, '62
Starbuck, Hal '32, '33, '34
Stark, William D. '32, '33, '34
Starkey, David Bruce '72, '73
Starling, Bruce Cordell '60, '61
Steele, Jimmy '28, '29, '30
Steen, Malcolm Everett '67, '68, '69
Stephens, G. H. '60
Stephens, Jimmy Ray, '73
Stephens, Robert Louis '71
Stephens, William B. '35
Stephenson, George Kay '66
Stevens, Kent S. '50, '52
Stewart, Jack '24, '25, '26
Stockton, C. A. '15, '16
Stolz, Charles '32, '33, '34
Stone, W. E. '17
Stoner, Ronald Eugene '61
Storter, Neil S. '09, '10, '11
Sullivan, Haywood C. '50, '51
Summers, Jacob Anderson '72, '73
Sumner, Kenneth Milton '51, '52

Sutherland, George '42, '46
Sutton, Clifford '46, '47, '48, '49
Sutton, John '10, '11, '12, '13, '14
Swanson, E. '19
Swanson, R. M. '20, '21
Swanson, T. J. '15
Swink, P. C. '17
Symank, John Richard '55, '56

T

Taggert, George Eric '70
Talbot, Randy William '72, '73
Tannen, Steven Olson '67, '68, '69
Tate, Charlie '39, '40, '41
Tatum, Earl '56
Tatum, Jim '56
Taylor, Earl A. '08, '09, '10
Taylor, James J. '52
Taylor, Ted '38
Tenney, Louis Earl '10, '11, '12, '13
Thomas, Clarence S. '17, '18, '19, '20
Thomas, Gary '64, '65
Thomas, Owen Jerome '51
Thomas, Philip E. '21
Thompson, Charlie '06, '08
Thompson, Harry W. '14, '15
Thompson, Jack Bernard, III
   '61, '62, '63
Thompson, John Clark '64
Thrasher, '09
Todd, Edgar R. '24, '25
Tolbert, H. L. '21
Trammell, Allen Raymond, Jr. '64, '65
Trapp, Richard E. '65, '66, '67
Travis, Larry Lee '60, '61
Treadgold, R. J. '31, '32
Trueheart, Harold S., Jr. '61, '62
Tucker, Charles '26, '27
Tucker, D. A. '16
Tucker, John '64
Turman, Lloyd A. '67, '68
Turner, James Morris '44
Turner, Jess L. '31
Turner, William E. '46, '47, '48, '49

Turner, William F. '33, '34, '35

U

Uspensky, Michael Nicholas '69

V

Vaccaro, Gasper V. '46, '47, '48, '49
Van Camp, R. K. '14
Vandergriff, J. H. '20
Van Fleet, Richard '08
Vangelas, Thomas '45
Vansickle, Dale '27, '28, '29
Vargecko, Paul John '59, '60, '61
Vaughn, Sidney '45
Vetter, Emerson '39
Vickery, Charles '29
Vidal, James H. '08
Vinesett, Jerry D. '68, '69, '70
Visser, Robert Henry '55
Vosloh, Robert Paul '54, '55, '56

W

Wages, Harmon L. '66, '67
Waggener, J. A. '10
Wahlberg, Joel David '56, '57
Waldron, Jesse C. '31
Walker, Garry L. '68, '69, '70
Walker, Ion '26, '27
Walker, Tom B. '36, '37, '38
Walker, W. S. '09
Walker, L. B. '38
Walton, W. L. '38, '39, '40
Warbritton, William Randolph '70
Ware, Charles Edward '50, '51, '52
Ware, Melton '34
Warner, Edwin R. '66
Warner, Henry '19
Warren, W. T. '34, '35, '36
Waters, Dale '28, '29, '30
Watson, Richard O. '52
Waxman, Mike '64, '65
Webster, H. Allison '47
Webster, W. J. '51
Wehking, Robert Jean '59, '60, '61
Welch, James John '69

Welles, Frank '36
Wesley, Larry Eustace '54, '55, '56
Westbrook, Jack Eugene '58, '59
Wester, William J. '51
Whatley, John '64, '65
Whiddon, Clifford '37
Whitaker, Glenn '25
White, Jack '44, '45, '46
White, Paul Edward '59, '60, '61
Whitehead, James Orlin '54
Whittaker, Glenn '25
Whittington, Arling '44
Wiggins, Lloyd Gregory '70
Wildman, Charles Frederick, '73
Wilkinson, S. A. B. '15, '16, '17
William, Buton C. '23, '24, '25
Williams, Angus '45, '48, '49, '50
Williams, Bill '36, '37
Williams, Bud '64, '65
Williams, Burton C. '65
Williams, Charles Broughton '42, '46
Williams, Daniel Marvin '69, '70
Williams, Donald E. '68, '69, '70
Williams, John David '72
Williams, Roderick Michael '72, '73
Williamson, H. E. '32
Williamson, J. D. '30, '31
Williamson, Kendrick Wayne '57, '58, '59
Williamson, Larry Cline '69
Willis, Frank '36
Willis, Kenneth '35, '36, '37
Wilsky, C. '21
Wilson, R. Borden '12
Windham, Joseph Nathan '56, '57, '58
Wing, Harry Fannin '52
Winne, Ross Wesley, Jr. '52, '53, '54
Wolfe, Stanley '26
Wood, G. P. '16
Wood, Sidney '42
Wright, Arthur J. '51, '52, '53
Wright, Joe Lawrence '50
Wright, Weldon '45

Wunderly, Joseph Alan, '73
Wuthrich, E. B. '17, '18, '19, '21
Wynn, Milton '44

Y

Yancey, Harvey '28, '29, '30, '31
Yancey, James '47, '48, '49
Yancey, James Mitchell '69, '70, '71
Yancey, Malcolm '19
Yarbrough, James '66, '67, '68
Yeats, James Melvin '55, '56, '57
Yinshanis, Frank '38
York, M. E. '52
Young, James Winston '59, '60, '61
Youngblood, Herbert Jackson '68,
    '69, '70